Karl Renz

May It Be As It Is
The Embrace of Helplessness

Karl Renz

May It Be As It Is
The Embrace of Helplessness

Edited By
Michele Brehl

A DIVISION OF MAOLI MEDIA PRIVATE LIMITED

May It Be As It Is: The Embrace of Helplessness

Copyright © 2011 Karl Renz

First Indian Edition: September 2011

PUBLISHED BY
ZEN PUBLICATIONS
A Division of Maoli Media Private Limited

60, Juhu Supreme Shopping Centre,
Gulmohar Cross Road No. 9, JVPD Scheme,
Juhu, Mumbai 400 049. India.

Tel: +91 9022208074
eMail: info@zenpublications.com
Website: www.zenpublications.com

Book Design: Red Sky Designs, Mumbai

ISBN 13   978-81-88071-67-8

All rights reserved. No part of this book may be reproduced or transmitted in any form or by any means, electronic or mechanical, including photocopying, recording, or by any information storage and retrieval system without written permission from the author or his agents, except for the inclusion of brief quotations in a review.

May It Be As It Is: The Embrace of Helplessness

Copyright © 2011 Karl Renz

First Indian Edition: September 2011

PUBLISHED BY
ZEN PUBLICATIONS
A Division of Maoli Media Private Limited

60, Juhu Supreme Shopping Centre,
Gulmohar Cross Road No. 9, JVPD Scheme,
Juhu, Mumbai 400 049. India.

Tel: +91 22 32408074
eMail: info@zenpublications.com
Website: www.zenpublications.com

Book Design: Red Sky Designs, Mumbai

ISBN 10   81-8807167-6
ISBN 13   978-81-88071-67-8

All rights reserved. No part of this book may be reproduced or transmitted in any form or by any means, electronic or mechanical, including photocopying, recording, or by any information storage and retrieval system without written permission from the author or his agents, except for the inclusion of brief quotations in a review.

Contents

Foreword	9
Awareness Is Just A Shadow Of What You Are	13
There Is No Bridge	50
The Song Of Wrongness	99
You Have No Business With Yourself	129
The Game Is Never Over	170
Such An Absolute Perfect Trap	212
It's All Self-Love	249

Other Books by Karl Renz

- If You Wake Up, Don't Take It Personally
  Dialogues in the Presence of Arunachala
- The Myth of Enlightenment
  Seeing Through the Illusion of Separation

Other Books by Zen Publications

- Redemption Stories: Unwasted Pain
- A Duet of One
- Pursue 'Happiness' And Get Enlightened
- Celebrate the Wit & Wisdom: Relax and Enjoy
- Pointers From Ramana Maharshi
- Enlightened Living
- A Buddha's Babble
- A Personal Religion Of Your Own
- The Essence of The Ashtavakra Gita
- The Relationship Between 'I' And 'Me'
- Seeking Enlightenment – Why ?
- Nuggets of Wisdom
- Confusion No More
- Guru Pournima
- Advaita and the Buddha
- It So Happened That... The Unique Teaching of Ramesh S. Balsekar
- Sin and Guilt: Monstrosity of Mind
- The Infamous Ego
- Who Cares?!
- The Essence of the Bhagavad Gita
- Your Head in the Tiger's Mouth
- Consciousness Strikes
- Consciousness Writes
- Consciousness Speaks
- The Bhagavad Gita – A Selection
- Ripples

Be what you cannot not be.
You are that Knowledge and that's absolute Knowledge.
But there is no knower in it, that's the main thing.

KARL RENZ

Foreword

'Whatever You Get From Me Is Wrong'

After many years of giving talks in Tiruvannamalai, as well as retreats in Ladakh, Rishikesh and Coimbatore, Karl talked in Mumbai for the first time in January 2010. In 1995 he met Ramesh Balsekar there for one day, and the next day he left for Tiruvannamalai, where Arunachala became 'the final cut': 'By that what I am, seeing that even the most superior awareness, which is pure light, is still imagination, and you are still prior or in spite of it - that takes the last hope of home away. If even the divine light of Shiva is just an imaginary light - what else can happen?' Since then he has been to Tiruvannamalai every winter where he has given talks for more than 10 years.

Landing at Bombay airport from Thailand after midnight, a small group of us traveling with Karl were more than curious about the first talk in Bombay. Sitting in a tightly packed living room at Cuffe Parade the next day it quickly became clear that the Bombay talks would indeed be something special. The talks in Tiruvannamalai had been attended by large crowds of Westerners, but only a small group of Indians from Tiru and Chennai. In Bombay there were as many Indian visitors as foreigners. Most of the people attending had been with Ramesh Balsekar for many years or met him briefly at some point. So there were many questions referring to Ramesh's concepts, as well as the 'teachings' of Nisargadatta Maharaj, UG Krishnamurti and Ramana Maharshi. More than in other talks around the world there was a focus on Advaita and other Indian concepts, symbols and techniques, as Karl kept surprising his audience with refreshing new twists on well-known traditions. The talks were high-energy and fast-paced with a lot of serious questions about spirituality, philosophy, science, psychology and many other topics. Karl says he isn't really interested in the questions but in the questioner revealing himself, but clearly the Bombay audience had good questions. There was a sense of urgency so the talks were argumentative, dense and most extended well past the scheduled two hours. Karl's irreverence, carelessness and infamous use of language in the face of Indian traditions seemed more shocking than in Western countries but didn't appear to offend anyone, even when it came to concepts like 'Advaita de toilette'.

What doesn't come across in the book is the incredible speed of the talks, and Karl's comedic imitations of the 'sick seekers'. 'Talks' doesn't really capture the full flavor of the experience except that there is a lot of talking going on. Karl calls them entertainment, and they are a much more colorful, unpredictable and chaotic performance than the usual question-and-answer satsangs. To me they feel like a mix of punk concert, circus, stand-up comedy and jam session - a mind-blowing, mesmerizing high-speed firework with words. It is a new way to experience language, a mix of poetry, rap, twisting and juggling, hammering and pounding and finally pulling the rug out from under you. Karl contradicts and changes meanings again and again until the mind is twisted into knots and all that's left is a refreshing sensation of blankness or hysterical laughter.

May It Be As It Is

Karl's brain doesn't seem limited by the usual laws of biology and doesn't stick to down-trodden connections between synopses, wildly creating new connections in all directions, unavailable to the normal brain. He constantly invents new words, doubling and tripling meanings, making word plays across languages, answering questions before they are pronounced and pushing every mind that tries to challenge him into checkmate. When someone called one of the talks in Mumbai a 'discussion' his reply was: 'Discussion? I am always right and you are always wrong. Is that a discussion?' No wonder he has been called the 'Advaita punk'. There is a total carelessness of talking, not the carefully pronounced statements and pointers of other spiritual teachers. There is obviously no one who tries to present any precious teaching or who cares about anyone understanding anything, but 'a loudspeaker who doesn't care what comes out of it'. Karl will claim he never said anything anyway. For him the beauty of language is its emptiness and he makes sure to take this freedom of words to the absolute limit. The listeners are bombarded with mind-twisting contradictions and every question is turned inside out ad absurdum. Any attempt to understand is drowned in endless complex variations of language which can feel beautifully hypnotic yet leave nothing to hold on to. The verbal destruction of everything that can be destroyed is painful when there is resistance or holding on to anything, but mostly people leave the talks with an amazing feeling of lightness.

Karl denies that there is anyone who has compassion and emphasizes that he is not our friend but our worst enemy. The experience in the talks is more the opposite. When called on it he just says 'What would you do if you see yourself suffering from a misunderstanding?' Some complain that he is too negative, but when after years of seeking and striving the last hope of ever reaching any spiritual goals is taken away, the sense of liberation is intoxicating.

The second year the talks took place in a home near Nepean Sea Road. Often his words were drowned out by the ever present honking of traffic and construction noises competing with bhajans from the apartment below, interrupted by arguments over the speed of the ceiling fans and the obligatory Indian cell phones going off.

After some time those who were still engaged in listening and talking could witness what someone in Mumbai called the 'nerve gas effect' – most of the audience lying on the floor motionlessly like empty shells, knocked out or in some kind of trance. And Karl sitting up front, looking fresh as always and continuing with endless energy, despite the heat, noise, pollution and jetlag.

I don't know what is really happening in these talks, I just know it is totally unique, a lot of fun, and the effect is an ease and carelessness that is dangerously addictive. Sometimes the mesmerizing variations of modern sutras remind me of Kaa, the snake from the jungle book and I wonder if the show that is going on is just a distraction while the brain is being re-wired and any understanding that has been collected in years of spiritual searching is deleted, including the seeker himself.

The talks in this book are a selection of seven from 26 talks Karl gave in Mumbai in 2010 and 2011. They have been slightly shortened with only a minimum of editing to preserve the original tone and Karl's free use of language.

Michele Brehl
June 2011

Awareness Is Just A Shadow Of What You Are

Q: Somebody presented me with a book on psychology. Is it possible to evolve spiritually when you have serious mental illnesses or serious mental problems?

K: Depends on your goal. What is the goal?

Q: Many people hold this belief that until you don't do your work, all spiritual seeking is pointless. Until you don't know about your own insecurities, until you don't deal with your stuff.

K: That's like Vedanta. Vedanta is a whole technique of making one purified and healthy and even able to face the truth. If that has to happen, it will happen. But still I would say you can never face yourself. You will never be ready for that. No one will ever be ready for himself. And the good news is, no one needs to be ready for himself. You can only be ready for some relative truth. Maybe high energy or intense experiences or something, but never for yourself. The Self never asks you to be ready for what you are. There is no need for readiness. So you cannot mix it. That's why I ask: what is your goal? If your goal is having a light body, being in a super natural 'Aurobingo' state, wonderful, then you can prepare yourself by whatever learning, by yoga techniques, by whatever. And then there are many teachers who can teach you how to do that. Whole Poona is full of it. The whole world is full of it. But there is no way that you get ready enough for that what you are. But still you have to try. So in a relative sense, to have a healthy body, a healthy ego, you can do something. That you can function in the world perfectly, in harmony with your surroundings, all of that can happen. But you can never prepare yourself for That. So yes, and no. If you have relative goals you can reach them.

Q: The line that really jumped up at me was that the belief 'I am not the body' is a sign of schizophrenia. But that's exactly what Ashtavakra is teaching King Janaka: 'You are not the body'.

K: Maybe it's not really translated the right way. You are not the information of the body. It says you are not the body, but you are the body. So you are not the information of the body but you are the essence of the body. So yes, and no. So the phenomenal experience of the body you are not. But you are that what is the body, in essence. So you are the heart of the information but you are not the information. So to say 'I am not the body' is still one phenomena too many who says 'I am not the body'. It needs only one illusion who says 'I am not' to discriminate itself. The discriminator is still phenomenal experience. The definer always wants to define. 'I am or I am not the body'. 'I am this but not that'. That needs a definer and already that is the phantom I, that is the defining me, that needs the definer, that always needs the differences. And by saying 'I am not the body' you are different from something, so it survives by 'not being something'. Even saying 'I am nothing' you survive by being different from something. It's all for survival. The ghost needs all that definition. Even in not defining he defines himself. No way out! And in that definition and in that defining is implied that you have to do something, you can do something, or you can not do something. Both come out of the same thought – the I-thought. So the idea that you have free will or that you have no free will is both definition and both is wrong. Having or not having a body – both is wrong. There is only wrongness, there is only falsity and the definer is defining false. False, false, false, false. So there is no escape in going from that to that, but that's the nature of the dream.

The dreamer wants to have a pleasant dream, and having a more pleasant dream means not having a body. 'I am spirit'. Then I am more in the comfort of spirit which cannot be touched by material diseases or something. So you define yourself as unborn. But even that one who defines himself as unborn is fake. So even the unborn is fake. The idea of unborn is fake. You are neither the born nor the unborn, nor anyone. But you are that. So if you are talking in that relative dream we can find all that 'terror-py'.

Q: You asked me what the goal is. I just got the goal as you were speaking. The goal is to have the complete authentic knowing from where you speak.

K: And that cannot be achieved by any relative understanding.

Q: The Advaita Vedanta still believes that you do something.

K: That's Vedanta. The end of the Vedas is Advaita. Where Advaita ends the Vedas start. You can not mix it. Vedanta is realization. And Advaita is nature. Reality is Advaita, that's the pointer of Reality, no duality, no second, that what is, that what is your nature. And Vedanta is the realization of it. And in the realization there are all kinds of goals, all kinds of learning and unlearning and doing and not-doing – that's all Vedanta

Q: And the expression Advaita Vedanta?

K: Advaita is the origin, that's Reality. And Vedanta is the realization of it. They are not two. You cannot divide them. Advaita is your nature, that's Reality, but Vedanta is your realization. So I don't mind the Vedanta, I like the Vedanta, but only because no one needs it.

Q: But they say you have to...

K: It doesn't matter if they say it or not! They have to say it! There is no way out for them. Why should they not say it? If they would say 'you don't have' it's false too. To say you have and to say you don't have is false. Both is false. Who has and who has not? All of that is the dance of what you are, and all of that is the realization of what you are. But by none of that realization you become more real, or less real. And then I can only say I try to make you so attracted to that what never needs anything, that by that you see this comes and goes. I try to make you absolute junkies for what is what you are, which never needs that what could be any junkie for anything.

Q: Is it the same for good company, that it also comes in the Vedanta?

K: No. Vedanta is not good company.

Q: Then what is good company?

K: The absence. The absence of any presence of any company. That's good company. The absence of the idea of good company, that's good company. But any Vedanta idea of good company is bad company, you go to bed with that, and you wake up with that.

Q: But it seems...

K: It seems, it always seems, seems, seems. Seemingly. It is not good to be with me, for sure not!

Q: Not with you, but ...

K: I don't even like to be with me, how can I say it is good to be with me?

Q: So is it the same with what appears to be good company, like sitting in talks with you...

K: As long as you are sitting somewhere with someone, that's bad company.

Q: And that is only relative, always?

K: Yes, that's relative bad company. And then you may get a relative good company. But both is bad company.

Q: But in spite of the bad company...

K: You have no company.

Q: But we sit here.

K: In spite of you not needing company you are experiencing company. But not because you need it. It's not because there is a necessity of company. You can not not have company because any moment you are awake you are in company. You are in the company of what you are. The big company. LTD unlimited.

Q: So what about this saying 'the highest tapas is good company'?

K: There are no tapas. That's the highest tapas. The tapas-lessness. The exercise-lessness is exercise. The exercise to be what you are, which never needs to exercise to be what it is. That is the highest tapas you can not do, you can only be. But any tapa you can do is Vedanta.

Q: So whatever you are trying is Vedanta?

K: Even not trying is Vedanta.

Q: So whatever you are doing is Vedanta?

K: Or not doing. Whatever you can name, whatever you can frame, whatever you can describe is Vedanta. The only pointer to your nature is Advaita. There is no two. That's all. Pointing to what is Reality which doesn't even know Reality. It is Reality. And there is no two. Whatever you can describe otherwise is Vedanta.

Q: So this is Vedanta?

K: I don't' know what it is. This is the realization of what you are. This is Vedanta. This is your absolute dream, but the absolute Dreamer cannot be found in it.

That's all. That's the pointer of it. You are not different from this dream, this is the way you realize yourself. But in no way of realization you can realize Reality. This is the realization of Reality, but Reality can not be found in it. As it was never lost in it. These are pointers in Vedanta to what is Advaita. But Advaita can not be achieved in Vedanta, thank God. So where Vedanta ends you start as what you are, and you end where Vedanta starts. So when you place yourself in Vedanta you commit suicide. You try to find

Reality in realization and then you make it relative. Self-guilty! What to do?

Q: Just be.

K: Just be is too much. 'To be or not the be' is not the question.

Q: So what is the question?

K: There is no question.

Q: Karl, I have never heard Advaita and Vedanta explained like this. Where did you get this from? This is amazing. This is beautiful. I never heard this before.

K: I don't know, I just know it. I know I didn't read it somewhere. It just comes. Because I see it. Because I am what is Advaita, and the Vedanta is the realization of that, that's all.

Q: So there is a recognition that you cannot escape Vedanta?

K: No, there is no recognition. It's too late. There is no recognition needed for what you are. Recognition is in Vedanta. Whatever you can name and frame is Vedanta. And where that all ends, what you are is.

Q: Maharaj says consciousness is all there is. And everything that comes in the relative is also part of that. It's not different. It's one.

K: No, I sit here and tell you can not not fall in love with yourself. And the moment you realize yourself you become the lover. The realizer. And then realizing and what can be realized happens. Out of that simply waking up. But what is your nature is already prior to that waking up what it is. It is never waking up by waking up. Because your nature doesn't start with realizing. So the realizer is already a part of realization. But not Reality. So your realization starts with the realizer realizing whatever can be realized. But whatever the realizer is realizing can not make the realizer more real as the realizer already is. So whatever you as an experiencer experience cannot make the nature of the experiencer more or less.

Q: You have pointed out that this realization is already full?

K: It is neither full nor empty. There is not even an idea of fullness. And no need for fullness.

Q: It's complete.

K: It's not even complete. It never needs to be complete. There is no need for completion.

Q: You did mention how could there be more knowledge...

K: The knowledge doesn't need to be complete. It is complete when it is complete and it is even complete when it's incomplete. It is that what is ignorance. It doesn't need to be knowledge to be knowledge. And that what needs to be knowledge to be knowledge is relative knowledge. It never asks for knowledge. It is never depending on knowledge. And that knowledge which is depending on knowledge is a relative knowledge, is false.

Q: So what you are and what you realize...

K: There is no 'you' in it. You are not that.

Q: But realization is not two, is one...

K: It's not one. One is one too many. When there is one, there is two. Where one starts, separation starts. Out of oneness comes separation. It's all Vedanta. Oneness is Vedanta. Separation is Vedanta. All you can do is Vedanta. It's all fine. But the only dream is that you can find yourself in Vedanta. That you can get more or less by whatever Vedanta is showing you. That's your only dream. And that makes you suffer about not being enough. And then you get never enough from Vedanta. Because you always have goals in Vedanta, higher, lower, deeper, whatever. And I am sitting here because you fall in love with an idea. And now you are in that trouble of being in love. And then what they call the heart knot has to be broken. So the relative love for yourself has to be broken. What does this mean? You have to see that by none of your loving or caring or anything you can ever reach that what you are.

So the beloved can never be known. And that breaks your heart. That breaks your imaginary heart that you have to know yourself to be yourself. That is your imaginary heart. Being in love with your beloved and imagining that you have to know yourself to be yourself. That there is even a self, that breaks your heart. This is already a fake one. Even the idea of self is fake. That there is even a self for you is fake. Self is imprisonment. Already the idea of self is the end of what you are. The purest notion of I - the end of what you are. It's not so bad. It's the best news you can get, that you can not be found in anything, because it means you can not be lost in it. You never lost anything in this whatever, your experience. And the best news is, you cannot gain back what you haven't lost.

Q: It doesn't sound so good Karl.

K: It depends from what position you look. For what you are, nothing is better than that. And for what you are not, it's hell. So there is a discomfort for what you are not, and there is a comfort for what you are. And then you better be what you cannot not be, because that is comfort itself. And the rest can not deliver the comfort you are. Thank God it cannot be delivered by any UPS. Ups! So it's good news for what you are, because there is no news. And it's bad news for what you are not. And I really don't care about what you are not. (Car alarm going off) There is always an emergency for what you are not. Only doctors care about you. Because they make business out of it.

Q: So Advaita is only up to the experience of awareness?

K: No. Awareness is already Vedanta. Too late. When you are awake you are already in your realization. Reality is never awake or not awake. Awareness already is an experience. The purest you can get, but even the purest cannot deliver what you are. So awareness or not awareness, who cares? Because in that what you are there is neither who or not who – you cannot find anyone there. Never! That is like deep deep sleep, because there is no one absent or present. There is just that what you are in the absolute absence of any presence absence presence whatever. Call it whatever. And no one complains there, and no one needs to know anything there to be what that is. That never needs any whatever you can imagine. Out of that all imagined dreams start, but it doesn't start when the dreamer is dreamed. So in spite of the trinity of Shiva, Vishnu, Brahma, or the creator of all of that, that what is para-Brahman, which is Reality, just Reality, which doesn't even have to exist to exist, you cannot even call it Existence, it's beyond whatever you can imagine.

Q: It's like deep sleep cannot be imagined without awareness?

K: Deep sleep you can talk about, because there is an awareness still. But in deep deep sleep there is not even awareness.

Q: Is there dreams?

K: Am I talking here? Or do I pee in the wind? You better go to Pune and do some tantra groups. Sometimes I advice people to go first to something else...

Q: I am too lazy to go to Pune.

K: The good thing is no one can comprehend what that is. There is no possible way of understanding it. Because the moment you would understand it, you would not be there. And whatever you do, you try against That. From that what you now believe in. The believer instantly wants to make even that a belief system.

Q: So it's all futile?

K: It's not futile. For who? It's wonderful! This is what you are, this is your realization of what you are and the next is the next. And as the last one didn't deliver, the next one will not deliver what you are. Wonderful! So it's all empty. It's all pffff – the next sip of coffee. The next, the next, the next. The next word flows out and nothing is said and the next listening happens and the next movie happens – and nothing happens.

Q: Ground zero.

K: Yes, you are the zero of the zero. You are what they call the groundless ground, the groundlessness. You are not even the origin, so why should you care about what doesn't come out of you? Nothing ever comes out of you! You never created anything. There is no creator in what you are. You are not even the source. You cannot even say you are the source. Of what? Who can say he is the source? Who claims to be the source? The source of what? So what to do?

Q: There is nothing to do! That's one of the worst things you keep repeating: 'What to do?'

K: No, 'what to do?' doesn't mean that there is nothing to do. It's just 'what to do?'. Whatever you do or don't do won't...

Q: ...deliver.

K: Whatever. 'What to do?' doesn't mean you cannot do anything. 'Poor me, I cannot do anything!' I am not pointing to that! I am pointing to the Almighty who says whatever is done or not done can not make ME more almighty than I am. I Am not talking to any poor me here, my goodness! See, you can only misunderstand it. Even when I say 'what to do?' you understand it like 'I cannot do anything'. I never said that. It's like: 'Karl said you cannot do anything!' It's like: 'Ramesh said I have no free will'. I think he never said it, to anyone. But you have to misunderstand it, because you want to survive. You interpret it your way, so that you can just do it your way again. And then you may claim: 'By my understanding I made it!' 'It was my giving-up!' 'My devotion!' What an idea! So I am not talking to this poor little pretender. 'Emergency, emergency, poor me, poor me!'.

Q: You are not talking to that, but that's what's hearing it.

K: No. There was never any imaginary I that ever said something or heard something. How can an imaginary object do anything? How can a dream object even listen? How can a dream object experience? How can a camera experience? Can you really say the camera is experiencing what the camera is recording? Can you say that? But that you claim! That I speak to a camera, and thinking that the camera understands something.

Q: But you can say that there is the impression of understanding.

K: There is not even the impression of the camera. The camera is pure energy. There is not even a camera in Reality. Pure energy, life put itself as a camera, recording something that is not needed. Even the camera is in its essence that what it is. But I don't expect the camera to understand that. And the camera doesn't need to understand that it's not a camera. It doesn't even know a camera.

Q: The camera is not infused with intellect, whereas the human being is...

K: Even the human being is not infused! You really think humans have intellect? Do you really believe in that? You really think you have consciousness?

Q: We have the so-called thinking-mind...

K: Humans have a thinking mind? Think about it! Who has what? Who owns what? Tell me! What phantom is owning what? What is yours? You have consciousness? Poor consciousness which can be owned by you! I would just destroy that consciousness which could be owned by you!

Q: The question was because Ramesh would often say that the human being has intellect which is what causes the ideas.

K: You claim that there are humans and that they have consciousness. I don't see any humans who could have anything.

Q: But there is consciousness, that's why you are alive...

K: But that's the question: who is here alive? Where are the beings? In Reality, where are the beings? In that realization there are maybe experiences of beings, but how can experiences own something? Consciousness playing a human being doesn't become human. Or does it? So are there human beings or not?

Q: No.

K: So who owns what then? Does consciousness own human beings or do human beings have consciousness? That's always this little shift. Consciousness plays a human being. And nothing is lost by it. And nothing is gained by not being a human being. But you imagining that you have consciousness - that turns it all around. That's the little suffering point, that you have something. That you claim to have consciousness – you make it two consciousness.

Q: Consciousness is there...

K: Where?

Q: In the six billion...

K: Does consciousness have a place? There is no consciousness in something! How can there be consciousness in something? What could contain consciousness? The container would be different from consciousness. Just ponder about what you say! How can consciousness be contained by what? How can it contain something?

Q: Isn't it that everything we can say can be negated? So for everything that exists there is the negation of it. The only thing is the negation of the negation, that is the only authentic thing, and that is also not true. So what to say? Nothing!

K: It never needs to be authentic. Who needs to be authentic? Who makes this bloody concept of being authentic?

Q: So every concept...

K: There is no concept! Show me a concept? Where is a concept?

Q: As long as I say...

K: There is no 'as long'! Who says 'as long'?

Q: Nobody says.

K: Nobody says? Who is this nobody?

Q: I am the nobody.

K: It's amazing! Whatever she says she goes deeper and deeper into the shit! You are like swimming in shit and then you try to keep your mouth above the shit. But the shit is what you are! And you think you have to keep your head on top of the shit. Everyone who puts his head out of the shit I cut!

Q: Good analogy!

K: Because that what is shit is chit. There is no difference between chit and shit. But you wanting to be on top of shit, you are the master of shit. So any moment you want to master yourself, control yourself, you are the master of shit. A shit master. Shit happens. And only shit happens. Because what you are never happens. But even to recognize that is too much, is shit. Fantastic!

Q: So are we coming here to be the master of shit?

K: No, masters of shit are coming, and I tell them 'what you try to master is shit'. And you are a shit master. Because you are a master of ignorance. Because there is no master in knowledge. And whatever you can be a master of is shit.

Q: Yesterday somebody asked me what you were saying. Maybe that's a good sentence to say! What

master are you? So now we will say you are the master of shit!

K: I would never claim – you claim, you tell me what I am. Everyone tells me what I am. I have no idea! That's why only so-called disciples make masters. Masters don't know any masters. There are only disciples who are believing in shit, so they are enslaved in shit. But the master will always tell them that there is no master. What else can he do? But the slave needs a master. And even shit is good enough for the slave.

Q: I have a definition for you: you are the master of the darkness we hope to keep hidden.

K: I want to put darkness over the light. I am not the Lucifer who wants to enlighten you. I show you that even the light is shit, is darkness. Because compared to the light you are even the light is dark. Too dark for you. So even the awareness is not enough awareness for that what you are. So to be the light, not knowing light, that's light. But the light you can know is just a shade of it, just a shadow. Awareness is a shadow of what you are. All the Vedanta is your shadow. You cannot get rid of it, that's all. Vedanta is your shadow, but you are the light which is realizing itself by Vedanta, by that shadow, as that what is light can never realize light, can never know itself. And the light it can know is realization of light but not what is light. I can repeat it and repeat it...

Q: You are talking to no one...

K: I am talking to that what is darkness, to itself. So I am talking to the Light which never knows the Light. There is only Self! There is only that what never knows itself. And now in action, in light, and now in vibration, and now it falls in love with some reflection of it, with some shadow of it. And now it became a shadow. What can I do to what I am, believing to be a shadow? Even believing in awareness is a shadow. What can I do? I can just slap it: 'Come on! Wake up from this waking up business!' 'Wake up from waking up!' 'Wake up from being awake!' Because what you are is never never awake. And there is never any experience of awakeness, what you call awakeness. It's not even awakeness.

Q: Is there a solid state, within that the moments are taking place...

K: Nothing takes place. In that there are no places, nothing takes place, there is no here and now, there is not even this moment – whatever you can imagine is not there. It is the absolute absence of any presence of any imaginary idea or not idea, or any sensational experiencer. It is the absolute absence of any presence – that's the only Presence, which has no presence, which is Presence. So the presence you can experience is already one too many. It's not too many, but where the presence starts you end. Where the experience of presence starts, what is the absolute Presence ends. Because the presence of a realizer, the presence of the seer, is already second hand. So the presence of the purest I, the notion of I, the witness I, even the witness I, is a shadow of what you are. You are neither the witness, nor the witnessing, nor what can be witnessed. You are that what is That. But that doesn't know That. But the witness, the knower, whatever the knower knows or doesn't know, can never deliver that. So the knower which is different from what he is knowing or not knowing or creating or not creating, can never become That. Because he is already That. He is not different from it. There is no becoming it. You are the seer which is not different from what it seen, in nature. But that is darkness for itself. So whatever is experienced is a dream for what you are. But still is not different from what you are. The only dream is that you try to find yourself in that what you imagine, and that makes you an imagined poor me. There is a misery of imagination, imagining that you can be imagined. And then you are in that pitiful I. Then you cry about yourself. That's the joke! The Almighty, that what is absolute Energy, feeling powerless. And you can not avoid it. You are even in the experience of being powerless that what you are. Because that will happen. This is one way of experiencing yourself. Experiencing yourself as someone who is born and now has a body and all of that, and all of that moment by moment is there. But I deny totally that by that experience of birth someone is born. No one is ever born and nothing is ever born. And Life is never born, and you are That. So by no experience you have lost something and now you cannot gain it back. So what can I do?

Q: To cognize something you need a cognizer?

K: It needs a cognizer.

Q: But you are saying it's prior to cognizing? And it's wrong even to say 'you are that' because there is no you in that?

K: There is no me and there is no you, there is no one who can claim to be that. Because there is no claimer in it. In that absolute ownership, being what is, there is no one who owns it. That's why: Who is witnessing the witness? Who is seeing the seer? That what is the absolute Seer has to be already there to see the seer. So the I of the I has to already be there before the I can be experienced.

Q: That's why it is the Absolute?

K: That's the Absolute which can never gain or lose anything. Absolutely. Because it is already what is. It cannot get more, or less. And as you are that, any moment you realize your-self. The next is just a realization, but there is no way that you can realize that what is realizing itself in that realization. And there is no need for it. Never demands any realization. And that what demands to get real is unreal, that's all. That what you are is never hungry. And the restaurant that offers you this buffet of realization doesn't have anything to offer. Your satisfaction is your nature. But you cannot get more satisfied by any of this - whatever experiences. And only that what thinks it's hungry can get satisfied. But you were never hungry, that's the problem. You cannot find anyone who is hungry, for anything. You can find a body who is hungry, you can find a mind who is hungry, you can find a phantom who is hungry to become real. That you can find. But you can never find that what is what you are in one of that.

Q: There is no need to find?

K: That's what I say. As you have never lost what you are, you don't have to gain it back. But still I say there is an experience of forgetting. But in the experience of forgetting there is no one who forgot himself.

Q: So it doesn't matter?

K: It didn't matter in the first place. In forgetting no one forgets. Because you cannot forget that you exist. Because that there can be forgetting and one who forgets, you have to exist. And then there is a remembering of the forgetting. So as there is a forgetting there is an opposite of remembering. But in forgetting no one forgets and in remembering no one remembers. So still forgetting happens, and remembering happens. There is this 'I am who?' and then 'Who am I?' But by the 'I am who?' no one went out and by the 'Who am I?' no one goes back. So you never went out, you cannot go home. But still you have an experience of going out. But by the experience of going out no one went out. And by the experience of going home no one goes home. There was never anyone who went out. Of what? You exist, and even to say 'I don't know' you have to know what you don't know. Even if you say 'I am not', you have to be. That's Ramakrishna's basic thing, even that you can claim not to be, you have to be. And that absolute Existence is in spite of all your whatever. But to suffer about oneself, that's the dream. That's really ignorance. Come on! It's a joke! This is really like a comedy, the Divine suffering about the Divine. But it happens. Look at it! You cannot avoid it. Even that experience can not be avoided. But even by that misery you can not find a me. There is an experience of misery, but who is miserable in misery? You have to say 'me'. But the me, what is the me? Part of the misery. The misery starts with the me in a miserable circumstance. The whole scenery is miserable. Because there is a me, because there is separation, there is mind, time, and all of that is misery. And that's the way you realize yourself. Or that's the way Reality is realizing itself. As an experiencer who is different from what he is experiencing. From a lover who is different from his beloved. And that's misery, and there is passion. Because out of misery there comes passion, to get out of the misery. So you are always moment by moment passionate enough to try to get out of it. But you cannot find any compassion in it. Where is the compassion? How can there be compassion in two? In that imaginary separation, in this love affair, how can there be compassion? When the lover is different from the beloved, how can there be compassion? And when there is no lover and no beloved there is compassion, but no one has it. There is compassion, your nature, but compassion can not be owned. It's an inexhaustible compassion, never never there. But that relative pity you show to others is only pity. When there is a difference between you and others you can only show pity, because you pity yourself. And when there is one who pities himself and pities others, where is the compassion in it? Impossible! So even a teacher is pitiful. Even a teacher is pitiful. Even the master knowing a master, being a master, is a pitiful master. He has to face his master first maybe, to get rid of his master. And then out of that pitiful master having pitiful disciples - my Goodness! What a pity. And then you expect out of that pity bliss. Ananda. That Ananda comes out of that what? Misery? You expect Ananda in misery? So you always look in the wrong place. You can only look in wrong places. And I am sitting here: be happy that you can only find wrong places and wrong findings. Wrong, wrong, wrong, wrong, wrong. Wrong looking, wrong finding, wrong not-finding – this neti-neti – I love it! Neither in this way nor in that way nor in whatever way, you can attain what you are. Be happy! Not that you don't have to be happy, that you don't even know happiness. The happiness that can be known is a shit happiness. No one needs it. And be happy that there was never anyone who was realized. No on ever realized his true nature. Because there is no bloody true nature, because even the idea of true nature is false. True nature! Fuck it all! Sorry. Am I sorry?

Q: No!

Q: You just realized you are in India, that's all!

Q: You are really showing a mirror to us.

Karl: Yes, I can only reflect. I never doubt what this is speaking. It is always wrong. No one can doubt that what can be said more than that what I am. Just by being what I am. So I don't need anyone who doubts that what I say because this one doubts it already more than anyone else can doubt it. So this doubtlessness - whatever comes out of this doubtlessness is doubting. So the doubtlessness producing doubts, because that what is doubtlessness can not be produced. So what? Does is make you different? You can only spit out what is not what you are. Because what you are can not be spat out. There is no 'core-splitting honesty'. Who needs that? There is only 'core-spitting honesty'.

So what about your consciousness? I always like that! 'I work on my consciousness'. Or does consciousness work on you? Undecided, hmm? Neither! I think.

Q: The problem is that everything I will say may sound nice for a split second, and then after you respond it turns into shit, and what you say sounds so on target. It sounds like suddenly it becomes transparent. And all I come out with from the relative point of view sounds like shit.

K: It has to, because you want to grab it, you want to have it. So you make it shit, immediately, when you want to own it. You make out of that what I say, which never is claimed by anyone, just by you claiming it, shit. You are the master of shit. For sure. Because you want to have it. For yourself. You make it shit. You make it something that can be owned. You make some understanding your understanding. Then that understanding becomes shit. Because only a shit master needs some understanding. Understanding talking, understanding listening, there is no one who claims to have listened or stores it somewhere. There is no need of storing it. I don't have to think before I speak, for sure not. I could not even try. I am much too lazy for that. You think that you think before you think. But you think before you think that you think before you think. Shit happens. So even if it's a split second after you think that you thought what you thought, it is still you thinking. Thinking, thinking, thinking. That's claiming. The collector. And what can be collected, what can it be? Can that what is life be collected by someone? Can that what is the treasure itself be collected? Owned? All this collection of so precious understandings and deep insights is what? Not worth more than a fart in the wind, for what you are? It stinks for a while but then it's gone. So this little me is like a fart, coming out of the Absolute. And the fart stinks for a while, maybe for 50 years, 80 years, whatever, but the stinker, which is just like a little smell, will be gone one day. But the Tastelessness, the Smell-lessness of your Nature, which is the origin of all the little smells, stinking stinkers, this Tastelessness can never be tasted in that. So your Nature is tastelessness, you cannot taste what you are. So you are Tastelessness. And whatever you taste, the taster, is already a taste. And whatever the taster is tasting is tasting bitter, compared to what you are. That's why they say you are the Sweetness itself. Whatever the taster is tasting is bitter compared to the Tastelessness you are, which can never be tasted by itself. So that absolute Tastelessness, the absolute Taste, of any absence of anyone who tastes or doesn't taste anything, that's the Sweetness of your Nature. That's the Sweetness itself. But you can never experience it, because whatever you experience is second hand. It's just a bitterness. It's bitter compared to what you are. Because all of that is bitter-field, the whole realization is bitter compared to the Sweetness you are. Any moment of experience, like every sip of coffee, whatever, a sunset, is not beauty, it is a reflexion of beauty. It's not different from it, but the Beauty you are, thank God, can never be experienced in any reflection of it. So enjoy it. Enjoy that you don't have to enjoy yourself in anything. And the joy you are can not be found or lost in any experience. I don't say don't enjoy it. I just say enjoy whatever. Because all of that is what you are. But the beauty you are can never be experienced by any of that in any relative sense. But the beauty you are is always there. The absolute experience that you are is never never. And that experience can never get more or less by any of this - whatever it is – Vedanta. I like Vedanta. But again, only because no one needs it. You cannot avoid it. But no one needs it. So if you cannot avoid it, what to do? That's the 'what to do'. You tried maybe everything to avoid to realize yourself, because you know there is a passion, there is suffering in whatever trying to know yourself. But you cannot avoid it. So there is an absolute final understanding: you cannot avoid yourself. So what? What to do? That peace can not be gained. It was always there. But by that understanding that peace can not be found, peace, which was already there, just is there. It was always there, but your attention just doesn't go out anymore by expecting something. The expecting may drop. But in spite of what you try to do in front of it. And that is like the Mahabharata in the hell, that this 'who cares' happens. And then there is no avoider anymore. And in no avoider there is no hell. There is only hell because you want to avoid something. You want to avoid yourself. But this is as much yourself as the highest superior consciousness as awareness or anything. This. Not more and not less as that. This is not something new. It was always like that. Moment by moment. Next, next, next,

next. Frame by frame. And you are framed by what you are. But who cares to be framed by what one is? You are absolutely framed. You are absolutely imprisoned to be what you are. And this is what you are. This is your absolute prison. And you are the one and only prisoner of your own imaginary prison. So what? You are self-guilty that you are imprisoned – by what? By your own imagination. Ha ha. And you can not get out of it because no one can get out of an imagination, because no one is in an imagination.

Q: 'This is That' sounds better than 'I am That'.

K: It sounds more neutral. It's like whatever your preference is. If that sounds better and you relax, why not? Normally they say 'I am that I am'. That's always missing. 'I am that I am' is more like 'I am that what is the I am'. But I am not the I am. To say 'I am That' something is maybe missing. So you have to say 'I am that I am'. So you are that what is the I am. But that what is the I am doesn't know any I am. So if God would pronounce that what is God, he would maybe say - I don't agree, because what is God doesn't even know any God who could say something - but if, just imagining, like a pointer, he would say 'I am that I am'.

Q: That is what is in the bible.

K: Yes, that's why an imaginary God would say, by understanding that he is an imagination, he would say 'I am that I am'. This is like the most consciousness can realize. Which is already a dream. Because consciousness is Vedanta. That what is - there is no consciousness. Consciousness is dream. Consciousness is already the realization of Reality. It's not different from Reality, but that what is Knowledge is neither conscious nor unconscious. It doesn't even know consciousness, never needs consciousness. It never needs to be to be.

Q: And it is written that the question was 'What is your name?' not what you are. 'I am what I am' is the name of God. It points to the duality already.

K: If God would define that what God is, he would say 'I am that what is the definer, but I am not the definer'. If he would say that. So that what is the definer is not the definer. 'I am that what is the I am'. Amazing. It's never finished.

Q: It appears that I am, so maybe..

K: It's all 'maybe'. And that there can be a 'maybe', there has to be that which is not maybe. So moment by moment even that there is a maybe, a doubtful doubter, that doubtlessness has to be there. It is always there. So maybe maybe, or maybe not. No I like this. It came - I don't know why it comes this Advaita, and then Advaita realizing itself as Vedanta. But it's just so natural, so simple. That what is, knows no second, is realizing itself in all these experiences of seconds. But it doesn't make itself second. Nothing gets lost in the way it's realizing itself. It's still no second. There is still that what is Advaita but in realization it becomes Vedanta. And Vedanta is not Advaita. But Vedanta is not different from Advaita and Advaita is not different from Vedanta. In nature they are not two. But still Advaita is only Advaita in the absolute absence of even the idea of Advaita. And when Vedanta starts, there starts the idea of Advaita. And then it creates these oneness ideas and all of that. One without a second and all that can be said comes then out of that Vedanta. And all that belongs to Vedanta. And what you are was never concerned about any of these concepts. Never any clarification of any Vedanta teaching or books - the whole Mahabharata is very nice, but still, it is only beautiful in itself because no one needed it, ever. Out of just pure entertainment it happens. Not out of any need or necessity whatever is is. Bible, Mahabharata, the whole Koran, is just there out of joy. These are all expressions of joy. The joy to be that what never needs to enjoy itself, that Joylessness of your nature, enjoying itself in infinite joyful or not so joyful experiences. In heaven and hell you experience what you are. And no way out of it. You can not miss one little aspect of realization of experience. You are the absolute Reality, Life itself, which has to realize itself in every possible and impossible way. You can not miss one little pain. Or one little comfort, or discomfort. So even this now sitting here, like trying to know oneself, you cannot miss. You have to experience yourself as a disciple or a seeker of truth. You cannot avoid it. No way out. Enlightenment, whatever it means, doesn't mean that from that moment on you are never suffering again, you are never unhappy. Enlightenment is actually the total annihilation of one who is or is not. It is actually the absolute drop of the unenlightened one. And then what you are remains. But this is not one who is enlightened or not enlightened. There is not even an idea of light anymore. And that is Light itself. The absolute absence of anyone who knows or doesn't know what one is. It is not one who now says 'I am nothing'.

Q: Because in deep deep sleep I can't say I am nothing.

K: Yes, there is no one left who claims anything.

Q: And in deep deep sleep all this means nothing.

K: It doesn't even know anything, not even itself. And now you know yourself and to know yourself as that which doesn't have to know itself and never needs to know itself. It's so natural. That's your natural state. To be what you are in whatever is and is not. You cannot not be. As you are in deep deep sleep what you are. I always like this pointer. It's not new, but I always like it. And that's really relaxing, because you don't have to be authentic, you don't have to be original to be what you are.

Q: You don't have to know anything or recognize anything or realize anything.

K: But the main thing you don't have to be original, you don't have to invent a new saying or something, you can repeat yourself infinitely and it's always new and fresh. It's always this freshness of what you are, absolute freshness. You can only repeat yourself, but it's always fresh, because the next moment you cannot even remember you said it. There is no one who remembers anything. So whatever you say is fresh the moment it's said. And being in this memory shit, you remember only shit and by shit you compare shit. And then you are in the comparison of shit.

Q: Me I am outside and I take it seriously.

K: And now you want to be inside?

Q: No.

Q: It sounded funny.

Q: Ok.

K: It's never ok. Don't lie to me. You don't mean it.

Q: There are doubts.

K: For what?

Q: For my understanding of what is.

K: There is your understanding?

Q: That's the doubt.

K: Yes, we can doubt it. It's amazing that one can say 'it's my understanding'. It's actually unbelievable. What an idea! It has to be demolished. Or this poor me sitting somewhere 'I don't understand'. Still claiming that he understands. It's his understanding that he doesn't understand. Who do you think you are that you don't understand? That's the devil, this arrogant me, it's always a devil who claims something. He claims to understand or he claims not to understand. Both is arrogance. First he claims he has done it and then he claims he has not done it. Ha ha ha ha. And by not having done it he can remain this little devil who has not done anything. 'I am not it'. 'I didn't do it'. And for sure whatever can be said will be taken by the devil in his advantage. Just to confirm his relative existence. Because he needs it. He needs moment by moment a little weight. And he always uses grammar to put some grams on his so-called shoulders, just to stay on earth. He needs every dogma, every grammar, every word, otherwise he is so fleeting. Any moment you don't give attention to it it is already gone. And then he has to remember instantly what was the moment before, he is really freaking out if he cannot remember. It's like a black hole. Like when you are driving for hours on the highway and sometimes for one hour no one is driving. As normal. No one drives anyway. And suddenly you wake up: 'Who was driving!' You freak out! 'Next time I will be more aware. I will moment by moment be the driver. It was really scary. Who was driving'? Everyone had that experience that there is no driver. But then the fear starts, and the fear is me. 'Next time I will be more attentive. More awake. Drink more coffee'.

Now she looks like Onassis (about someone in the audience with sunglasses). No, she looks like the Indian Prime Minister. People are always amazed that I hit on nationalities. You have to slap anyone who thinks he is American or German. Or Indian. Or universal. Or cosmopolitan. All this esoteric bullshit. Or anyone who thinks he is not German or Indian. Because that happened in Poona. All the Germans came and burned their passports. 'We are not Germans anymore'. 'From now on I am not German anymore'. Ha ha! They became Sannyasins. This idea that taking another name makes you free or takes your story away. Then you just create another one, a no-story. But for that I like it. Existence makes these Vedanta pointers that you think you try your best but it doesn't deliver anything. You really give your best and you believed in it because the trap was made totally perfectly. That something can be done, and that by dynamic meditation you can become like dynamite and know yourself. And that by having sex every night you can free yourself. Ha ha. You just get exhausted, that's all. You get bored by the next and the next one. And then they think if you get bored by the body experience then you go to the higher spirit. That's all Vedanta.

Q: But many of the meditation techniques are aimed to exhaust the you.

K: Yes, but that's already false. That's the Vedanta. That by teaching you can exhaust the ignorance. Nice idea. Nice to try. But if you ask me, thank God it's futile. Imagine existence could be controlled or achieved by a technique. What kind of existence would it be, which could be achieved? And one could be the chief of it. 'I am the chief of existence'. Like an awakened one sitting somewhere 'I am the chief of existence. And now you are all my Indians'. This is the beauty of emptiness. That's the beauty that Beauty can never be expressed. And whatever beauty is expressed is merely a shadow of Beauty. The same with Knowledge. I like these shadows, as they are empty. They can neither make me more or less as I am. The knowledge that I am can never be gained or lost by one of these shadow experiences. So what? And the shadow knowing more or less and the shadow taking himself as a German, ok, you are German. You are a germ anyway. And one day the germ will be gone. And something else comes. The next never stops. The realization never ends. As you never end, the realization never ends. So the next comes. It's like Nisargadatta when he was dying: now with this body organism all the tendencies go, and there is still no one who cares. Good pointer.

Q: Then they speak about the Maha-Samadhi, after this goes.

K: But Maha-Samadhi is already there. It didn't happen. That's why I like it - Maha-Samadhi can not be attained. That's why they put Ramana in a sausage, mummify him and think when they walk around him they gain something. They think by making a race around a sausage they can gain themselves. All that is Vedanta. Why not? I like it. It's like a truth race. Who is the fastest, who is the slowest, who is the most serious walker. Pradakshina, Pradakshina, Pradakshina. You turn around your self. And if Ramana is a sausage you turn around a sausage. What else is this body? A sausage machine. You came out of sausage, and you will become a sausage.

People always ask 'what do you think about unknotting the karmic knots? That's Vedanta. Your tendencies - unknotting them by techniques, by meditation or something. You come to me, we are doing the opposite! I put so many knots in your bloody brain that you cannot even imagine that they ever will be gone. It's all knotty-knotty. Because succeeding by unknotting knots makes the first knot, that there is one who has knots, stronger and stronger. No,

I go the opposite way. I make so many knots for you, maybe there is a point of giving up even trying to unknot them. Because then laziness is there, your nature. The laziest of the laziest. So that you can even go from the relative to the not relative oneness, and then even to awareness, you are succeeding in something. That makes you even more trapped in that. It's not less trapped. One who claims to have awareness or is now established in choiceless awareness, is in a bigger trap. It's even more difficult to get him out of that trap. There is one who feels not so bad. And out of that nice dream of being awareness - who wants to wake up? Who wants to drop that? This here, here plays the music, here is the entertainment! And if you cannot be here what you are, and you need that comfort of awareness, who can that only be? Only the devil needs the comfort of being in heaven. That what is relativity, that what is this, never needs to get out of it, and can not get out of it. And who makes these differences? So whatever advantage is a disadvantage. Any advantage. And whatever advantage comes by understanding is a misunderstanding. Because the advantage to be what you are, which never needed any advantage, is always there and never needs any understanding. And any advantage which comes by understanding is relative. And just feeding the me.

Q: What about the advantage I feel about knowing this concept about not getting an advantage?

K: But I didn't say that! You repeat it, but I never said it. I said 'having or not having an advantage is part of the phantom'. That advantage which never needs any advantage which never knows any advantage is always there. And by no having or not having an advantage it can be attained. So that advantage of a me not needing an advantage, is one advantage too many he doesn't need. So even not needing an advantage - that advantage is one advantage too many. So that advantage - the Absolute, which never knows or doesn't know itself even, the total absence of any need of advantage, cannot be attained by one who then sees an advantage in having no advantage. That's the trick.

Q: So therefore either getting a feeling of 'this is an advantage' or 'this is not an advantage', is irrelevant?

K: Absolute irrelevant. It's always one who discriminates.

Q: What else Karl? 'No way out'. 'One too many'. 'Too late', or 'too early'. What else?

K: Shit master. Wherever there is a master there is a master of shit. The nature of shit is chit. But the chit cannot be found in shit. Nothing else.

Q: That's why it's always 'forget it right away, whatever is said'?

K: I didn't say that. You can remember it or not, it doesn't matter. I never say 'forget what I say'. I never said anything, how can you forget it? You see, that's the way it happens! 'Karl said I should forget what he says'. I never said it.

Q: I don't know if it was you. I heard that.

K: Don't defend it! 'I heard it. It's not my fault'.

Q: You see all the defense mechanisms instantly!

K: Yes, you are a warrior. You defend. You want to stand guard. You are a guard for whatever you know because you are in the military. It's a 'me-litary'.

Q: Yes, I am governed by Mars.

K: You are what? Excusing herself because her stars are like bullshit! 'I am only an asshole because my mars is in taurus'. Fantastic!

Q: 'My mars is on my ass'.

Q: What about defending our dead master?

K: It's all dead masters. Dead masters, dead disciples, all dead. There are only dead masters and dead disciples. I know it's not so easy for one who believes in a master and needs a master, to say all masters are dead. But I have to say it. Any master from the beginning is dead. Dead knowledge. Dead master. Dead disciple. Dead understanding. But that's the beauty of it. None of that can reach That. Never ever anyone reached That. Never anyone lost That. That's the main thing. That never lost anything. So there never was anyone lost in anything. And now someone reading something – out of that one who never lost anything? Ramana always talked about the spider - the spider will always spin, spinning a network of consciousness. He even called consciousness a phantom, a spider. Always spinning a network and trying to catch itself, and by understanding it cannot catch itself in its own net, just withdrawing the net. And the instant it is withdrawn, it spins again. Never ending spinning and withdrawing. Spinning and withdrawing. And only consciousness can be identified or non-identified. Being identified relative consciousness, being not identified cosmic consciousness. Only consciousness makes a difference. So only consciousness is a phantom. That is Vedanta. Consciousness, Vedanta, being identified, not-identified. Teaching consciousness being identified is wrong, being non-identified right. Impersonal good, personal bad. That can only happen in relative consciousness, which is already an imagination.

Q: Consciousness is always duality.

K: The idea of consciousness creates duality. God knowing himself there is consciousness. He is conscious to exist, there is consciousness. Already there is duality.

Q: And the root is the desire.

K: Out of that duality, the doubtful God, comes the doubter. And out of the doubter comes all the doubting and what can be doubted. The false is already there, that God can know himself. God can be conscious about that what is consciousness. Or God. There is two. Consciousness being conscious about consciousness is two consciousness. Already the dream starts. So consciousness waking up, becoming aware to be conscious, or to be the purest consciousness, already is separation. There Vedanta starts. There consciousness starts to teach itself. It becomes its own master and disciple, it's own lover and beloved. All that realization happens by that. But by none of that realization it can know itself because of this precious consciousness. Sounds good. No one needs it. So precious. So powerful. But powerful in what? Can it create something? Can it destroy something? I am always waiting that lightening hits me when I say God is powerless, cannot touch what is what I am. And that what I am never needs any God. And never knows any God. God oh God. Creator.

Q: What you said about the impersonal and the personal always being part of the dream, but the impersonal is preferable because there is less suffering than in the personal.

K: Yes, there is suffering and no suffering. And for sure you have a preference which is no suffering.

Q: Sure. But it's still in the dream, and you can't get out of the dream.

K: Yes, and when there is no suffering, the opposite is suffering. So out of no suffering, it will go back to suffering.

Q: So how to be not in the picture?

K: The only absolute solution is being the picture. And the picture doesn't know any picture. Being out of the picture is still part of the picture. The picture doesn't know any picture. And by being the picture the picture cannot suffer about the picture. But you trying to get out of the picture, you place yourself in the picture.

Q: When you say the picture doesn't know any picture, are you talking about being so totally present in the picture that...

K: There is no need of total presence!

Q: So what does it mean?

K: Just to be that what never knows itself, in anything. Neither knowing or not knowing anything. It doesn't mean anything. There is no 'me' in it, and there is no meaning. Only the me needs a me-ning.

Q: There is no personal knowing...

K: There is neither personal nor impersonal. That what is the impersonal doesn't know any impersonal and that what is the personal doesn't know any personal. And that what knows the impersonal is still personal. So that what claims 'now I experience myself impersonal' - Oh! Who is experiencing himself impersonal? And takes it personal? And thinks the personal is better or worse than the impersonal? Who defines what is finer?

Q: So what to do with this 'who'?

K: I don't know. You cannot kill it because it's not there. You only give it life because you think it's too much. For who? It plays two. One is too much for the other. But the one and the other are both phantoms. One phantom confirming the other phantom. And one phantom saying to the other phantom 'without you phantom I would be as a phantom better off'. That is a schizophrenic me saying the me without the me would be better off. So the me tries to kill the me because the me imagines without the me the me would be better off. That keeps him running. That's the loving-caring me. The lover who thinks 'if I would be in unconditional love, if I just could accept my beloved totally, I would be in the best of impersonal loves'. So he makes a condition of this love. So impersonal would be better than personal. 'If I would just accept my beloved as the beloved is. Me'. And maybe there is even a moment of oneness with the beloved, an acceptance that everything is all right, and everything is perfect, but even that is fleeting. Just the opposite of not perfect. So the perfect love is still imperfect. Because there is one who needs a perfect love. The impersonal acceptance of the beloved. So you maybe reach that by whatever. And then? Amen. Then there is a man, one man too many. A-men. Or woman. Two men too many. Because there is more man in a woman than can ever be in a man. It's like you are puzzled, because you want to find the last puzzle for the absolute Puzzle. You are so puzzled because you imagine you get out of the puzzle and then you look at the puzzle and there is always one piece missing. And you are always wondering what is missing? And you are always looking at that puzzle and you know, you always see something missing. And you always want to find it somewhere. You want to re-puzzle it, you want to rearrange the whole puzzle, and still there is one piece missing. Even if it is complete, the total thing, something is missing, the puzzle is not complete. And then suddenly, by whatever event, you get totally sucked into the puzzle, and there is no one puzzled anymore. There was never any problem. The puzzle is always the puzzle and never is puzzled about the puzzle. You are only puzzled because you see the puzzle. And the moment you see the puzzle you are out of the puzzle. And then you are puzzled by the puzzle. So every night you get sucked into the puzzle, and you are the puzzle in the deep deep sleep, and who is puzzled in being the puzzle? No one. And every morning you step out of the puzzle and look at the puzzle and then you are puzzled by the puzzle. Then you try to arrange the puzzle again the way you like the puzzle. But every night that puzzler gets totally sucked into the puzzle, and then the puzzle is just a puzzle. Very simple. Every morning you just imaginarily stepping out of the puzzle and you become separate from the world. And every night you have no energy anymore to be the puzzler so automatically you are the puzzle. Because your imagination makes you so exhausted. Then every morning you step out again. Because you are fresh. You are exploring again: 'Yesterday I could not puzzle it, but today I will make it'. You promise yourself every morning 'today I will make it'. 'Today I will meditate 10 hours about my puzzle'. You even try to sink into the puzzle. But trying to sink into the puzzle you place yourself outside of the puzzle. You want to go deeper into the puzzle but trying to go deeper into the puzzle you are out of the puzzle, you are part of the puzzle. And when you are part of the puzzle you are puzzled by the puzzle. Fantastic puzzle. What else can this little puzzle do? He wants to be the puzzler. And sometimes he is even achieving that he is the puzzler himself, the creator, he creates all the puzzle: 'I am the center of the universe, from me everything comes. I am the origin. I am real and everything else is just my imagination. My imagination. Everything is illusion. Not me'. So it goes on and on and on. So this realization, this Vedanta, these variations of ignorance, continue. And whatever is different from something else is ignorance.

Whatever is Vedanta, whatever can be experienced, is too late. Even the purest awareness, the purest I, is too late. It's just a dream that you can find yourself in your own realization. That's too much.

Q: Can the absolute express itself or is it too late?

K: Did I say anything?

Q: Who can say that the first thought...

K: What 'the first thought'? The thought is already after the thinker, the first imaginary potential I, there is not even a thought.

Q: Can not be what is...

K: How can it be what is? Because it is different from what comes then.

Q: Because...

K: Because there is a because. Because that has a cause it cannot be real.

Q: Why does it have a cause?

K: Is it always there?

Q: No.

K: You see. How can it be real? Reality can not be sometimes, sometimes not. And that awareness is sometimes, sometimes not. Where is that awareness in deep deep sleep? If it would be real it should be uninterrupted. Only the Existence that you are, that Knowledge that you are, is even in deep deep sleep. Because without that Knowledge that you are there could not be any rising of any awareness I. So what you are is Causelessness. And that what has a cause is off-course. The cause doesn't need any cause. Only what is off-course needs a cause, and then needs to find the cause.

Q: Is that the play, is that the entertainment?

K: It's a realization.

Q: But the absolute doesn't need that, it's just...

K: It has to! In spite of needing or not. It's doing it, look at it! It's no question of needing or not needing. It has to, because it cannot otherwise. It's there. Buddha called it 'divine accident', it happened. The divine woke up. So now it started to realize itself. Now trying not to realize itself is too late. Now trying not to realize yourself is part of realization. It's too late. It's all too late.

Q: Can you say that the absolute is pure energy?

K: You can say whatever. You just said it! You can say the absolute is pure underwear. You can say it. It means nothing. It doesn't make the absolute known. You can say it, the absolute doesn't care. You can call it a cup of tea. The absolute pure cup of tea. It never minds to be called anything. You can call it shit, it doesn't mind. Imagine the absolute would mind if I call it shit. I could not even pronounce it. It never minds anything. But whatever you call it for sure is not it. But it's even not not it. So even to say it's not it, is not it. So what else can you say?

Q: So it's like when zero was created or the concept of infinity was created...

K: No, zero came to know zero. Zero woke up, became aware of zero. So there was zero zero. The zero of the zero. And there are two zeros. That's the beginning. And out of zero comes one. I like this 108 – zero is like a zero, and when you turn it around from the side it is one, and if you bent it it becomes the eight, the infinite. It's only zero – taking the oneness and the infinite – but it's all zero.

Q: Zero was created...

K: It was not created!

Q: Ok. The concept of zero was created as a reference point, but really no one can say what a zero is. Mathematicians can not say what a zero is.

K: They can say what a zero is: a zero is the absence of any presence of any number or no number. I can say it. If I can say it, scientists can say it. One can say it.

Q: It doesn't capture it.

K: I capture it. It can be said. What can not be said?

Q: Anything can be said.

K: Who tells you that you cannot capture it?

Q: I know.

K: Just by being what you cannot not be you capture it absolutely. You can just not capture it relatively, that's all. So you can neither say you can or you can not. You can not not know yourself. You absolutely know yourself by being what you are. You cannot not be what you are. So absolutely you know yourself. The only thing you can say, you can never know yourself relatively because there are not two. For relative knowledge there would have to be two, that's all. But you can neither say you know or don't know yourself. You can only say whatever you know in any relative way is not that what you are. But even that you can say 'I don't know what I am', you have to know what you are. You have to be that.

Q: You are saying that being what you are is being That.

K: Be what you cannot not be. And that is knowledge. That's absolute Knowledge you can not not know. You are that Knowledge and that's absolute Knowledge. But there is no knower in it, that's the main thing. No knower and nothing what can be known. And the moment there is a knower, there is relative knowledge, because only the knower is relatively known. And whatever can be known is not delivering that Knowledge you are because you never lost it. So it never needs to be delivered. You cannot regain it. As you have not lost it. So you have an experience of a loser, the knower, which is the loser, and then trying to gain knowledge. But whatever the loser-knower is gaining is relative knowledge, and will never make the relative knower into that what is Knowledge. Thank God, the relative phantom-knower can never become what is the absolute Knowledge, because already in his nature he is absolute Knowledge.

He is not different to it. So even as a relative seeker you can not become what is the seeker, because already the seeker is that what is the seeker. And being that what is the seeker is knowledge. So the nature of the seeker is knowledge. That you can even be a seeker you have to exist. You have to know that you exist. And that knowledge is uninterrupted. And then experiencing yourself as a seeker seeking what can be sought doesn't make you less or more. So no seeking has to stop for anyone. No seeking has to be dropped or no search has to be called off. All of that is Vedanta, all of that is relative teaching that something has to happen. It's more than easy to be the ease itself. But you cannot have it. You can not be at ease. You can never be at ease. That one who needs to be at ease, is a phantom. You are ease. And nothing is more easy than to be that what you are. And that is never never that what is ease. And that dis-ease of one who wants to be at ease is a disease. Whoever wants to be healthy must be sick. But you never became sick, how can you be cured? You are not any part of any purification game. You never know any pure and impure. It needs one who knows purity and impurity, and already that is fake. Thank God no one ever was and will ever be pure enough for that what he is. Never ever. So never ever anyone, by whatever he is doing or knowing, can know that what he is. In any relative way. But in another way, you can not not know yourself. You are That. What keeps you away from it? Nothing! Nothing can keep you away from you being what you are. No one can pull you out of what you are. No one can put you back. Not even your self. So only an imaginary self can be pulled out and put back into something. Only an imaginary knower claims to know something. What you are never needs to claim anything because it's already what is. There is no need for claiming. You can not get more or less as that. You are the absolute owner in that sense. By being that what is. And that can not be hungry for anything.

Q: I am exhausted. I don't know how you feel.

K: Imagine I would be exhausted! How can one be exhausted by talking about what one is?

Q: So how come this is exhausted?

K: Because you want to grab yourself. You are after yourself. You are already exhausted just by attempting to know yourself. How can knowledge exhaust itself? How can energy exhaust itself? How can meditation exhaust itself? A meditator can be exhausted by doing meditation. What an idea! 'I am going to meditate'. Just to say that! Ha ha! What a joke! One who claims that he can meditate.

Q: I don't know what meditation is.

K: You are meditation, you don't have to know it. Moment for moment realizing yourself. The experiencing of what you are is meditation, moment for moment. There is no moment without meditation. So you claiming not to know meditation, that's a joke. You are meditation. You are the Absolute meditating about what it is in whatever possible way. And there is no special way. It's just moment by moment the realization of what you are, which is meditation. And then it's even playing a meditator, making a special meditation. Even that is part of it. But not special. Even that special meditation is not a special meditation. It's just one aspect of meditation. But the next sip of coffee, the next breathing in and breathing out, the next whatever, is always that. Meditating about what you are. Experiencing being the experiencer, experiencing what is the experienced. There is no difference in all the experiences of differences. They don't make any difference. And any moment, only because you expect something coming out of that, you are suffering about being unfulfilled. And that's stupid. That's ignorance. Otherwise there is no ignorance. Suffering about yourself, that's ignorance. Suffering about the idea that you need to be fulfilled to be what you are. That creates this little sufferer. And it's always suffocated. Not getting enough air. Not getting enough anything. And then even that is meditation, imagine! Even that can not be different.

Ok. That was enough.

THERE IS NO BRIDGE

Q: I was interested in Maha-Shivratri. Could you explain a little bit more about Shivratri and how we understand it?

K: Me?

Q: How we in India interpret Shivratri as the union of Shiva and Parvati. How do you see it?

K: You can do it on the mundane level. Then there is Shiva, a man, who gets married to his beloved, and then they have a happy marriage. But normally the Shiva moon - Shiva marrying Parvati - is like Parvati and him dissolve into that what is beyond. To the darkness. To the no-moon. So Maha-Shivratri you celebrate the absence of a relationship between Shiva and Parvati.

Q: The absence?

K: Yes, there is no difference in nature between Shiva and Parvati. So in that absolute no-moon there is no husband and no wife. There is just Existence. There is just Nature. In the absence. And then the next is the next light of the moon, then the whole circle starts again. Then the relationship starts again, the relative love affair and all the drama starts. Until full moon, then the absolute ego is there, the Jiva. And then it declines again until the no-moon. Every month. So it is realizing itself in that light, but it is an artificial light. Then they go back to their natural state, and both dissolve into that what is their nature. That is the marriage actually, the idea of marriage, that the relationship dies. There is no one who relates to someone else. So both are that what they are, without any difference. And then they are realizing themselves again in differences. So then there is Shiva again, experiencer experiencing himself in all that.

Q: And this cycle keeps repeating.

K: Keeps on and on and on. Never ending. That's like the biggest pointer on the sky. Every month, the ego is blowing up, like the moon. The artificial light of the sun you see is an absolute ego. And then it declines again. And then, when it's the end of it, the absolute absence of any presence of any separation. And then the presence of separation starts again, and the whole drama starts again. And you cannot avoid it. So Shiva, not knowing Shiva, is Shiva. And there is no Pravati and there is no relationship. But then it starts to become the light of Shiva. And that is like Adam in Christianity, and then Eve, and then all this relative information comes out of it. Unavoidable. It's like the I and the 'I am'. The lingam and then the space, the yoni. It's always this trinity, which is the way you realize yourself. But reality is always beyond and prior to that. So every Shiva-moon Shiva dissolves into his own nature, not knowing Shiva. And then knowing Shiva again. And by knowing Shiva he creates the space and then the whole universe, and destroys it again just by declining again. So it's a wonderful symbol. I like it. It's a very nice theater every month.

Q: You mentioned some reality prior to Shiva.

K: Prior to the light of Shiva.

Q: Not prior to Shiva?

K: No. Shiva is Self, Shiva is Para Brahman. That what is Shiva is Shiva. But the light of Shiva, Shiva becoming aware of Shiva, then he becomes relative. A relative experience of light. He becomes aware of himself. Becoming aware of himself, being awake, that's the light of Shiva. But the light of Shiva is not Shiva. It's the light of Shiva. And then comes the space of Shiva and then the whole universe of Shiva. But that trinity, which is realization, is not Reality. It's not different. That's the way Shiva is realizing himself. But it's not that what is realizing itself. So it starts realizing itself as the light of Shiva. As being aware. And then 'I am'. And then whatever comes.

Q: So the light of Shiva is something like creation?

K: It's the first phenomenal experience.

Q: The first stage of creation.

K: The first stage of creation.

Q: Creation of time and space.

K: That's the beginning.

Q: So Reality is before that?

K: That what never starts and never ends, is prior, during, and beyond that experience. Prior simply means it is in spite of it. In spite of the presence of light, Reality is. In spite of it, not because. So the cause never needs any even being awake, or aware of itself. So it's not different. I don't say there is a difference in it. It's just your reality is already there before one who is realizing is there. So before an experiencer is there, that what is the experiencer is already there.

Q: Is Shiva a concept of human beings or is it something independent of human concepts?

K: It is a Self-made concept. Humans can never create any concept. A concept cannot create a concept. No, Shiva, the Self, whatever, starts to talk with itself. At first sight. Being aware there is a dialogue starting. I, then 'I am', and then what, or who. So it is always starting inquiring, and then by that he creates even an idea of himself. He is imagining himself. He gives himself a name,

Shiva. But only a Jiva gives himself this name, Shiva. But a Jiva is not different to Shiva. So whatever is, is Self. There is no one else to blame than that what is Self, and that is what you are. For anything. Whatever is, is Self.

Q: I was wondering whether Shiva and all these things are just a concept, some idea of humans.

K: No, human beings cannot create anything. What already is a creation cannot create something else. Everything is created by that Para Brahman, or Shiva, just starting to dream. You cannot blame anyone else. There is no concept in anything. Every experience, even now this world, are experiences of what you are. And the only concept is, the dream is, that you as an experiencer take yourself different from what you experience. That's the only dream.

Q: Is this an intuitive knowledge or is it something that has some basis in science?

K: The scientists they say they cannot find matter. So they created an idea of matter. But if you look for it, it's not there. But you have to exist even not to exist. Even that there can be no matter, you have to be that what you are. So it's like a total confirmation, moment by moment, even that you can not know yourself, you have to know yourself as That. This is not like what you can doubt. Even that you can doubt to doubt, you have to exist. Prior to the doubter. And beyond the doubtful I, you are. Because otherwise there could not even be a doubter doubting himself. Concept or not concept, I have no idea. I just ask anyone, whoever I meet, to meet myself, be what you cannot not be. And without that there would not even be a doubting, not even a concept could arise. Even the word concept cannot be there. Even that someone sees 'everything is a concept', only a concept can see there is only concept. So I have no idea. Only illusion would claim 'everything is illusion'. For me there is no such thing. But otherwise you can say, out of fear you can say, maybe the idea of God arises.

Q: Going back to science's idea of evolution, creation, the big bang and all that when the creation started. Do you find any parallel between the big bang and Shiva being prior to the creation?

K: Buddha called it the divine accident, that would be the big bang. The divine, Shiva, waking up, becoming aware to exist, that would be the big bang. But you cannot find it. Because for me even that big bang never started. That would be like making something the beginning of something, but for me Reality and realization is not two. So there was never any big bang. No evolution or anything. There is no before.

Q: What do you mean by Reality?

K: Reality is that what is this. Reality knows no difference. In the absolute absence of the word reality and any imaginary reality there is Reality. And there is no difference between Reality and realization for what is Reality. And now talking about what is Reality, you make it an image. You make it an object. And then it becomes a religion. The Reality religion. Or the Truth religion. And then you create all these religions about imaginary so-called images. And we can ask where they come from. In Buddhism they say the purest idea of existence creates fear. And out of that fear there is a creation of all possible ways out. Or compensations of that fear. And that is maybe what you can call humanity, or relative existence. A doubtful I creates doubtful images of doubtful Gods who maybe can save him or help him. But all of that is realization. All of that can not be avoided. This is the nature of misery. The nature of one who exists is in the misery of being different from what he is. And that is unbearable. Because it is unbearable, you automatically look for your nature. Any moment you are not what you are, you are missing what you are. And by that missing you create an image about what you could be. So you start to imagine what you could be. And you start to imagine how it would be if you would be what you are. Automatically. So any moment you are not what you are, you are dead. And by being dead you want to become again that what is not even born. What has not even an idea of life and death. So that's the inbuilt seed of anyone. This longing. And I can only sit here: 'The misery cannot stop. Any experience is misery'. Misery of the experiencer being different from what he is experiencing. That's the misery of being different from something else. That's called a me. Just like a me which is different from something else. There is me and others. All of that. Instantly there is separation. And that misery cannot be killed. It cannot be avoided.

Q: Misery is illusion?

K: Misery is the illusion that the experiencer is different from what he is experiencing. But not the world is illusion. Only that illusion that you take yourself as someone who is different from something else. That's the only illusion we can talk about. That Shiva becomes a Jiva who is different from his nature. And then he is like a human, Jiva. Then he tries to become Shiva again. But any moment he tries to become Shiva, he confirms that there is one who needs to become Shiva. But that is an illusion too. You cannot become what you are. By whatever you do. So whatever you try to become what you are is like a contradiction. You confirm one who needs to be what he is. It's a fantastic trap. And absolute trap. You are trapped by yourself. You are trapped by your absolute intelligence. And the intelligence of what-is is always more intelligent than you think you are. This intelligence will always create another trap in front of you. Another image, another God, another truth, another reality, and deeper, and understanding – all of these traps are made by yourself. And no one else can make that trap so very well that you can step into that trap. And the absolute trap is that you fall in love with yourself. You were falling in love, at first sight, with yourself. And now you have a love affair, which is unavoidable. So you become a lover, and you have a beloved. A beloved outside, or a beloved inside. Doesn't matter. There is one who wants to know his beloved, himself. And by wanting to know him you make yourself different from your beloved. This little intention, wanting to know yourself, coming out of a doubtful I who thinks I have to know myself to be myself - an absolute trap. So an accident happened, you fall in love with yourself. Love at first sight. Love at first being aware, the first purest mirror, you fall in love with that mirror of yourself. And then you started doubting that mirror. Because it is the nature of doubtfulness. You are an image. And any moment you are an image, you doubt the image. And then you start all this seeking. Inquiring. So what to do?

Q: So the million dollar question is: how does one know what one is. Who am I?

K: Yes, and I would say, how can you not know what you are?

Q: The question is, can you know?

K: Yes. But not relatively. Absolutely you know already what you are by being it. That what you are is Knowledge, and can not not know Knowledge, because it is Knowledge. But that one now who tries to know himself, is imagining Knowledge. So whatever he gains is imaginary knowledge. And not what he is. But even that that can happen, you have to know yourself. You cannot not know yourself. You have to pretend to be outside of yourself. You have to pretend to be awake. There is a pretending it. An imagination happens. You have to imagine yourself as one who is awake. So there is a little effort there, of dreaming. And then out of that you think 'now I have to make more efforts'. So it's like a wish happened, and now you have the wish for wishlessness again. But the origin of any wish is wishlessness. There is a wishlessness of that Absolute, which never needs anything. No necessity at all. And out of that comes a little wish, waking up. And the wish is already wishing for wishlessness. Because any wish is too much. Wanting to know is too much. So you want to get rid of the wish. Wishing for wishlessness. Wishing for knowledge. The ignorance wants to know.

Q: Wants to know who I am.

K: Yes. So it pops up. It came, and it will be gone one day. But not by any wish. The wish can never reach the wishlessness. That what comes out of wishlessness can never go back to wishlessness. It came like a flower and will be gone one day. But in spite of your trying to reach something by that wish or not. Whatever is reached by that wish is temporary, and relative.

Q: So in other words, no attempt should be made to understand...

K: No, no. You can do whatever. Worry and be happy. You cannot not inquire. Every morning you wake up your intention is happiness. Every movement is for happiness.

Q: For all that I don't know what is happiness.

K: Whatever you have done in your whole entire life, any movement, was for happiness. So if any intention is for happiness, and it comes from happiness, what's the problem?

Q: So what is this happiness I am not able to know? I agree with you. Everybody is trying to be happy. And there is this concept of happiness. And it is difficult to understand, to me.

K: The me makes a concept, the me says 'without the me, I would be better off'. The me imagining that without the me the me would be better off. That is like whatever he is doing is trying to get rid of these preferences or tendencies, which is like a hindrance. So it tries to dissolve problems.

Q: So is happiness trying to be what one is not?

K: No, trying to become what one is. But it is futile, thank God. That you cannot control yourself.

Q: So happiness is trying to be what one is?

K: Yes, because that is ease.

Q: One cannot help being what one is?

K: No.

Q: So there is no need to do it.

K: In spite of no need, it happens. Things happen. You brush your teeth in spite of you knowing that they will be gone one day.

Q: I don't know if things happen or illusory things happen.

K: Yes, but that - illusion or not - is not my field. Whatever movement of the whole universe is for happiness. There is no 'your movement' at all. And there is no illusion in it. All of that is a play of energy. And this play of energy is the intention of happiness. Of a joy. The joy in action. So even the wish, coming out of wishlessness, is in its nature wishlessness. So it's a dance of joy. There is no illusion. All of that doesn't help, to see it as an illusion.

Q: Everything that is happening is the way it is supposed to happen?

K: It is what you are.

Q: You just have to accept what it is.

K: You don't even have to accept it.

Q: No question of accepting it?

K: No. You don't have to accept it. You just are what you are. That. What is this.

Q: No inquiry?

K: There is inquiry, but no inquirer. You cannot find anyone who is inquiring. You can experience wishes, but you cannot find one who is wishing them.

Q: How can there be inquiry without an inquirer?

K: That's the wonder. That's the miracle. There was never any seeker. There is seeking. But where is the seeker? Try to find the seeker.

Q: I always think that maybe both, inquiry and inquirer, are a human imagination?

K: Humans are an imagination already. How can an imagination imagine something else?

Q: Second order imagination?

K: No, no, no. The whole dream is dreamed by the absolute Para Brahman, the absolute Dreamer. And whatever is in the dream cannot dream anything. But the nature of the Para Brahman cannot influence what is the dream. It is all Para Brahman. It is all the Dreamer dreaming himself. There is nothing but Para Brahman. And Para Brahman dreaming himself as a dreamer, still that dreamer never dreamed anything. The dreamer, the dreaming, what can be dreamed, is all dreamed by that Para Brahman. That dreamer, which is already part of the dream, never dreamed anything. The experiencer is already experienced by that absolute experiencer you are. There is no experiencer as a me who is experiencing anything. How can that be?

Q: So experience is nothing but some interpretation made by oneself?

K: All is self-made.

Q: Imagination.

K: All images. All phenomenal images are coming out of the Noumenal you are. And the Noumenal itself is just dreaming itself in all possible phenomenal experiences. And none of that phenomenal can create another phenomenal. The cause it what you are, and whatever is this, is off course. But that what is off course is not a cause of something else. So you cannot blame anyone. There is no me to blame, there is no you to blame. There is blaming, but who is there to blame?

Q: Let me ask you a question which is really bothering me. So you talk about phenomenal and Noumenon. Para Brahman, and Reality. Maybe you equate Para Brahman with Reality?

K: You can say that's the only Reality.

Q: The question is: is Reality something independent of human thinking or is it a creation of human thought?

K: The words, the idea of Reality, came out of relative reality. Because for Reality there is no Reality. That you can say. The idea of reality is only part of relative reality. The idea of truth is only part of relative truth. All of that is part of the dream. So even the idea of reality is part of the dream. For sure. Because that what is not a dream doesn't even know a dreamer. So whatever can be known or not known, whatever you can imagine, whatever you can give a name to, is all dream. And whatever in that dream can be dreamed and you can experience, can never lead you to that what is the absolute Dreamer. There is no bridge. Thank God that what you are can never be reached, not even by yourself. As it cannot be reached, it cannot be affected. By anything. So there is no cause and no effect in what you are. And that's Advaita, because Advaita means there is no second. And when there is no second, there is no effect from anyone. Who can be affected by what? It needs two for being affected. And effects are only in the dream. So only dream objects are affected by other dream objects. And that continues, like a chain of reactions. Effects, effects, effects. But you cannot find the cause. The action you cannot find. Energy cannot be found. You can only experience the effects of energy. And not by one of these effects can energy be controlled. Only effects controlling effects. Very effective sometimes. But who cares? So when I say you have to know yourself in the absolute absence of any presence of anyone who knows or doesn't know, that you do every night. So it's nothing new for you. You know yourself in the absolute absence of any presence of any absence of any knower or not knower in deep deep sleep. To know yourself as that what never needs to know or not to know itself, that is ease. Because no one complains there. There is no complainer. And every morning you wake up there is a complainer. Who wants to make it more plain, more harmonic. Naturally he wants to have a harmonic life, a happy life. Let him do his job. But he can never reach that harmony you are. Because that harmony, that there is no second who can disturb you, that harmony which has not even one who can be disturbed, that happiness which never needs to be happy or doesn't even know happiness, that joy which never needs to enjoy itself, can never be reached by anything. So as it can not be reached by anything, you cannot lose it by anything. No losing, no gaining, in all of that. None of that can make you more or less as you are. Wonderful. A bomb explodes - does is make you more or less as you are? Cancer, or this or that or whatever you imagine as the most horrible event in your life. Or your wife leaves you, or your husband is going with another one. So what? It hurts a while, and then? It all comes and goes. Welcome, wel-go. Hello, good-by. Already. And you are still what you are. In birth never born. And in dying never died. So what to do? If none of what you have done or not done in your whole entire whatever, never changed what you are, never made you more or less as you are, what to do? Let the dream be as the dream is, and just enjoy the silence you are. Which can never be disturbed by any explosion of any disturbing mind or anything. So mind, no mind, who minds the mind? Never mind. So the peace you can reach in this life is a false one anyway. But you cannot help it. Because whatever you try is to be in harmony. That what is an object naturally tries to be in harmony with its surroundings. It's a natural tendency.

Q: So harmony, peace, what you are talking about, 'just enjoy yourself', they are in the relative?

K: No, it's all absolute what you are.

Q: In the Absolute, in the Advaitic terminology, there is the one, there is no second.

K: There is no one.

Q: There is no second.

K: Yes, but that means there is not even one.

Q: In 'there is no second' is implied there is only one.

K: No, no. It's not implied. Ha ha ha. That's already a false conclusion. There is just no second.

Q: So in Advaitic language, there are two ways of living, there are two realities. One is the absolute Reality. And the other is the relative reality. So we in every day life live in relative reality. That is a reality of the laws of nature. Science. Everything happens according to some laws which nobody can change. So that is a different level of living, that is relative, where maybe all the ideas of harmony and long living happen. And the other one is this absolute Reality where only the Para Brahman exists, and there is nothing more one can talk of. Every word you use is loaded with concepts. So you are imposing something on Para Brahman.

K: For me there is no problem of talking about anything, because as I said before, none of that talking concepts or anything can make you more or less as you are. So you can talk and talk, and that's the beauty of talking, that it cannot do anything. I just point to the beauty of talking or anything that can be done or not done, as it can not make you more or less as you are. But I agree, you are relative when you imagine by birth being born. All of that is real what comes out of that position. That becomes a reference point, and from that reference point you have all of these rules to follow. All of whatever cause and effects and all of that what is a relative happiness is your world, your realm. And I have no problem with it. But if you look for the ease you are, we can talk about it that you cannot find it in that. And the only case is what you are. And the dis-ease will always be there. So as someone said, what is for you Advaita and what is Vedanta? Advaita is Reality and Vedanta is the realization of it. But the so-called dream starts when you, by starting to realize yourself, become a realizer who is starting to be different from what he is realizing. Already the realizer is false. Because the realizer belongs to Vedanta. But the end of Vedanta is Advaita. And only in Advaita you are what you are. And the moment your imagination takes you out into Vedanta, into all of that field of knowingness and whatever can be known, whatever can be realized, any moment you want to get out of it, you have to stay there. Whatever you do then, for sure is a disease. Because every moment, even to exist, is a dis-ease. You are not at ease. There is no ease. And from that moment on you want to be at ease. And whatever you try is like an intention for that ease. So I can sit here and say there is no bridge. From there no one will go back where he belongs. There is no going back. I can only sit here and say in the beginning there was no beginning for what you are. So in that first imaginary dream of one who is realizing himself, you already were there. And you will be there when this one is gone. And the most simple is, every night you drop that, and every moment it pops up by itself. So I am pointing to the helplessness of Advaita. Of that where there is no one who can help himself. There is an absolute absence of any presence of any possibility to help yourself. And that never enters that Vedanta. It never goes out of itself. But only that is your longing for. No one can explain why you long for that what you are. But it happens. And I can only say this is the way you realize yourself. It will always be the way you realize yourself. You will always realize yourself in misery. Because the happiness you are can not be experienced. And whatever you experience is misery. So you have to be in spite of that misery what you are. Because there is no end of it. So now you can decide. It's not your decision. But you are anyway what you are. But what is the ease and what is the dis-ease?

Q: How to know?

K: You don't have to know that. You just have to see that whatever you can see you cannot be. Not more. And the seer is already part of the scenery. The seer, the seeing, what can be seen, can be seen. So it's a scenery. But that there can be a scenery, you have to be prior to that. Without that what is prior, there is not even a possibility of a scenery. So Reality has to be with and without. And already is with and without a scenery of experiences. And I can just talk to myself and say 'come on, did anything happen since you were so-called born or remember to what you are at all?' Nothing ever happened. There are events happening, there are things going on, but there is still that absolute Presence of what you are, which is an absolute Absence where the relative presence appears in. So dream-like events happen. A dreamer starts, and dreaming starts. But that absolute Absence of any presence was never never. So you already are That what is never never. So we are talking out of fun. This is not because of anything. This is entertainment.

Q: So pain and suffering is also in that?

K: It's all your dream. It's all what you are. And you cannot escape it. You cannot avoid what you are. So you cannot even avoid the smallest pain or the biggest pain. All of that is what you are and you cannot not realize yourself. You are Reality, and this is your realization, there is no difference. And what you are is easy, to be that what it is. Because in that experience of pain there is no one who has pain. There was never any ownership in anything. That's the main thing.

Q: So I understand you correctly when you say you cannot be what is realizing itself, you mean one is already realized?

K: You already realize yourself. This is your realization.

Q: So everybody is realized?

K: No, there is no 'everybody' in that. Everybody is a realization of that what is everybody. But there is no everybody. That what is everybody doesn't know everybody. So that what you are is no-body. And neither is a body or a no body. It is neither something nor nothing. Even nothing is too much. Or too less. You are that what is nothing, and you are that what is everything. But you are not nothing and you are not everything. And you are not even beyond. You are that what is the beyond. And you are that what it this. You cannot find what you are not. But you can never find yourself in what you find. This paradox is not for any simple me trying to understand it. Because that is not an understanding. This is being what you are. And that is in spite of understanding, in spite of all this tralala. I like this tralala, this bla bla bla, because no one cares.

Q: So the whole exercise...

K: It happens anyway. In spite of you...

Q: Surrender or...

K: Surrender the surrenderer and be happy. There is no 'mine' in it. There is no anyone's belonging. What belongs to you? The body? Piece of meat? The me-steak? Family?

Every night, I like it absolutely, the deep deep sleep, every night you are absolute what you are, absolute at ease, that what is ease. And every morning this happens, in spite of your wanting it or not. You cannot even help waking up. Now wanting not to wake up is too late. So you woke up. And by waking up you realize yourself. In this little one and the big one, in unity or in oneness, all of that is what you are. You can even make seven states out of it. You can make a piece, piece, piece of cake. And you can slice it and slice it but by slicing you cannot slice it. You cannot get a piece out of peace. Whatever you do, you cannot make it more or less that peace you are.

Q: As a student of science I have one way of looking at this making pieces and pieces...

K: There is no end to it...

Q: So all of us are what? We are nothing but bundles of these particles and fields. Everything is just groups of particles and fields. Which has a dubious faculty of thinking one exists...

K: It's all imagination of something.

Q: What I see is because the mind is constituted in a particular way.

K: It's all fiction. Science-fiction. That's why it's called science-fiction.

Q2: He is a nuclear physicist.

K: I call it science-fiction. That's the beauty of science, that science can never control existence.

Q: By science you also reach the same conclusion: there is nothing but some field which you cannot define.

K: I always like to say: science could not find matter, so it may not matter. Scientists are the biggest seekers. They are seeking happiness. Like in Cern in Switzerland, that they want to make anti-matter and matter, and the marriage of that. That is like Shiva and Parvati marrying.

Q: I worked in that field.

K: Yes, and then suddenly there is that light there. Pure light. Pure light just for a split second, and then it divides again in space and form. Formless and form. But they try it. So even the scientists want to be enlightened. They want to control themselves. But thank God it cannot be controlled.

Q: They don't want to control, they want to know...

K: Yes, but that's controlling. Wanting to know is wanting to control it. Wanting to know the beloved, and if you know the beloved you can control him. It's control, what else? Love is control. Any relative love is trying to control the beloved. There is a lover and a beloved. And there is a fear that the beloved is not yours. And then you try to control him by knowing him. Every little tendency of him, you want to know him. Even if you become a scientist of energy, you want to know energy. You want to know what is energy and you only want to know it because before energy controls you, you want to control energy. All controllers! But thank God that there was never any scientist who could even control himself.

Q: So he wants to know who he is.

K: Yes, but for what? Because he wants to control happiness.

Q: He wants to know why this element of control is coming into the picture?

K: And the 'why' is always misery. I sit here: why not? Let him do his job. No danger. That what is Knowledge can never be known by anyone. And that what can be known is just a dream. The scientist is a dream, that what he is looking for is a dream, whatever he finds out is a dream. And it is all a temporary reality he can find, he can lose again. So it's nice entertainment. So it's fun. Enjoy the job. Enjoy that you cannot find that what you are looking for. Enjoy the not-finding. You cannot not look. Any moment you are awake you have to inquire into your nature, that's your nature. To inquire into that what is your beloved. That is your way of loving yourself. But enjoy the not-finding. Enjoy that you cannot control it. Enjoy the unpredictable. Enjoy that what you are.

Q: The joy is in the search, in the journey. There is no destination.

K: There is a search without expectation of finding. The action without an actor. There is intention but without anyone who has it. There was never anyone who had any intention. So the whole universe is intention. But you cannot find anyone who owns that intention. The Totality has the intention to inquire into Totality. And Totality can never know Totality as Totality is. So whatever Totality is inquiring is inquiring into some imaginary totality. So what? Let it do it. What's the problem? No ending of that inquiry. And no risk of finding it.

Q: There is no end. Because everything that is created is not satisfactory.

K: Thank God you cannot get satisfied. Be happy that nothing can satisfy you. If there would be something that could satisfy you you would depend on that bloody thing.

Q: Then you would be dependent.

K: Then you would depend on someone who can satisfy you, or something. Some truth, some experience which can satisfy you. That is hell that there is someone else already. Two! And that one can satisfy you. My goodness!

Q: So unhappiness is built in the duality?

K: It is misery. Any moment you experience yourself you experience misery.

Q: Is it possible to live in unicity? In Advaita?

K: No. No one can do that. There was never anyone who could not do it, and there will never be anyone who can do it.

Q: I don't get the first part.

K: There was no one in the first place. How can that one who was not there in the first place live Advaita? Thank God Advaita can not be lived by anyone. Who would that be?

Q: So there has never been anybody?

K: There was never anybody. Where is even the question of living Advaita, living a good life? What's the question about a good and a bad life?

Q: It's a contradiction.

K: Total madness!

Q: So reality, what is true, the criteria can be human reason?

K: You can say energy takes the form of a so-called human, and then creating another form which is not different, and then having a dialogue, about itself. It's like a self-talk. It's like every morning you wake up, there is three waking up - me, myself and I. And then asking 'how are we?' You already wake up in a hospital, in a madhouse. This is your hospital. And there are always doctors who are as sick as you. And the sick doctor wants to help a sick patient. And both are talking about their sickness, infinitely. And everyone is competing who is the sickest. Or someone is even competing who is the healthiest. But the one who competes in health, he must be in hell. Any competition is in hell, in separation. There is one competing with someone else.

Q: So deep sleep is closest to Advaita?

K: Deep deep sleep. Deep sleep is still awareness. Deep deep sleep simply means That what is the deep sleep. That what is the awakening, and that what is now awake. You can go on. It is not that the deep deep sleep is what you are. You are here now what you are. But in the deep deep sleep you can say there is no complainer. So your knowledge is in the presence and absence of that complainer, which is unavoidable. You cannot avoid this. There is always something wrong. And if something is not wrong, you call it oneness. But even that is wrong. That there is one who is not wrong. So for me everything is wrong. Wrong, wrong, wrong. It's the song of wrongness.

Q: This is too much above my head. So I want to ask something else. Ramesh says that you are the ego. I am struggling with that. I feel that ego is totally different. If you have the sense of doership, that is the ego, if not, you are not the ego. But Ramesh always said 'You are the ego. You will die as an ego'. That concept is something which I am not able to accept. Could you enlighten me on that?

K: What is meant by it is you are that what is the ego, but that what is the ego doesn't have an ego.

Q: I didn't get you.

K: Yes, if you would get me, there would be no ego anymore. So the ego fights for his schizophrenic idea of me. There is an ego who has an ego. And that means duality. A me who has a me. There is a me-me. And then what Ramesh is pointing to, you are that what is the ego. And the ego came and will be gone as that what is what you call ego. But the ego doesn't know any ego. Only in ownership there is two egos. And then one ego wants to get rid of the other ego.

Q: I cannot understand, there are not two egos.

K: But it needs two egos to know an ego.

Q: Something I can't get into my head. Is it I and the ego? If I feel I am not the doer, somebody else is the doer, then they say the ego is not there. But as long as they feel 'I am the doer', that is the ego. Ego is something which is different from you and it doesn't exist at all. You imagine it exists. But I was told by Ramesh 'you are the ego'. That is the way the contradiction is coming. Until then I have accepted that I am not the ego.

K: That was what I was talking about. That one who is not the ego is still the ego. That's why I said there is two egos. One who is not the ego and sees an ego. There is two. One who is different from the ego. Then there are two egos.

Q: The other one is an ego, I am not an ego.

K: But that are two egos!

Q: This is my downt-to-earth question, not an imaginary one. What I heard from so many people is 'you are different from the ego'. And if you are feeling that you are doing something, that is the ego that gives you this feeling. But this is what I am trying to practice now: I am not the doer, somebody else is the doer, that is what I have been told. I am trying to accept that. If I am not the doer, but I am feeling I am the doer, that feeling is considered an ego. I want to know if that is correct thinking or not correct thinking. That's all I want to know.

K: Whatever you understand now is depending on one who needs to understand. That's called ego. There is a need, a needy I, which needs to understand. That's called ego. That's an experience. You experience one who is needing some understanding to get rid of that ego, because there is a dis-ease, a not-pleasurable experience. Because there is a me which is always longing for something. There is always something wrong with it. So that's called ego. And you are right: what you can experience you cannot be. But that experience you cannot get rid of. It will be there. That experience of a me which is misery, the me-sery of the me, which is the ego, will always be there. But the me, which is an experience of misery, which is an experience of one who is doing something, is sometimes there and sometimes not. So who is there without it?

Q: Normally I feel the ego comes in only when I do something great. When I did something horrible I try to pass it on to somebody else.

K: That's a tricky ego.

Q: In other words I always feel it's not me who did something. It's some other force, call it Reality, call it whatever in the skies, but that is what is making me do that. Ultimately I am trying to feel now that I don't do anything, somebody else does it. If I do something wrong, I am not wrong. Somebody else has made me do that.

K: It will be more and more, because you are already in the grace that it takes you away as one who is born. This experience of being born gets weaker and weaker. And then the doing just happens by itself, just by natural understanding. But it doesn't happen by any relative understanding. You go more and more to that where there is no one who can claim anything. It's a natural tendency. Just to go to that what is the absolute shelter, the absolute comfort, which never needs any comfort. And whatever happens otherwise, what needs comfort and all of that, gets less and less attractive. So only that is attracted to itself and by that attraction to itself, just being itself, all of that is a dream anyway. So not by any understanding of you understanding something, doer or not doer, that happens. It's a natural tendency. And if that happens it happens. But not by anyone's wanting or not. As you, by whatever tendency, went out, and you fall in love with this ego, you fall in love with that what you are. And you took yourself as a doer and all of that happened, it was just a happening. And now there is a happening of you withdrawing again, this letting go just happens. And then it just happens because it happens. You don't even have to know why. That's the final thing. You don't have to know why it happens. So this will happen anyway. And then you are neither detached nor attached. Because there is not even one who is left who is detached from anything. Because you don't even have to call it anything. It just happens. So you become like a canvas where all the projections are dancing, and the canvas was never affected. Like this old analogy. It's a natural tendency. So we are talking about that no one can give you anything. This cannot be transmitted. It cannot be anything that can be taught. It just will happen. As it happened that you went out, you go astray, by becoming a doer, by feeling misery. And then by natural tendencies you withdraw from that. And then you are again in that glory of ease, which you never left in the beginning. But it seems like by going out you went out. And then there was another experience of going back and withdrawing from it. But even in the beginning no one went out. And in the end no one went back. Because there is an experience of going out and an experience of going back. But in going out no one goes out, and in going back no one goes back. But still there is an experience of it. So there is an experience of doership. But you cannot find the doer. There is an experience of non-doership. But you cannot find the non-doer. There was never any doer or non-doer in both of it. It never led you away and never leads you back. You are always That. What you cannot not be. So in a dream you go out, in a dream you go home. But what you are never left what it is, home itself. You are what is home. But there is no one at home. And as there was never anyone at home, that one who is not at home cannot go out. So it is a dream of going out, a dream of one who goes out. And there is a dream of one who goes back. Naturally.

Q: I got another one. This has been worrying me for a long time. Ramana Maharshi used to say 'question who am I'. He thinks it's very easy. I found the most difficult one is that!

K: It's more than easy. If you want to do it, you cannot do it. If it happens, it's more than easy.

Q: What do you mean?

K: That's the trick. Ramesh would say 'if it is meant to happen' it is easy as a piece of cake. If it is not meant to happen you can try the 'who am I' for ten hours a day and just get exhausted.

Q: What Ramana Maharshi is saying is every time you have a question you question 'who am I'. I am consciousness, that ends there, it doesn't go anywhere further. What is it that he meant, I can't understand. He has realized, I always think 'how did Ramana realize it? Why am I not realizing it?' So many people have been to Ramana Maharshi, they talk so highly about him, but none of them are realized.

K: If you read all of Ramana's books, when he was asked 'are you realized?' he would always say: 'how can that what you see as Ramana realize Reality'? What is Ramana is Reality, and this is a realization of it. So there was never anyone who was realized. That was his pointer. There was never anyone who was realized. And that means there was never anyone who was not realized. So why are you asking 'why him and why not them?' There was no him.

Q: I agree. From his point of view. Not from my point of view. Ramana always said that everybody is realized. He has no doubts about it. But I have doubts.

K: The 'who am I' is always a nice thing, because if you really do the 'who am I', the world drops by who, am, and then the I is the last thing you can experience. But prior to that I is what you are. So that question 'who am I?' is always pointing to the origin of whatever is and is not. So just to be that, this is like a pointer to that.

Q: So theoretically I accept this thing, but when I get practical I don't get anywhere.

K: No, it will happen when it happens and then you have to do it 24/7/365.

Q: Pardon?

K: If it is by the grace of yourself withdrawing from whatever, it will happen 24 hours a day, 7 days a week. Without that whatever you do is futile anyway. But if That is involved, just by its nature it will always concentrate on itself. And that is a concentration camp that it puts itself in, the concentration camp of that question 'who am I?' will always be the answer to that question. And in that question there is no questioner. That's all. In that absolute answer, in that absolute what is questioning, is no questioner. There is an absolute answer, but no one who gets answered. You are the answer. But no one can claim that. There is no claimer of that answer. But your tendency now is you want to have it.

Q: Whatever you are talking about, the books I read also talk about this. But my feeling is I am not realizing. That's all my question is.

K: Yes. And you are right. And I can say you will never be realized. Forget it!

Q: I want something positive! I don't believe that. I want to struggle. If I die without that, I....

K: You see, that confirms there is always one who will struggle. The inquiry will never end. And as long as there is one there will be inquiry.

Q: Maybe. That I accept, but...

K: And taking oneself as special, 'when my inquiry is ending then...'. You will never end! You are not different from your neighbor. You are not different from 7 billion others, and 7 billion others is what you are, struggling for what they are. For happiness. And it will never end. Taking it personal, 'I want to be enlightened', that is really the suffering part. In realization there is no realizer. That's the main problem. But one wants to be a realizer. He wants to be the realizer and then he is suffering not being it. And he can not feel it and all of that. So suffering ends when there is realization, but who is the realizer? And who is not realized? There was never anyone who was realized or not realized. So you are right, you cannot realize yourself. And be happy that you cannot realize yourself.

Q: They said Ramana Maharshi realized.

K: No one says that! Only phantoms say he was realized. He never claimed that. Ramana was a rare case, he never claimed anything. He even renounced renunciation. He devoted devotion. He always went back to that ownerlessness. So who says he was realized, and now makes him a banana? Only monkey minds make Ramana a banana.

Q: Ganapati said that he is a realized person.

K: Then he was not realized. If one says another is realized, then he was not realized. Because anyone who says someone else is realized for sure is not realized. Then he claims himself to be realized and there is always one too many. One who confirms someone else confirms himself. And being depending on that it is possible to realize himself. Fuck them all! Kill them all! Send them to hell! They are as non-realized as any chair sitting here. Do you ask this chair 'are you realized?'

Absolute - 'who cares'.

Q: You are talking about something very impractical.

K: I am not here to make anyone happy. That's not my field to make anyone happy. I am not in that business.

Q: I am not convinced. A chair and a human being - there is a difference.

K: Then it's a difference. That is your field, and then I have no interest in your field.

Q: I am expressing my feelings.

K: And that's maybe the problem.

Q: Ramana said, if I remember correctly, 'there is no Ramana'.

K: There is no Ramana. Ramana was the biggest lie on earth.

Q: The question of Ramana being realized is meaningless. We are in a dream state. We are imagining Ramana to exist in our dream. And in that dream we dream that he is realized.

K: And then you compare yourself with Ramana. When you think there was a Ramana you think you exist and Ramana exists, and then you start comparing. And then you want to be like him.

Q: My father used to tell me that if you sit there (with Ramana) you will not ask questions at all. So much peace, that doesn't come with anybody else. That's why I say he is realized. Quite a number of people who were there have told me 'when you sit there, you forget everything, your questions are automatically answered'. When someone asked Ramana when he had cancer 'how is it that you are not feeling the pain?' You know what he told him ? 'When the pain comes I take my mind off the pain'. That is why I said he is a realized person.

K: But if he would be Reality he would still be sitting there and doing the same thing. That's the whole point. Whatever is different is dream. I don't deny what happened there. I never deny anything. For what? But whatever can be different from something else is dream. That's all. And I agree, Ramana was different from anyone else. But that doesn't make him different. There was no one who was different. But as a phenomenal experience he was different from any other phenomenal experience. Like Arunachala is different from any other mountain. For me Arunachala is the origin of the universe. The light of Shiva. But that what is Shiva is prior to that light, that you shouldn't forget. The light of Shiva is not Shiva. So the dream of Shiva starts with Arunachala, with that light of Shiva. And then Ramana - embodiment of that light. Wonderful. And then whatever happens around it. All of that is wonderful, all can happen in that dream. Even that you are in the presence of someone and you feel at peace, something is solved immediately. All of that, but if that would be Reality, it should be uninterrupted. It should not be in one case and not in another case. So whatever you can make a difference has to be different. And Ramana was always saying in Reality there is no Ramana. So Reality never needs to know anything and Reality never needs to stop its mind, because Reality has no mind. And whoever claims that he felt more or less in some presence, I don't deny it. But it's a fleeting shadow of what you are. There is a fleetingness in it. So even the deepest peace you can experience in whatever presence, is not it. Is a relative peace. So it's not bad, I don't want to talk it away. But I just say the peace you are, it can not be compared to any experience at all. And only to be that is ease. The rest is coming and going. And can maybe temporarily calm your mind. Temporary peace of mind. And I have nothing against it. If that is your goal, do whatever. We can talk about how we can maybe by understanding appease our mind that we don't have this notion of doership and all of that, fine. But if you really want to be that ease, none of that can help you. So yes, everything that can be done can be done. But for what you are, all of that is futile. And I like Nisargadatta, I like Ramana, because there is always this contradiction. Do the 'who am I', and if by that 'who am I' you become a peaceful man, a peaceful mind, wonderful. But even by that 'who am I', the biggest pointer ever, you can not attain what you are. That I like most. Yes, sattvic living, don't eat garlic, don't do this, don't get involved with this action or that action. You may sleep better. But don't think by not eating garlic you can be enlightened. So yes, and no. For the relative dream whatever you can do there will be something, more peace or less peace. You have to meditate anyway.

Q: That is a dream peace?

K: That is a dream peace. Yes. And if that is your goal – whatever. But if you ask me for what you are, and how to attain what you are, I can give pointers to that. But no one can transmit it. And no one is able to have a presence, because That has no presence.

Q: How do you look at Ramana considering Arunachala as Shiva? He even took rounds year after year.

K: Yes, he took a stroll every day. He always said I am walking around myself and the Self is unmoved. This is the symbol of Arunachala, the Self, unmovable. So the light of Shiva, unmovable. The origin of whatever is can never be touched, disturbed, or anything.

Q: It's not an attempt to answer this question 'who am I? So are you implying that Self is the answer to this question?

K: Self is the absolute answer to the question 'who am I?' But the Self is not calling itself anything. There is an absence of any presence of anyone who calls himself anything. So the Selflessness is what you are.

Q: Are Self and Shiva and Para Brahman the same?

K: You give it different names.

Q: Self is used in English language...

K: Because there is no religion involved.

Q: So the Self, or the way you use it, is in the sense of Para Brahman?

K: Yes. The Self not knowing the Self. That's Para Brahman. Brahman not knowing himself, that's Para Brahman.

Q: When you say consciousness, is it the same?

K: No. Consciousness is the dream of that.

Q: And awareness?

K: The superior consciousness, which the dream starts with.

Q: I didn't get it. Consciousness is awareness?

K: The highest consciousness, pure light, awareness, superior consciousness, there the dream starts. That's the light of Shiva, the supreme light of Shiva.

Q: So awareness is the light of Shiva. And consciousness?

K: Consciousness starts with the supreme consciousness, as awareness. All of whatever is, is consciousness. So there is a high consciousness, a middle consciousness, and a lower consciousness. It's like the absolute supreme light, and then the space-like spirit, or that emptiness, and then comes everything of information, matter. But it already starts with awareness. It's like a dream. It has different states. Consciousness shows itself as awareness. And then consciousness shows itself as emptiness, as spirit, as ether, and then as form. But showing itself in different forms or non-forms, it doesn't make it different. It is as light already what it is, as it is as space or as form. All of that is consciousness. All of that is Vedanta, you call whatever, realization.

Q: Awareness is the Para Brahman, or Self?

K: No.

Q: Awareness is trying to be aware of oneself?

K: That's already a dream.

Q: So consciousness of self trying to be aware of self?

K: Consciousness trying to know consciousness. And that would be the closest. But the closest is not close enough. Awareness is still an experience, of being awake. Even the purest notion of awareness still is an experience. And then it ends. And then where that ends, that what you are starts.

Q: Maybe the Self, or Para Brahman, is the purest form of consciousness?

K: No. It is Consciousness. But that what is Consciousness doesn't know Consciousness. It is Awareness, but that what is Awareness doesn't know Awareness and doesn't have awareness. And it is the World but it doesn't know any World. It is Knowledge but it doesn't know any Knowledge. But when we talk about consciousness we talk about a consciousness we can experience. And that is a dream. So Consciousness having a dream about consciousness. So that what is consciousness is Reality. And then Consciousness having a dream about consciousness, which is a realization of consciousness. So Consciousness realizing itself in awareness, in I-amness, and then the world. But even Consciousness realizing itself as whatever, doesn't become the way it is realizing itself. So you dream yourself in many ways.

Q: When you talked about three levels of...

K: The trinity of Shiva.

Q: Three levels of consciousness.

K: There are three different ways of experiencing yourself. There are even seven. The first three are relative. And the last four are not relative. That's all. But by none of them you can know yourself. You can neither know yourself in the world, being in the world and being like a man. You cannot know yourself as spirit. You cannot know yourself as awareness. And then you go to the beyond, to the fourth state. Then in the absolute absence you don't know, because there is no one who doesn't know himself. And then you start as awareness, you are awareness. And then you are not relative, you are what is I-amness. And then you are what is the world. You are the absolute man, you are the absolute spirit, and you are the absolute awareness. And you are even that what is the absolute beyond. But the absolute cannot know itself in one of them. It is realizing itself in seven different ways. Seven different ways of dreaming what you are. But the Para Brahman cannot be found in one of them. You cannot find the Dreamer in one of them. Only the first three are relative. And you may say there is suffering, the experience of suffering. And then there are four states where there is no suffering. And for sure you have a preference of no suffering. But you cannot avoid that you have to experience yourself even in the first. You cannot avoid one of these experiences. So you have to be what you are, even in that misery you now experience you have to be what you are. If you cannot be in that misery what you are, you will not become it in any other state. And that what has to be in a different state, and claims only in a different state it will be better, that's called ego. But it's called ego because it goes anyway - 'e-goes'.

Q: So there are seven levels of enlightenment?

K: Seven ways of realizing yourself. But Reality can not be known in one of them.

Q: Reality is unknowable.

K: Yes. For itself. And that's Advaita. Reality knowing reality is relative. Reality, in an absolute absence of any knowing or not knowing itself, is Reality, and that never needs Reality. Never needs to realize anything. Only the unreal needs to realize. And the unreal being realized or not realized, is still the unreal.

Q: The unrealized can never realize.

K: No, it can realize, but not the Reality.

Q: Not the realized Reality.

K: No. So it's like an unenlightened one getting enlightened. There is a phantom unenlightened one. And then the phantom gets enlightened. Ha ha ha. It's still a phantom. Who cares about a phantom who is unenlightened and then becomes a phantom who is enlightened? Only another phantom. Only consciousness cares about consciousness. That what is consciousness never cares about consciousness. So only in the dream consciousness cares about consciousness. So consciousness in the dream is a phantom consciousness. Because you can only experience yourself in a dream. As what you are you will never experience yourself.

Q: So the paradox is only for the phantom?

K: All you can talk about is phantom talk. That's why it's fun.

Q: Depends on how you look at it.

K: No it's fun. If you are not the phantom it's fun. If you are the phantom for sure it's tom-tom. You are in the diffi-'cult' of differences. When you are what you are it's 'fun-tom'. That's fun. If you are not what you are, you are in misery. Any moment you are not what you are, you are in a misery of missing what you are. No way out. Instant misery. When we talk about Ramana, he said the only suicide you can commit, any moment you are not that what you are is misery and suicide and you are dead. Because life can not be known. But any moment you take yourself as something that is alive, something that can be experienced, you are dead. You are a dead experience. And that's the only suicide you can commit. Not being what you are. And by being mortal, and being whatever, for sure in that instant you have a tendency to become immortal. Naturally. But whatever you do then is futile. It's a wonderful trap. A wonderful absolute trap. And no one is trapped. That's the beauty of it.

Q: That's very depressing.

K: But depressing is the closest to deep rest. When one is deep-pressed, he is the closest to the deepest possible rest. The deep-rest.

Q: Good way of looking at it.

K: If grace is after you, if that depression happens, because there is a senselessness happening, the world makes no sense anymore, marriage makes no sense, money makes no sense, nothing can satisfy you, you become depressed. But that deep rest is because grace is already after you. Because you coming closer to that what is peace, and that never needs any sense of life, there is no meaning in it. It never needs any meaning. And if the Self wants to be that again what is Self, not knowing anything and not needing anything, you will be depressed. The closer you come to that what is rest, you as a phantom will be depressed. I take it as a good sign.

Q: Can you please repeat what are the seven ways of realizing oneself?

K: Seven ways of dreaming. The most common dream is like this daily life dream. This being in a world, being born, having a body. That's a way of experiencing yourself as one who is born and may die again. And then you have all these problems with daily life and how to survive and all of that. That's the most common dream. And if you are very lucky, there is a shift of perception, from the perception of being a relative personal dream, to an impersonal oneness dream of I-amness. Can happen. Then you experience yourself as not different from anyone. Then you already think you are awakened. Some claim to be realized because they are not different from the world. Before there was a difference and now they shifted to the oneness. They are unified again. That's the second only. Even that, they have an experience, and the moment you want to stay in that second, you are out of it, you are back in that world. So then they try again. It is a ping-pong happening. A ping-pong of being in form or non-form. The doer or the non-doer. And then by luck, you see both is futile. Both is temporary. Then you already become a Jnani. The awareness, that neither the formless or the form can deliver what you are looking for, the peace which is not interrupted. So both is futile. Then already you are in the awareness that neither form or non-form can make you happy. That's already the samadhi of awareness, the choiceless awareness. The third. But even from there you never know, it is still a most subtle maybe, that you can end up in the world again. So you have to make an effort to stay there. You have to be moment by moment in that presence of the presence. Holding your breath. 'Don't get involved anymore! Stay there!' And when you are totally lucky, then you even go to the fourth state. And then there is no coming back anymore.

Q: That can happen only after death?

K: No, no. Jesus is a total symbol for that. He got crucified on the world, and pierced to the heart, and even forgetting everything. He went through the realm of the dead, which is actually the absence of that what you call life. But still he was what he was. That, his Nature, could not be killed by the absence of the world or any dream of this body. This is like the initiation of the fourth state, the Christ state. From Jesus he became Christ. And from there he became: 'Me and the Father is one. I am the Father. Me and the Spirit is one, I am the Spirit. Me and the world, the Man, is one, I am the Man'. The absolute Awareness, absolute Spirit, absolute Man. These seven ways, he went from Jesus, the son of Maria, to the Oneness, the teacher of love, then he went to the awareness, and then the beyond, and then he resurrected as that what is Life, experiencing itself as Awareness, as Spirit, or as Man. So you are the Absolute in whatever. Experiencing itself in seven different ways. But the Absolute can not get more absolute than it is. Or less. So you can neither become more or less what you are in one of them. But it may happen that perception shifts to whatever. So the absolute Seer experiencing itself in seven different ways, doesn't make the Seer different. By all the differences you cannot get different. But as I say, you have to be what you are in this first, as you have to be in the seven. There is no advantage for you, and that's the absolute advantage. And that what needs an advantage in one of them, will always only get disadvantages. Because being one who needs an advantage is in its nature already a disadvantage. That's called ego. The ego who thinks in a different state it would be better off, that's called ego. But it came and it will be gone again. And the Absolute cannot help it. And doesn't need to help it. Because it doesn't need anything to change. So when I say you have to be in spite of the way you experience yourself, I point to that what is already in spite. Not because of anything.

Q: What is the advantage you are talking about?

K: Like a personal advantage that you have more money. The first state. Then the second would be a spiritual advantage that you would be in the oneness. And then the next advantage would be that you even go to the Aurobingo advantage, to the super-hero, superman. Then you have three numbers right. Bingo, bingo, bingo. Because you know them all. Then you go to the beyond. Then you think 'I am beyond everything'. But who claims to be beyond? Another phantom. All phantoms claiming being in whatever state. Da Free John, Adi Da, he claimed to have reached the seventh state, 'the only one ever'. He claimed to be the first one: 'And now consciousness can rest, because I made it'.

Q: So this ego comes and goes...

K: Yes, it's a ghost. It's a ghost experience, because it came and it goes. Whatever comes and goes is a ghost. Karl is a ghost. This body is a ghost.

Q: So this is only when the body is there...

K: And then comes the next one. There is no end to it. You think this is the end of the story? Ha ha. The next will always be the next. And the next is just something different. There will always be a unique experience of the next. The next moment, even in this relative world, is always different to the moment before. Always unicity. Absolute moments, getting destroyed that the next moment can flower. And then this gets destroyed, the next one. It's always moment for moment absolute experiences of what you are. Here and now already. There is no need. It may happen the shift to the oneness, and then to awareness. Why not? But no one needs it. And you have to be anyway here now what you are. If you cannot be here now what you are, what kind of Absolute would it be who needs a different state to be? Only a relative needs special states. And that's the realm of hell. There is a devil who needs a better hell. There is only a better hell, but the hell is not good enough. Because hell is differences. And hell is separation. But what to do?

Q: Would you say that these different states are in increasing order of happiness?

K: Maybe they are more relative ease. But the relative ease doesn't lead to the absolute ease.

Q: You talk of ease, not of happiness.

K: For me it's more like ease, as in peace.

Q: So absolute ease is only in the Self?

K: Only the Absolute which is the Absolute but doesn't know any Absolute. Just by being absolute and there is no idea of even a second, because there is not even one.

Q: So it is that ease which doesn't need that ease?

K: Yes. That ease which never needs to be at ease. Never. It doesn't even know ease.

Q: And doesn't need any proof of it.

K: No. It never needs to improve or prove anything. And that what needs to improve and always needs to prove, that's called ghost. And the ghost always needs a proof to exist. Only a ghost needs a proof of existence. Existence itself never needs to prove itself.

Q: Doesn't even need to exist.

K: Doesn't even need to exist to exist. So that is the end of Vedanta. Because that what doesn't even have to exist to exist, that breaks all of what you can imagine to know or not know. That what is beyond all imaginary ideas.

Q: Existence is also an imaginary idea?

K: Absolutely. Only in relative existence there is an idea of existence. There is a new book on Zen, it says 'Zen, the biggest lie ever'. I like this. Like 'Advaita, the biggest lie ever'. Even to call it non-duality - you can only call it non-duality in duality. When there is non-duality, there is duality. So even that is no way out. And who needs to go out of what one is? Who is imprisoned? By whom? So what to do?

Q: Thanks a lot.

K: Enjoy yourself, because it will take a while. An infinite one. Never ending story. And whatever has a story is his story. Who cares about his story. This is the story of the body, then the story of God, then the story of the spirit, the story of whatever you imagine. So it's not your story. Who cares about it? It's his story. And there is no storage in the self. There is no self-storage. Only in America, there is self-storage.

Q: So all spiritual books are his-story books.

K: They always go to the lie-brary. They are lies buried in lies. That's the beauty of all the books. So enjoy the lies. The Self talks to the Self and it buries the lies in lies and it lies and lies. Lila.

To be ease itself is more than easy. It's an effortlessness of that That, what cannot not be what it is. And the rest cannot bring any rest. Thank God the Rest cannot be brought or transmitted or experienced at all. And the rest you can experience, ok, it's a fleeting rest, it comes and goes. So you are in rest and in not rest what you are. And thank God you cannot find any home or place to lay down your head. Because there is no place for you. For what you are, where can you rest? You try very hard to rest somewhere, to find home. Ha ha. No way.

What else can I not do?

Q: Can you say something about your story, how you started talking to people?

K: Sitting at Arunachala and having a coffee and just chatting around, just having fun, like now. And then comes one and then comes another one, and that one tells 'there is one'. And I always said 'I will never sit in front of people and make an official talk'.

Ha ha! Always said that. 'Fuck them all! How can you talk about Truth? Truth cannot be talked about'. That's what I said. Look at what I am doing around the world. Maybe I already knew what will happen?

Q: Did you have a personal teacher?

K: Yes, my grand-ma. My grand-ma is my lineage. She was my one and only teacher. When you are three years old and you lose your toy, you cry for a little piece of wood or something, because you think it belongs to you. You claim that ownership. The heart is bleeding, as if you lose the biggest love of your life. It's not different. Then the grand-ma comes and says: 'Son, come here. Sit down. Close your eyes. What do you see now'? 'Nothing'! 'That belongs to you'. 'Ok'. You get up, open your eyes - absolute ease. If you ask me, that was the absolute teaching, my grand-ma. Showing me you are with and without that. Seeing or not seeing. What is yours? What belongs to you? No belongings - no longing. Absolute ownerlessness. There is no one who owns anything. But your heart is bleeding for a little piece of wood. What a joke. Or some beloved is leaving you. Or your girlfriend is going with someone else. This self-pity. Where does it come from? Because you think you have something to lose, or to gain. That's self-pity already. You are the absolute owner of that what is, you are that already. And now you are in the self-pity that you can lose something? Poor me? The Almighty imagining that it can lose something? What an idea! So in that sense I try at least not to feed the pity. Being ruthlessness. But sometimes I can, sometimes I can not. Even that I cannot do.

Q: You have been to Arunachala so many times.

K: Fifteen years.

Q: Have you met any disciples of Ramana?

K: Yes. The nephew.

Q: Any interactions which were helpful to you?

K: No. I am absolutely grateful that no one could ever help me.

No, Arunachala was the final cut. Of all the strings. Because I was able, by whatever before, to go with the perception on a journey to places. So I go into the cave and go into that light of Arunachala, and really experiencing Arunachala is the origin of the whole universe. Out of that pure light all whatever, universes, milky ways, coming out of that light. And then it hit me: so it's an experience. Shit. Even that is not it.

Q: Have you ever wondered why this experience is localized there and not anywhere else? Or everywhere else?

K: Yes, I tried. It's like a camera who is wondering why the camera is not everywhere. The perception is not different in anyone. The preceiver is different. The perceived perceiver is different, that's the reference point. But perception is not different. Can you find a difference in perception? Absolutely not. You can only find differences in perceivers, which are reference points of camera positions, perceiving from different positions. But perception still is perception. Having infinite camera points, infinite reference points, looking at whatever, is not different. You cannot make it different at all. And being perception, which is prior to a perceiver, that's all. The perceiver is already perceived. But you cannot find anyone who is perceiving. You can just say there is perception.

That's why they call it the absolute Seer, where there is no Seer. And the Seer you can experience is already experienced. And that comes and goes. But that what is, is never never. So in that sense you call it in-no-sense. That's the innocence of your Nature. And whatever the innocence is sensing is not different from it, but is not that innocence. So your Nature is absolute innocence. Senselessness. Whatever comes from there can be sensed. And the first sense is the sensor. And then the sensing what can be sensed. But already the sensor is sensed. By what? You will never know what it is, but that is maybe what you are. The absolute Dreamer which is already prior to the dreamer you can dream. The dreamer can be dreamed, the dreaming and what can be dreamed, but who can dream the dreamer? So you cannot find that dreamer you are in the dream.

Whatever you find is only a dream. And whatever you can count is not the counter. You can count the counter, the counting, what can be counted. But that one who is counting the counter, the counting, what can be counted, cannot be counted. As there is no one who counts anyway. That's the tenth man. You always only count what you can count, but you never count the counter. And the counter is never never. But you are not an accountant. Who makes a story about some precious insights, precious spiritual events or understandings?

Q: If you come from that part of the world, have you ever been influenced by Western philosophers?

K: A little bit. Wittgenstein and Kant. But only a few pages. Because they were much too complicated.

Q: Are any of these closest to the things you talk about?

K: It's like Wittgenstein would say what you cannot talk about you should be quiet about.

Q: That means you can't talk...

K: No, I can talk infinitely about what I am.

Q: No, that what you cannot talk about better to remain quiet.

K: No. That doesn't help. I say so many words, and have never said anything. This is a paradox.

Q: You are referring to the Para Brahman when he said that. That is the thing you cannot talk about.

K: But to remain quiet there is one too many who remains quiet. You have to say without saying something. Meditation is words, talking without a talker. There is action without an actor. But that one who is quiet, he still talks too much.

Q: Nobody else hears.

K: It's like if you meditate for peace, ha ha. You want to make more peace out of peace. Meditation is your nature. But there is no one who gets anything out of it. That's the joy of meditation. The peace you can gain by meditation is a fake one. Meditation itself is peace. But not claiming 'now I meditated five hours, now I am more at peace'. But it happens. All of that is futile, thank God.

Q: This idea of Wittgenstein was quite appealing to me when he said like whatever you talk about, Reality or whatever, is something you cannot talk about, because any words you use are going to be wrong. So talking about that, talking about Para Brahman, or about Self, is futile.

K: Yes. But that's the fun of it. That's the joy in it. We are sitting here and talking and talking, and maybe in one split second you see it's all bullshit. Whatever can be said, whatever can be not said, is all bullshit. Can not make me more or less as I am. So it was good for something. That it didn't give you anything. That it doesn't give you anything, that's the good thing about it. That nothing comes out of it. That's the good thing about it. So we can talk and talk and talk. But this is the meaning of good company. There is no one who wants to change anything, and still talking like hell - this paradox, this living paradox.

Q: It does not add to the knowledge nor takes away ignorance.

K: No. It is ignorance. It is the nature of ignorance and it is the nature of knowledge. And it makes no difference. The Absolute in knowledge is the Absolute in ignorance. Nothing has to come, nothing has to go, for you to be what you are. So bla bla bla or no bla bla bla. You don't have to be quiet to be what you are, come on! And that what has to be quiet and thinks that is an advantage, let it have one. Be generous.

Q: You have been a musician. Music helps in this?

K: No. Painting didn't help. There is too much pain in it. Pain-ting. The word says it, it's pain. Because there is one who thinks he can create something. And then you always doubt what you do. Is is good enough? Is this really art? Oh my goodness! But if it happens, ok. But the moment you take yourself as a creator, you are in the pain of doubting. So God knowing himself as a creator, he doubts what he is doing. He becomes a creator and a doer. But that doer could never have done anything. The dreamed creator can never create anything by himself. It's all by the grace of call it Nature, call it Life. So there is a doer, and there is doing, and there is something that can be done. But the doer never has done anything. So nothing ever happened.

Q: What are your views on meditation? Is it something you recommend?

K: Drinking coffee. The next sip of coffee. The next breathing in. The next whatever comes. Because that is.

Q: It's just an activity?

K: No. Just experiencing what you are, that is meditation. No expectation that something can go away from you and something can come to you. You just enjoy the next, as you are. As the next can not bring you anything, as the last could not take anything from what you are. So the next will always be the next. There is no expectation. Or any regrets. There is no expectation in the next and no regrets from what was before.

Q: No expectation of peace?

K: No. That is meditation. So you are shanti. But you cannot get more shanti. Trying to get more shanti, you are in trouble. Trying to know shanti, you make it an object. Then you are in trouble. So shanti, shanti, shanti. That's the meaning, out of shanti only shanti is experienced. Shanti can only experience shanti. The Absolute can only experience the Absolute. There is only the Absolute. So the absolute experiencer, the absolute experiencing, and the absolute what can be experienced. All is the Absolute realizing itself, in an absolute realization. Moment by moment. That's peace. Peace not knowing peace, and there is no second who can disturb that peace. There was never anyone who could disturb that what is the Nature of existence. Come on! So there is uninterrupted peace. Peace, peace, peace, peace. But no one has that peace, thank God. And no one can ever own it. So it will never be your peace. That's the beauty of that peace. And the peace you can have you can lose. And already you are in the hell of ownership. That's why they call it 'ownership knot'. The heart knot. That you have a heart. That you can lose a heart. That you have to open a heart. All that which comes with having a heart. Oh my goodness! So that what is Heart doesn't know any heart. Doesn't have any heart. And no heart to lose. Or to gain. But having a heart. Oh my goodness. A pump pumping, that's ok. But having a heart, a spiritual heart, ui ui ui. No, it's all between an owner or that what you are. The relative ownership, being different from what you own, or being the absolute Owner not having anything to gain or to lose at all. There is no between. And any moment you are not that, there is suffering. Missing that what you are. And there is no between. The only fulfillment of that what you are looking for, is to be that what never needs to be fulfilled. So it's a paradox. And that what needs to be fulfilled will never be full enough. It's always too full or too empty.

Q: It's like desiring desirelessness.

K: Yes. It's impossible. There is only a wish because wishlessness is there. So it comes out of what it is, the wish is rising from wishlessness, and will go back to wishlessness. Automatically. Naturally. There is a natural rising and going again. And the wishlessness is uninterrupted what it is. So the realizer starts and whatever is realizing, and then it will be gone one day. But by that dropping of the unrealized one, no one becomes realized. So there is enlightenment, but in enlightenment there is no one who becomes enlightened. There is just a drop of the unenlightend one. Naturally, as it was rising, it will drop again. It is already gone now. It cannot even drop anymore. It never rose, that's the problem. So we can talk about realization. Realization may happen. But it never creates any realized one. And then just to be that what you cannot not be is just the drop of the idea that there could be one or is one at all. That cannot be done by anyone. You do it any night anyway. It's more than natural. Every night you happily drop the world and the body and whatever can be dropped, just to sleep. And no one fears that something may happen there. And every morning this pops up again. But if you could avoid it you would happily stay there, where no one is.

Q: Is it possible to stay there, being a realized one. Or there is always coming and going?

K: You always have to realize in the next. The next frame of the movie, which is what you are, you can not miss. You can not avoid what you are. You are that. How can there be an end to it? And if there is a next, like a daily life next, there is a daily life next. If there is no next, as in the oneness, there is no next. There is a finite and there is a infinite. So you experience yourself in the infinite, and in the finite. But the finite doesn't make you finite and the infinite not infinite. Because both are experiencing yourself in different ways. So you are neither infinite nor finite. Or whatever you claim. So what to do with it?

Q: Infinite and finite is your own...

K: Imagination. Even the infinite is imagination. Because if you say something is infinite, you create duality. Because if something is infinite, there is something that is finite. If there is something that is always, then there is something that is not always. So you better be that what never even knows whatever is or is not. But how can you not? You start again. Because you cannot not wake up. And then you fall in love again. And then the love affair starts. The passion starts. But the compassion is still there. Out of compassion there is a passion of love. Compassion, your nature, is never never. You are compassion, you are acceptance. And out of acceptance comes one who is or is not accepting. So what? So you realize yourself in that relative way of sometimes you can, sometimes you cannot accept. But acceptance has to be already there. Or peace. Call it whatever. That there can be even an experience of Existence, Existence has to be. In shamanism you are what is Existence, the absolute Self, and you have two absolute sides. The manifested imaginary side, and the non-imaginary non-being side. The non-being and the beingness. So you experience yourself in the beingness and in the non-beingness. But neither the beingness nor the non-beingness makes you more or less as that. You are never more or less. In whatever beingness experience you experience yourself, you have nothing to gain, and in the absence of any beingness experience you have nothing to lose. And there is only beingness and non-beingness because you are. And that has no cause. But whatever you expect to be better off there or there, you are off course. You are not what you are. And then we can talk about it. The Abstract can not know the Abstract. Whatever can be abstracted, you have to abstract to be the Abstract. All of that can happen. If it's meant to be, it will happen. If the Jnani way leads you to that, ok. If the Bhakti way leads you to that. But in the end you are that what you are. There was never any Bhakti, there was never any Jnani for what you are. But when there is Bhakti there is Bhakti and when there is Jnani there is Jnani. You cannot talk it away. You cannot say 'I am already what I am'. No! You have to go through all that whatever you have to go through. Even if you already realize 'I don't have to, because I am already...', you have to do it. You can not avoid one single misery. Ignorance. None of that can be avoided. All of that is what you are. No end to it. There is no happy end. That's the beauty of it. Happiness can never end. Imagine there would be a happy end. And that of a me!

Now I stopped going to Tiru and talking there, because it is too much. There are now too many Ramana disciples. The one who always said there are no disciples of the Self, there is only Self, the one who claimed I never had any disciple, and no one was ever his disciple, who never took any disciple. Now there are thousands of disciples who claim 'I am a Ramana disciple'. And making themselves special in it. He, the one who was destroying all the special things, there is only I to I, Self talking to Self, there is only Self, there is only Reality, now disciples making him a banana. Thinking 'we have to be like him, this is our master'. Then they put his photo behind them, and some other masters. And then having a big back-up. 'Ramana said, and I am in the lineage of Ramana'.

The one who said himself he has no lineage, and whatever is a lineage is unreal. They make a lineage out of him. What to do? You cannot avoid it.

Q: Lila.

K: Yes. Fantastic! Or Buddha. Buddha said there was never any Buddha walking this world. There will never be any Buddha walking this world. What comes out of it? Buddhism! As if you could develop, cultivate, your Nature. Happens. Like Advaita. There is no way to know yourself. What comes out of it? Vedanta. Then comes Advaita Vedanta. Then even Vedanta claims that by Vedanta you can attain Advaita. There is only Vedanta because there is Advaita. But they want to turn it around, totally. They would say in realization you can realize Reality. No! Reality is realizing itself in realization. But not in realization you can realize Reality. This is like this little illusion. I am amazed by it. Jesus - they all said it. And in spite of it there comes Christianity. Having a German pope! A Jew who created a German pope! Isn't it a joke? That's fun. I really found it funny. Imagine you could foresee what will happen with what you say. You really should shut up, if you could. It will always be misinterpreted. Whatever you say is a misinterpretation in the beginning. And whatever comes later is a silent post, only can be more wrong, wrong, wrong. False creates false. Infinite reactions to false. But I like it. That that what is not false can never be found in the false. False false false. I like this neti-neti-neti more than anything. If you could just stay in the neti-neti, no problem.

Q: Why do you call it misinterpretation? It could be the person's perspective?

K: Yes, but it comes out of the me, and whatever comes out of the me is a me's-interpretation.

Q: But others...

K: Yes, but when there is others it is already a misinterpretation.

Q: But for himself it is a perception.

K: Yes, but even that is a misperception. Wherever there is a perceiver is a mis-perceiving. There is a missing, there is a miss-perceiving. Missed in action. It's all wrong. I am not the first, I don't have to invent it. Ramana was a rare one who said it starts false, it ends false. And what is not false will never be found in the false, that's all. Whatever you can experience is falsity. So I can make pointers to that. But even to say everything is falsity is false. False, false, false, false.

Q: Your words saying it is false are false?

K: Yes! So the one who says everything is a lie himself is a liar. Wonderful. Let the liar lie. Be my guest. Like you are home itself, and there is a guest coming, a liar. What can the liar do? He lies that he has a home. He has no home. It's not his home. He claims to have a home. Ha ha. Ok. Be generous. Let this bloody guest stay for a while, he will be gone one day. He comes and goes. But not by your getting involved in his comfort. He will rearrange the whole house. But this house still doesn't mind. He thinks when this room is empty, then I will be better off. 'Emptiness is my home'. Ha ha ha. And then the rooftop. 'Nothingness is what I am'. Then he claims 'I go to the cellar. When I don't know what I am, I am what I am. I am the not-knowing'. He always walks through the whole house and always claims 'that is now my home'. Because he didn't feel so at ease there. So he always looks for ease and cannot find it. Rearranging the whole house. Making it more modern style, or abstract, or anything. But still, not happy. So the guest will never be happy. Never. There will always be something else what is better. The next one. The deeper realization. The higher one. Or whatever. Never ending story of consciousness trying to find a better place. Something better than consciousness. Wonderful. So even consciousness is a dream. Cannot help itself. And you expect consciousness to help you? It cannot even help itself.

Q: Listening to you I was reminded of similar ideas of one Indian so-called philosopher, UG Krishnamurti.

K: I met him 1995 in Saanen. One hour.

Q: Did you talk to him?

K: I met him, but I didn't talk to him. We avoided to talk. But I like him. He was a barking dog. And I agree, God knowing himself he becomes a dog and whatever the dog is doing is barking. I totally agree with that. Whatever comes out of this god-dog now is barking. God never says anything in his Nature. He doesn't even know a God. But any instant God knows God, he becomes a dog. Like god-dog. And then he becomes dog-matic. Dog-ma coming out of it. And then comes all the rest. The big dog-ma, creating all the bla bla barking around. So what else can a dog do? You cannot even blame him. He talks. He has a dialogue. The logo has a dialogue with the logo. Dia-logo. Always trying to get so sharp that it can even cut itself. It will never cut itself. Because for that it needs two. Even the intellect, there is no second intellect. As there is no second consciousness. So it can never cut itself. Can never know itself. So even as absolute Intellect, no way of knowing yourself. So if even the absolute Intellect can not know itself, who else can know himself?

Q: Even the absolute Intellect is limited?

K: Yes. The Absolute doesn't even have to be absolute to be the Absolute. And that what needs to be absolute to be absolute is not absolute. Fantastic. So even the purest, absolute purity, is not pure enough. That needs to be pure, to be purity. What a fantastic Nature of what you are, which doesn't even have to be Nature. Doesn't need to be natural. Never needs any natural state. It is Nature. Never knows any natural state. And any idea of purification is the dirtiest you can have. What's dirtier than purification? Instant dirtiness. You are dirty instantly when you try to purify. Makes you a dirty bastard. I like shit shit shit shit. Chit can not be known. Knowledge can never be known. But whatever can be said, enjoy the shit. Shit happens. And only shit happens. I am a farmer, so I like this way of talking. If I would be a professor of something I would maybe use different words. But I like this basic whatever. I would always ask, why could this little farm boy, this cowboy from the countryside in Germany, milking cows, ever come to this sitting in Bombay or sitting somewhere else talking about all that abstract whatever? Unbelievable! But things happen just as they happen. You cannot predict it. You cannot predict it. You cannot put someone into the right school and train him. I enjoy the helplessness as nothing else. There is no conflict in anything. Where is the conflict? With what? How can you be in conflict with something? It even needs an effort to be in a conflict. I am much too lazy for that. I am even too lazy to be lazy. That's my problem. Otherwise I could not sit here. Because trying to be lazy is much too much effort. I rather let the words flow, like being the flow and the words come out or not. There is a carelessness of talking. I don't know. Not to talk would be much too much effort.

THE SONG OF WRONGNESS

Q: I have this sense of great discomfort with being self-conscious, being conscious about whether I am doing the right things. From what you say, in enlightened living there is no self-consciousness, there is just the event and there is nobody to be conscious of what's happening. Would that be right?

K: Yes, there is no self who could be conscious. To be what you are, there is no self. There is no necessity of consciousness at all. The beginning of all trouble is the 'I am'.

Q: Being self-conscious?!

K: The beginning of all trouble is the I-am. Being self-conscious, then the trouble starts. The false starts. That's why for me there is no Sat-Chit-Ananda. Because it is interpreted like the self has to know itself and be in the happiness of knowing itself. For me it's never happened. That's already a pointer which doesn't fit. It's too much anyway. For me it's more like just Sat. That's it. Or Chit. Or Ananda. But not three together, then you imagine that you have to be conscious or aware of what you are to be happy. Then it's pain and then I call it such-shit-ananda. Then it becomes like a condition, that you can only be happy when you know yourself. You are what you are in spite of anything.

Q: So the idea of knowing yourself is...

K: It's a never ending story. That's Vedanta. That is trying to know yourself. That will never end. When the 'I am' is there, the 'I am' will always want to know what the 'I am' is. There is no way out. So the easiest way to be what you are is to be prior to that.

Q: And there is nothing you can do to be that?

K: No. By none of what you can do out of the 'I am', you can attain that what is prior. It's absolutely in spite and independent of all doings or not doing or knowing or not knowing whatever can be known or not known. So the Para Brahman doesn't know any Para Brahman. And what can know the Brahman and the Para-Brahman is already too late.

Q: But then that takes you away from even trying to better your personality?

K: No, it doesn't take you away from anything. There is no effect by that. It doesn't do anything.

Q: When you say 'be in That'...

K: No, I don't say 'be in That'. There is no one in That. There is no 'in' in That.

Q: I understand what you say, there is no one in That.

K: There is not even no one. One or no one is one too many. Whatever you say now, it's too late. Whatever you try now to make That something, it's too late. You already imagine what it would be. No. It can never be imagined by anyone. It's not an image. You cannot make anything out of it. No advantage or disadvantage. Whatever you say, it has to be in the 'I am', coming from there and trying to have an advantage or disadvantage. And then always checking: 'What would it be for me'? 'How would it be if I was enlightened'? 'What would happen'? But this is already too late. That will never end. The unreal will always try to become real. And already the 'I am', the purest notion of 'I am', is unreal. From that root-thought 'I' all the rest is following. So false creates false.

So even the creator is false. Whatever can be created is false. False false false false. So now trying to make that what you are part of that falsity, my Goodness! Of course you try that. Because you are in love with yourself. But it will never happen.

Q: Control or change, it's the same thing.

K: It's the same. You love yourself and by loving yourself you want to control yourself. Because you want to own your beloved. But you cannot own your beloved. In ownership there is suffering. Even the imagination that you can own yourself is suffering. That you are something that can be owned is dependency, is unbearable.

Q: I was just thinking, instead of asking a question and you answering the question, is there something you would like to say, which is not question-dependent? Is there some message you would like to give to someone who is sincerely seeking, and struggling?

K: Yes, I can give you a question!

Q: I want the answer without any question being asked!

K: It's an old technique: Try to find something which is not a hearsay what you picked up from someone, and try to find a question which is your question. Try to find a question which you haven't heard from someone, you have not read somewhere, no one has given to you, which you have not learned. See if that what you are has any question which is not second-hand. Try to find that question of yours. Any original question. Try it. And if you come up with it, show it to me.

Q: I don't know if it is original or not.

K: That would be the question. What is not what you have learned, what you have read, or your mother or your guru told you? What is that? What would you be without that hearsay, without that learning? Not even nothing you can claim. So that would be my advice: try to find that question which is yours, which is not second-hand. That would be the direct path. And I tell you, that what you are never had any question, never needs any answer for anything.

It's questionlessness. It's answerlessness. It's the Absolute. How can that question itself? And that questionable 'I am' which is always collecting some questions and answers will always collect question and answers. That's why I call it his-story. Who cares about his story? The story of him will always continue asking himself 'who am I?' or 'I am who?', 'I am who? Who am I?' - up and down like a spider spinning and withdrawing the net again. But even by withdrawing it's spinning. This spider 'I am' will always spin. Spinning, spinning, spinning. That Brahma that spins the whole world, that creator, always spinning whatever can be spun. And then withdrawing it again, just to spin something else. So you are that spider, or you can be what doesn't even know any spider, doesn't even know any spinning or anything. So you make your decision. For me that what is beyond that spider, just transcends that 'I am', which is the spider, by just being what you cannot not be. You will be without any question fine as you are. And there isn't any possibility of getting finer. And that what never can be finer can never be defined by anyone. So you are the finest of the finest. But the finest of the finest doesn't know any finest. There is no finest. And you are the highest of the highest. But the highest of the highest doesn't know any highest. Or lowest, or anything. But anyone who knows, that knower which starts with the 'I am', always wants to get more. It's never satisfied by anything. So now you can make a decision, whether you are this unsatisfied bastard you think you are or that what never even knows itself. It's not in your hand, but that you are anyway. For that there is an effortlessness of existence. Just to be that is an ease and nothing is more easy than just to be that what you cannot not be. And for the rest - the rest can not give you the Rest you are. So let the restless 'I am' do whatever the restless 'I am' is doing, it will never find rest anyway. Because the rest you can find is a temporary one and doubtful and will start something else. What to do?

Q: So the questions that one needs to bother about are those which are not caused by the conditioning, is that what you are saying?

K: No, I am saying that what you are never had any question. So you looking for some original question is already one question too many. And that one who is looking for that original question will never find it. In not finding that origin - who cares?

Q: All the questions are based on thinking.

K: On hearsay. You don't blame thinking. It's just someone who heard something from someone who heard something from someone - silent post. You know where it starts? With that what we are just doing. This is the beginning of the last moment of hearsay. This is the effect which creates all the other effects of that what is even the last effect. The last moment is created by this moment. Hearsay. This is the beginning and the end of that what was just behind you. The effect of realization of what you are. But you cannot find yourself in that realization. And the realization will always be a love affair with yourself, and in this love affair you want to know your beloved. The inquiry will never stop. So you better be in spite of that inquiry. Because the inquiry will never end. There will not be any happy end in it. And be happy that there is no one who ever knows himself in any relative sense. And that Knowledge you are you cannot lose anyway. Or gain in anything. What to do? So there is that absolute Ease, and whatever you can experience is a dis-ease. And you expect in the dis-ease to find the Ease? That's a sickness. It already comes with the first 'I am'. The sick one. The potential sick one then is seeking health. The seeker. The 'sick-er'. No one is sicker than a seeker. The seeker seeking that what is the seeker. It's just being in a misery of missing oneself. But what to do? It happens.

Q: So the seeker seeking the seeker is a trap?

K: It's not a trap. It happens. It's just the way you realize yourself. The 'I am' is a seeker. And then the I, already being a doubtful 'I am', out of the doubtful 'I am' comes a doubtful seeking what is a doubtful image. A doubtful image trying to seek a doubtful image, thinking by that he can get real. You cannot even blame it. The unreal is unbearable. To be unreal is unbearable. Even to exist is too much. It's unbearable. And from then on you want to get rid of that burden. It's like an inbuilt seed of misery. Whenever there is an experience there is an experiencer and something that is experienced, there is two. And this is unbearable. So you seek a way out of that. And that will always happen. And then there are seven billion others who are seeking. Everyone takes it personal: 'Maybe I can call off the search'. Ha ha ha. Still seeing seven billion others who are seeking, 'But I called off the search! I made it! I am awake now and I can show you how you wake up'. It's all part of that, false. One claims something and then wants to share it with someone else. So what can I do? I can just point to the false. To what you are I cannot point. This job is more than easy! Whatever you say is wrong!

Q: Did I get you right when...

K: No, that would be wrong. Whatever you get from me is wrong.

Q: When you used the word 'disease' I was wondering if inquiry is a disease.

K: Inquiry is already a dis-ease. Has to be. Who wants to wake up from a nice dream? If the dream is nice and no one is bothered, why do you inquire? There has to be a dis-ease. An automatic dis-ease. Any moment you know yourself you are in a dis-ease of knowing yourself. That there is a knower who is different from what he is. That is already a dis-ease. So there is a misery of separation, automatically. And there is no way out of it. And it starts very early. The very purest notion of 'I am', being awake, already there the false starts. So even that purest notion of awareness is not closer to what you are. And who wants to be close to what you are? You want to be what you are, you don't want to be close to what you are. In the closet, with yourself. Close-up.

Q: So what you are appears to be really enigmatic, very complex, unknowable.

K: No. It's so easy and so known by what you are, because you are that. Nothing else you know more than that.

Q: That is a paradox. I don't know what I am.

K: You know it absolutely. That you now can say now 'I don't know what I am', you have to know that you exist. There is an Existence which is Knowledge, which allows that one to say 'I don't know what I am'. Because that you can say 'I don't know what I am', you have to know what you are.

Q: And this knowing is not by inquiry?

K: In spite of inquiry you are. That there can be inquiry you have to be That. That there can be one at all, you have to be prior to that one. That there can be an experiencer at all, that what you are already has to be there, that this first experience can be there. And that never demands anything.

Q: I have this tendency to question 'Is this correct or is this an illusion? Is it something I imagine or is it something real?' This I always question for everything.

K: That is called dream. The dreamer dreaming about the dream, about a real dream or an unreal dream. Only when there is a relative dreamer he has a real or unreal dream. For what you are this question never applies. It only applies to one who is already false. Good and bad and right and wrong only applies to one who is already false. So that what is goodness and doesn't know any goodness and never doubts goodness. Now the doubter will doubt everything. And he doubts himself, and then doubting whatever he can doubt. Let him doubt. He will never stop doubting. Whatever he claims, whatever he can reach, is doubtful. Sooner or later he doubts it again and then comes something else. And deeper and higher and more awareness and another awareness and deeper realization – never ending story. So that story of that phantom which is sometimes unenlightened, sometimes enlightened, is a phantom story.

Q: You said yesterday a basic pointer is to be the Self.

K: Whatever you are looking for is for that which never has to look for anything. All you wish for is for that to be which never wishes anything. But by no wish you can reach that wishlessness which is what you are.

Q: And what you are implies you are Self?

K: I said you are Sat, and that what is Sat is Satisfaction itself. And never gets more or less satisfied. Its Nature is Satisfaction. But that what is Satisfaction doesn't have any idea of Satisfaction. It simply is that what is Satisfaction. It can never get more or less. And that what can get more or less satisfaction is satis-'fiction'. Very easy. There is fiction and there is satisfaction. So in that fiction you will never get satisfaction. So in that fiction there is a fiction of Sat. An idea of Sat. But for that what is Sat there isn't even an idea of Sat. It's just that what is Sat. But I can repeat it and repeat it, it won't make any difference. Because you forget it right away anyway. So whatever you can understand is a misunderstanding. Whatever. And I like it. All that misunderstanding is beautiful. By none of that, whatever is understood, can you ever attain what you are. It will never be good enough. And that's good enough for me. And all your heart is longing for is to be Heart without any idea of heart. To be Heart which has no heart to lose or to gain. Now that you have a relative heart, there is an ownership running you. This relative heart always longs for that Ownerlessness. That freedom of Heart, where there is Heart but there is no one who has any Heart or can claim any Heart. That what is Heart and can never be more or less Heart. And never needs to open up or close down, because for that Heart you are there is no idea of being closed or open at all. So all that applies to the relative heart of an ownership heart. 'My heart' - which is more or less open. And that one who thinks 'I have an open heart' is more closed than anyone else. I always like this heart business. It's very hard. To be heart is so easy. But to have a heart and then working on your heart, and wanting to make an open heart surgery. Then there is someone else you have to open your heart to, what a business! And then you claim for yourself 'I have an open heart, and someone else has a closed heart'. What an open heart is that, who sees others who have a closed heart? And then by whatever event it can be closed again. If it is not the way you like it, you close it again. 'I open my heart, I close my heart'. Sounds good. But it only sounds good. It is never sound enough. I don't believe in any heart. Questions about heart? I like heart. Valentine's Day! I like to destroy that fake heart, wherever I meet it.

Q: So you don't believe that there is anything called love?

K: There is something called love. But what can it be? False!

Q: Then it takes away the very essence of living.

K: I hope so!

Q: If there is no love, why would I want to live?

K: Jump out of the window! I don't hold anyone back. If you still think it is in your hand to jump or not to jump, jump! You cannot even lift your little finger without the acceptance of Totality. Without that what is already there. Who needs a sense of life? Who needs this love and who needs a meaning? Only the me. The me is still thinking that he can be loved by someone else without any condition.

Q: So what is unconditional love?

K: There is no unconditional love!

Q: How would you talk about a person like Mother Theresa? She had so much unconditional love.

K: No, she didn't have it! Come on! I liked her a lot, because she was the rare one who said in her letters 'I only do this work just to cover the darkness inside. I am not doing it for anyone else, I am just doing it for myself'. There was no one who was loving anyone. So don't claim that Mother Theresa has a loving heart. Selfish as everyone! And at least she admitted it, pure self-love, and not for anyone else. You just want to get out of the misery. And you think by doing good you can cover up the misery.

Q: When I see the portrait of Ramana Maharshi, that's a symbol of...

K: Shut down! It's all a hope. You think it's possible, and that makes you survive as a little one who thinks one day I will maybe be like Ramana. That's why I call it Ramana banana. The monkey mind makes even out of Ramana a role model how it has to be. In that sense I have to destroy even him, as Ramana destroyed Ramana, because he always destroyed that body, this image. No one can have compassion, not even him. And he was always pointing to it. Compassion cannot be owned. You are compassion. But compassion cannot be shared. And compassion never shows. That compassion that is showing is pity. You are pitiful now as one who sees Ramana as special. That's pitiful, because you pity yourself. It's all self-pity. Coming out of the pitiful me, and thinking one day I may be like him, and then and then and then. Postponing your so-called nature to whatever future event when it will be possible for you to be like Ramana. He was the first one who destroyed all the images! And now, what does he become? Ramana-ism, another religion in Tiru. That's maybe why I don't go back there anymore, because there are too many disciples running around who claim to be a disciple of someone who never took any disciples. What a falsity, running around this mountain now. But the mountain doesn't care. Someone claiming to be - I could... But I am too lazy for that. I have no interest in cleaning up. Otherwise I would have to destroy the whole universe. But I did already. How can I destroy what is not there? Just by being what you are you destroy everything. Whatever you can imagine is destroyed. What is there? There is only what you are. And just by being what is what you are, there is not even an idea of falsity anymore. But when we talk about how you can reach it, it's all false. So if you ask me what you can do – false! If you ask me whatever – false, false, false, false! But if you ask me what you are – you are That and this is this, and there is not even an idea of falsity. So yes, there is falsity in whatever we talk about.

And whatever I do is trying to destroy the falsity in front of you. But the instant you are what you are, there was not even an idea of falsity. Or right and wrong. Or something that has to be changed. Even someone going to Ramana and claiming to be a disciple, who cares? For that there is the absolute 'Who cares'. But if you ask me, that relative one, and I see myself being trapped in that idea that he can attain himself by just behaving like Ramana, then I have to hit him, or myself, because I don't see anyone else. So if I hit someone I hit myself. So if I destroy all the teachers, I destroy all my own ideas of teachers. It's not that I see any Ramana or someone who is false. I just see myself in that delusion of suffering about an image. So I rather destroy it. I do my best, but still I don't expect anything to come out of it. It's all futile. So it has to be more like fun. It's an entertainment. I cannot take it seriously. But the moment this energy is there, it's very serious. But it's an empty seriousness, it's an empty energy.

Q: So you have no ideals and role models...

K: I have many. But they are all empty. I still have an image of a girl I never met. Thank God. I never met that girl which would be fitting to this guy. Nothing has to change. I don't claim anything. I am as stupid as I was before. I still shave, I still dress in the morning, I brush my teeth which are not there.

Q: So no idea, no ideals?

K: I have no idea about no ideas. It's all what I am and I can not avoid what I am. So the next moment is just experiencing what I am. But by these experiences I cannot gain or lose anything. So there is no gainer, no loser, that's all. But that is your misery: you are a gainer or a loser. In that instant you committed suicide for what is the absolute owner. You become a relative owner, and now you get never enough. And you don't even have to give it up. I still have my bank account. All of that is there. To be what you are nothing has to go. You don't have to renounce anything. That I like about Ramana – the renunciation of renunciation is what you are. You cannot renounce what you are. So you renounce renunciation and just be that what you are. You devote devotion, because there is nothing you have to devote to anyone. Who can devote something to himself? And who needs that? So if you ask me, Ramana for me is like as I am, That. But to make him a role model I destroy him right away. So I have to call him Ramana banana. And only for the monkey mind it is so appealing. Let the monkey mind be busy. Always making role models and all of that holy holy business. He needs a holy business, because he is unholy. He is insane, so he creates an idea of sanity. So any moment there is something holy, you create the unholy, in the same instant. Holy shit!

Q: So when you say 'be what you are', and that's all you can be, that means be the contradictions, be the dis-ease...

K: Whatever. You are that what is ignorance, you are that what is knowledge - there is no second. That's Advaita. Non-duality, or no second, means you are That. And when there is ignorance there is ignorance. So you are absolute. Absolute means there is no second. And the absolute can never be attached to something else because there is nothing it can be attached to. So the absolute detachment, there is no one who can be detached from anything. There is not one who sees the world as an illusion and then is detached from the world. Just by being what you are, which is That, there is a total detachment. But not any relative detachment of one who is detached from something else. That's always like this little misunderstanding that there is one in realizing, creating one who is realized. Never happened. The unenlightened one drops. The little owner drops. Just by you being what you are, which is the absolute owner. But the experience of the relative owner doesn't have to go for that. That's the beauty of your nature: nothing has to be changed. It never asked anything. Never demands anything. Never needs anyone to be different. So there is an absolute acceptance of that what is. Just by being what you are. But not by any achieving any relative acceptance. So it will never be your acceptance. There is no ownership in acceptance. When you are what you are there is a compassion beyond your imagination. But this cannot be owned. So you cannot claim 'it's my bloody compassion'. Where there is a me, the mind, there is pity. There is only one pitiful I pitying another pitiful I. Self-pity. So it's very pitiful. That's why the Buddhists want to achieve this compassion. But in compassion there cannot be anyone left. So it will never be achieved, it can never be cultivated by anyone. But still they try. And I agree, they should try. Why not? Let them try.

Q: But why is the misery of separation felt very acutely only in some people?

K: No, it's in everyone. More or less. But it's in everyone. Even the one who claims to be happy is fearing that the happiness can go again. Fear runs everyone. The moment you exist you fear. There is an existential crisis already. And that crisis is like a doubtful I.

Q: But the misery of separation is felt very acutely by some people only. Others are happily enjoying their lives.

K: You think! You imagine. Because you think 'I am miserable and everyone else is happy'.

Q: Yes.

K: Yes. That's self-pity! Everyone is like that, if he is totally depressed: 'Everyone is better off than me!' And if you are claiming to be happy: 'I wish everyone would be as happy as me!' Always this reference point. And thinking no one is more miserable or more happy than me. That's the nature of it, this arrogant devil inside who wants to run hell. This little child, which is already there, being loved or not loved. And the world is doing what the child wants or not. It's like a little God inside, the little creator God, the little Godchild who is now creating and never pleased by his creation. And if he is just a little bit pleased, he thinks 'I am the biggest, I am the top of the world, the number one'. And if it is not behaving like he expects it to behave 'I am so miserable because my existence doesn't behave as I like it!'. What a game. So even the little one knows he is the Almighty, but then he asks himself: 'Why doesn't the world behave as I like it?'. There is this knowledge already, this is a natural knowledge, that you are the Almighty. You cannot deny it. Everyone thinks he is like this little absolute God. So God becomes a little one. Still being that God and thinking: 'Everything should be according to my will, but why isn't it like that? Why do I wish something and it is not just happening?' And then you do all these Avatar trainings and all of that so that you can claim that power back that you may have lost. With all the siddhi masters, concentration camps of siddhis, you think you can claim your power back, your almightiness. Because you want to rule, because you are in love with your beloved. Love is running it. And then you want your beloved to behave as you like it. And if the beloved is not behaving as you like it you are miserable. So it's never behaving totally as you like it. There is no happiness in anything, thank God. You cannot find any happiness in any relative experience. And it can never be owned by anyone. And when there is happiness there is no one left who can enjoy it.

Q: Why do some people come to people like you?

K: Because there are rare ones who are so fed up with the world and all the misery that they already turned their vision to that what is that what they are. And that is a natural tendency. When that is involved what is the Self and wants to be that again what is without a self, it will kill moment by moment what is in front of it. It's just reducing. It's like the absolute Abstract abstracting. First it goes out, and then abstracting again whatever can be abstracted just to be that absolute Abstract again which cannot be further abstracted. Or the Substratum, substrating whatever can be substrated just to remain in that absolute Substratum which can never be further substrated. So if this is involved - that is why everyone is sitting here. There is a tendency of what you call seven billion others to go out and look for happiness in the world. It's a mass tendency. And then in very rare cases like this, it turns around. Because that one is totally fed up. It tried everything - relationships, Mercedes, gold, houses, all material things that don't work, still feeling miserable. And then there comes the spiritual experiences. Then you go for the blissful I-amness, for the oneness experience. And then you have little bliss moments by whatever little understanding. And then you are miserable again. These little orgasms happening by understanding. Then it's like Kundalini rising or something, 'Oh yes, I feel it already in my back! My master told me, if I feel it there I am already on the right path'. And then 'Oh yes, now it's in the shoulders!' And then there are teachers: 'You have to open your crown chakra'. And then near death experiences, you have to leave your body. And then you leave your body, but back again: 'Shit! I have to leave it again!' And then you have this burning and you think 'Must be an opening of my third Eye. I can see clearly now!' And then suddenly you can say what you have never dreamed about, because this chakra opens here. You are so amazed that you can speak out of the blue, without any speaker. And then you say 'Now I am the oneness of existence, now I made it! Because my heart opened, because now there is heart without heart'. But even that is fake. Even that experience is false. Wonderful! You expected so much of the Kundalini, being in that flow of the Kundalini. But it was killing you, because if it really works on you, you will be not there anymore. So you cannot even harvest. You cannot harvest what you are. There is no harvesting. There is just what you are, and that is harvesting moment by moment. It was already there. You are permanently harvesting what you are by experiencing the next and the next. That was never different. This is not something new. So I don't deny the processes of anything. But you are moment by moment harvesting what you are. Experiencing what you are. And it is nothing new. So even experiencing a me in a misery is harvesting. You are experiencing what you are. So what? Does it make you miserable? No. What you are cannot be miserable by anything. How can that what is the absolute Seer get miserable if there is a happy or unhappy me? So all these experiences are there or not. They are always different. But they can never alter your nature. They can never change what you are. There is no possibility of changing. All of that is just there for entertainment it seems. Enjoyment. So you enjoy whatever is there. What is there what could be done to you?

And suffering about yourself, that's ignorance. Because this is what you are. How can the Self suffer about the Self? It needs two Selfs to suffer. When you are what you are, there is not even one Self. And how can the absence of any presence of whatever absence suffer about anything? That's the absolute end of the sufferer, which was never there in the first place. But any moment you want to make that sufferer happy – ha ha ha! It's like an infinite business. Some other questions? I always try to finish in five or ten or 15 minutes. But there is no danger that the questions ever run out.

Q: So what is this doubt?

K: You! You are the doubt. And the doubt is doubting the doubt. Whatever exists is doubtful. Any existence is doubtful. Because whatever exists, because it has to exist, it's doubtful. That's why they call it the direct path: just start doubting the doubter. And whatever the doubter is doubting is doubtful. But that there can be a doubtful doubter doubting whatever is doubtful, you have to be there. That's why it's called the Omnipresence, which has no presence, which is presence. Without the absolute Presence of what you are there is not even a doubter doubting what can be doubted.

Q: So the absolute Presence is characterized by the absence of the doubter.

K: No, the absolute Presence of what you are is in spite of the presence or absence of the doubter.

Q: So there is no concept of a doubter or no doubter. There is just the Presence. But that doesn't need to be talked about?

K: No, we can just say: without that there could not even be a doubter doubting something else. That you can even doubt your existence, first you have to be prior to that doubtful existence. You have to be that absolute Existence that there can be a relative existence doubting its relative existence. And that absolute Existence never demands any absence or presence of any whatever.

Q: Which manifests itself in living as total ease of existence?

K: Total ease? No. The Ease cannot be experienced.

Q: Which cannot be experienced, but which is the Ease itself.

K: But that is not an experience, that is your Nature. It's not an experience. Whatever is 'ex', it's an ex-ternal dream. But that what has no inside and no outside cannot be experienced.

Q: It is pure existence.

K: Even to call it pure Existence is still doubtful. Whatever you call it, it's not it. 'The Tao you can talk about is not the Tao'. It doesn't have to be pure. What existence has to be pure? Only a relative one. Existence doesn't know Existence. And there is no necessity of being pure. There is not even an idea of anything. All these ideas are in dream. Only in the unreal there are ideas of real or unreal and pure or impure.

Q: So when this consciousness of this small self comes in, then all these ideas come in.

K: The moment the 'I-am' is there, it is already the potential of all that falsity. You are the absolute Reality, but you can only experience yourself in unreal experiences. That's the nature of it. You can never experience your Self. So Reality can never be experienced. But I don't deny experiences. So the absolute Reality can only experience itself in unreal experiences. That's why the absolute Dreamer, which is Reality itself, can only experience itself in a dream, in a dream-like experience. But the dream-like experience never makes that absolute Dreamer more or less. However the dream is dreamed, or whatever happens in the dream, cannot touch that what you are. How can it be touched by its own dream? And now thinking that you can suffer about your own dream, how can that happen? Only what is in the dream is suffering. Only in the dream there is seeking. There is a me. Getting, losing, having too much or too little - all part of dream. What are we just doing here? Dream! This is an experience of misery. I don't deny that. And it doesn't have to go for you. For who does the experience of misery have to go? Only for you, for a me. What you are never cares about it. That's the question: 'Who cares?'

Q: It doesn't matter.

K: If there is matter or no matter.

Q: There is no matter.

K: No matter is still too much matter. There is no one who cares about matter or no matter. Matter, no matter? Does it matter if there is matter or no matter? Mind or no mind? Who minds, that there is mind or no mind? Never mind. What is that what is never minding anything? That what you are never minds at all. And that what minds is only the mind minding the mind. Let the mind mind the mind. It's his-story, and mind already is consciousness. And who needs that consciousness? Only consciousness needs consciousness. What you are doesn't need consciousness. So forget consciousness and be what you are. If you could do that. But you cannot. Because consciousness always pops up again. 'Hello, hello!' Hell-oh!. It's all hell! So hell means light. And when there is light there is this Lucifer-I, this little devil who lives by that light. And then he wants to teach himself, he wants to learn something. So God knowing himself, he becomes his own devil. And life – which is evil – when there is life, an experience of life, the opposite is evil. It's already misery. Same word – life is evil. So you better be that what doesn't even know any life. But the life you can know is what? Relative life. And that is separation. That is what is called the nature of evil – separation – two. And you cannot help it. You are Reality and you cannot help yourself, you have to realize yourself in separation. But does that experience of separation make you separate? Absolutely not! So Reality has nothing to gain or to lose in the way it is realizing itself. And you cannot realize yourself differently. You have to realize yourself as a lover, loving the beloved. The seer, seeing what can be seen. The experiencer experiencing what can be experienced. Even to merge them is too much. You confirm that there is a separation. Even to create oneness is separation. Whatever you do in that realm of that so-called scenery of a seer seeing what can be seen, even that you recognize yourself in that what is seen, is one recognizer too many. What you are never needs to recognize anything. That what needs to recognize something, understand something, is always a misunderstanding. Trying to control the beloved. Even by recognizing himself in it is one too many. It's all false.

Q: So there is no obstruction?

K: No. You can not be obstructed by anyone. When you are this, you are always obstructed. Even by being that you are obstructed. But by being what you are, what is Heart - how can Heart be obstructed? By what? It needs two! But if the dream starts there is a dream of two. Automatically. There is a dreamer and a dream. But already the dreamer is part of the dream. The dreamer you can dream is not what you are. So the dreamer, the dreaming, what can be dreamed, is all a dream. What you are is in spite of the dreamed dreamer, the dreaming, whatever can be dreamed.

Q: So the misery really is trying to take the obstruction away, that's where the two happen?

K: There is no bridge between this one and that. No bridge. You cannot attain in that what is false that what is not false. Whatever you try is just confirming that there is one who needs something. The phantom will always try to become real. So the phantom 'I am' already tries to become real. But it cannot happen. The unreal will never become real. And that what is already real doesn't need to become real. So there is no bridge. So there is no way to become what you are. As there is no way to become what you are, you never lost it. Just see the beauty of that, that you cannot reach yourself. That is a happiness. So whatever you can know, the knower who can know something or cannot know something, let him, it's his story. Let him be enlightened even. Who cares? He can claim whatever. He cannot claim anything. Because a dream claimer claiming a dream object, even enlightenment, who cares? Before he claimed to be unenlightened, and then he maybe claims to be enlightened. Ha ha ha! Wonderful. But what can he take away from you? Nothing. He is a thief who has nothing to steal. Only by you giving attention to him you make him real. And now you already paid attention to the first 'I am', you fall in love with that first 'I-am'. Now you pay attention. So you pay.

Q: So when the 'I am' does not exist...

K: It was never real. It never existed. It was always unreal. Because what is Reality is always prior and beyond that 'I am'. There was never any reality in 'I am'. And you cannot destroy it. That's why you cannot destroy it. Because there was never any 'I am' to destroy. And for what you are it never needed to be destroyed. Only the 'I am' needs to destroy the 'I am'. But who cares if the story ends for that phantom? What can end starts again. In ending there is no ending, in starting there is no starting. So let him imagine that now he made it. Ha ha. Be generous. Be absolute generous and let the dream be the dream and just be what you cannot not be. That's all. Nothing of that dream can deliver anything what you not already are.

Q: So all those who claim to be enlightened are all dreamers?

K: Absolutely. Only in the dream there is an enlightened one and an unenlightened one. That's the beauty of it. Let them be enlightened! Or claiming to be realized. I meet many of them. And I have fun just hitting them. But not because I want to do anything. It's more like I have a hammer and the hammer has to hammer. And there is a nail who claims to be enlightened. So I hammer the enlightened nail. But what to do with it? It's like a rubber nail. You hammer it down and you just turn around and the rubber nail - tick - back again. So how to destroy what is not there? You just hammer something that is not there, and then you turn around and it is back in business. I should be the most frustrated guy on earth!

Q: So they are happy dreaming that they are enlightened?

K: No, they are not happy.

Q: They imagine they are happy.

K: Don't get jealous of enlightened ones. Because they are as unhappy as you are.

Q: So all these things are just concepts to be relatively happy?

K: Relatively unhappy. There is no happiness in the dream. There is only more or less unhappiness. That's all. So no need to be jealous of anyone. But you see it all the time, that thank God there is no one who is enlightened, because they all have their little failures. Thank God no one was ever happy. There was never anyone who was happy, ever. Neither Buddha, Jesus, or Ramana, or anyone, was ever happy. That's the beauty of that.

Q: Less unhappy.

K: Even that not. If you really see it there was never anyone who was happy. And there was never anyone who was unhappy in the first place. If there really would be one who was unhappy, there would be a possibility of being happy. But there was no one in the first place who was unhappy. How can that one who was not there in the first place, which is the dream unhappiness, become happy? So there was no one in the first place who was unrealized, so how can that what was not there in the first place, become realized? That's the beauty of that there is no enlightenment for anyone. If you really see it, there was never anyone who was enlightened. Then there was never anyone who was unenlightened.

Q: Both are concepts.

K: Both are unreal and not real. So if you see that there was never anyone who was enlightened, that just takes that one away who is unenlightened, that's all. Very simple. It is not something that is a big deal. It's just a split second. You split all these ideas of gaining something in the dream just by being what you are, by just seeing there wasn't even anyone here. So if this is gone, where are all the others? There are only others because there is one here. No one here, no one there. But there is no bridge between it. You cannot fake it. That's the beauty of it. You cannot fake the absence of a presence of separation. You cannot fake it. And anyone who tries to by recognition of anything and then claims 'I am in the oneness'. Ha ha. 'My peace'. Ha ha. It's always fun.

Q: Is it possible to be what one is with or without baggage...

K: It's impossible not to be it. It's impossible for you not to be what you are. You always need a slight effort not to be what you are. You have to pretend you were born. You have to believe in your mother, you have to make an effort, just for that.

Q: Just by ceasing the effort, one can be what one is?

K: No. Just by being the laziest of the laziest bastard you cannot not be. Which you were never. You are laziness. And the laziness is even too lazy not to be lazy. If you ask me, I am so lazy I am even too lazy to be lazy. So I talk. Because automatically energy is dancing and if I would try to be lazy, that would be really a big effort. So I am too lazy to be lazy. So let the dream be dreamed and the dream is an effortlessness of dreaming. Because the dream is already there. The next moment is already dreamed. The last moments are still there. Nothing happens anyway. So there is no effort needed. Because it is a block of silence. Nothing ever happens in it. Everything is already there and never never.

Q: But you have a sense of being a witness?

K: A witness? No, I am sensing a witness, but I am not the witness I can sense. So who is witnessing the witness?

Q: So you have a sense of being the witness?

K: No. I didn't say that. You misinterpret what I say, because you want to become a witness. I said I sense a witness. And I sense witnessing and I sense what can be witnessed. But whatever I can sense makes no sense. What a sensation. What a circus! How many clowns do we need? Never enough. And then there are some clowns who claim to be directors of the circus. Avatars. And then some others claim to be beasts. And some others are musicians. Never ending circus.

Q: What's the definition of an Avatar? It doesn't make any sense.

K: No, it makes sense. Because Avatar is Krishna, and Krishna is God the creator who cannot change his creation. But he tries.

Q: But when they speak about certain people being Avatars, what do they mean?

K: It's not people Avatars. It's just aspects of Krishna. Aspects of consciousness.

Q: What's unique about them that they are named Avatar?

K: Who names them Avatar? Consciousness plays these roles. It's 'his story' – he makes this whatever happen. And in these stories there is consciousness with more energy, more siddhis, and it can produce Swiss watches. David Copperfield should be the biggest Avatar. He can produce whole airplanes, and no one calls him Avatar. Everything can happen in this dream. What can not happen in this dream? You can fly to the moon, you can fly to the next dimension. All of that is there. So in the dream there are Avatars. So what? Ali-babas. And I always think why is lightening not striking me? If there really would be an Avatar, he would be so powerful, if I make a joke about him he could just shut me up. But every word I speak is on the demand of Totality and cannot be avoided, not even by me. So there is no doubt in any word. The words are just doubtlessness. They are just by the total demand of what is, by what is the next moment. So no one speaks anything. There was never anyone who spoke any word. So all is empty. As the Avatars. There was never any Avatar with any siddhis. But still they are there in this dream. But you don't doubt a butcher who is butchering pigs, do you? It's the same. It's the same dream objects. And if you have 5 million followers you are not a bigger one. Then shit would be the biggest Avatar, because so many flies cannot be wrong. If the amount of disciples count. Sorry to be so basic. The farmer speaks. Because I had to step into cow shit so often. And the tails of the cows were beating me up so often.

Q: You talked about the three different states...

K: Three different ways of experiencing.

Q: And you said 95% of the day you are in...

K: Everyone is. If you are more than 5% in the state of being disturbed, you already end up in the madhouse.

Q: What is the disturbing state?

K: The me. The misery. If you are more than 1% or 2% or 3% of the day in the misery of the me, you end up in the madhouse.

Q: So people in the madhouse...

K: They too have an open heart. Because they can be disturbed easier than someone else who has a big armor around him. So a healthy ego is rarely disturbed. Because he is full of himself. But if the armor gets weaker, then all the information from outside gets into that, and then the disturbance is much more often. So the weaker your armor is, the ego, then the information is coming into that so-called system of me. And then you get disturbed much more often than one who is in his solid block of ego. And then you end up in the madhouse. And then the doctors want to build up a healthy ego again, an armor around it. That's why it is called a disease – it is an easing of the armor, the heart opens, the ego cannot take it. If it is a weak ego the heart opens, the armor - armor and amore - it's the same – then love happens. Someone is entering you and if that one is not doing what you like, you get disturbed. Every moment your heart is burning, because the beloved is not doing what you want. And then they call it romantic-schizophrenic paranoia. And I agree! Because your beloved is not behaving as you like it, it disturbs you moment by moment, the whole day. You cannot even take your attention away from it. 'What is she doing now? What is happening now?' And then you want to get rid of it, and you drop everything, and you end up in the madhouse. And then they start to build you up again. It's not for everyone that he reaches the armorless, this oneness state where there is no difference anymore. (Cell phone rings). Something is calling. In the cinemas now they block it. But not here. Yesterday everyone was speaking on the phone. The movie was running, heads are falling, werewolves dancing, and everyone on the phone. That are healthy egos! In India there are more healthy egos than in America. Indians I think have not so many problems with getting crazy, no? They are crazy anyway, they don't mind. Whole India is a madhouse, where should you go? Look at the traffic and everything!

Q: To have a healthy ego, an armor, or to be without armor, which is more advantage?

K: For the misery of what you think you are it's better.

Q: To be what you are?

K: No, there is no possibility of getting disturbed. Only the relative me can be disturbed. And then the relative me needs an armor around it and needs all these techniques for survival. For that we can talk about a more healthy ego.

Q: So the one with the healthy ego is more relatively happy?

K: No. Just relatively less disturbed. Not happy. Don't mix it. Less disturbed. There is always a tolerance limit for everyone. There will be a circumstance this will be disturbed.

Q: I wanted to know which has more advantage.

K: That would be your relative advantage, having a healthy ego. That's a relative advantage.

Q: That's why there is a saying 'Ignorance is bliss'.

K: Yes. There are relative advantages, I don't deny them. But this is hell. Being one who needs advantages is already hell. I am talking about the absolute advantage to be what you are never knows any advantage at all. Never needs any. That's the absolute advantage. But any relative advantage is doubtful, and for sure there will be someone who is crossing the line, and you will be in hell again. You can be the strongest guy on earth, the healthiest ego, there will be one who is stronger than you, who will beat you up when it is most unexpected. It comes from the side you will never be prepared for. Maybe your mother or your mother-in-law, or you fall in love again. All these big egos, when they are in love, huu! There is no security. There is no secure place in anything. You cannot find home. There is no secure home that you can find. Even awareness is temporary, you have to leave again. All the seven ways of dreaming cannot deliver the home you are. Thank God home cannot be attained. So as it cannot be attained you cannot lose it. That's the beauty of it. As you have never lost what you are you cannot attain it. So be happy. Worry and be happy. The worrier wakes up in the morning and the worrier worries. What else can the worrier do than worrying about the worrier? The self-love happens every morning, there is a worrier worrying about himself, being in love with himself, and then loving-caring about what will happen to me. And then seeing someone who is relatively more happy, and he already calls him enlightened Or someone who can be quiet. 'Oh, he doesn't have to speak anymore. He must be enlightened!'. What an idea! Or someone who can go to the Himalayas and not say anything to anyone for 20 years. Then you already call him a holy man. Because you know you cannot shut up. As much as you try. It's like the people who meditate. In meditation they can be as peaceful and in the Buddha position and wonderful, and the moment they come out the fly on the wall is disturbing their peace. They just reached that peace of inner harmony and they come out, the slightest sound: 'Better go back to meditation!' What kind of peace is that which can be disturbed? 'My peace'. So it's a piece of cake.

Q: They examined the brains of those who meditated for a long time and they found some changes. Maybe you should...

K: Me? Maybe the system would collapse! There is no silence there. Why should there be silence? The silence you can detect is a fake one. For me it's more vibrating energy. What is this thinking that you can sense silence somewhere? This is hell! That you think there is silence you can sense. How can silence be sensed? If there is a sensor sensing silence there are already two, and that is already not silence. It's a dream silence. So let them claim the dream silence by meditation, a different vibration in the brain. My Goodness. I like it. What a competition – who has the most peaceful brain? What an idea! But this is humanity. Olympic games of consciousness. Who has the most peaceful and the most active brain? And who is the biggest sufferer and who is the biggest enjoyer. It's always competition running. If you sit somewhere competition starts. Then you have to defend your position.

Q: But there might be a rare case who does not participate in this.

K: You cannot not participate, you are that. You have to participate without being a participant. You have to participate anyway. But if you participate without any participant, then it's fine.

Q: So these are the rare cases.

K: This is the absence of a case. Because everything else is being a nutcase. That's the absence of a case and that you cannot count. Because there is no one to count then.

Q: That is like a rare case...

K: That is like a case who doesn't know any case. That would be the rarest of all cases, because this is what you are. It is so rare, you cannot even find it. It is more than rare. It is so common, it's everywhere, but you cannot find it. So this is like a wonder-bar, you are sitting in front of it and you are that what you are, and you claim that you are thirsty. You are a fish in the water and you claim there is no water. But even the fish is not different from what it is drinking. So when you drink you have to go (to the toilet). What you are is never thirsty, that's the beauty of it. No urination possible. Drinking without urinating. There is no digestion possible. You don't have to digest yourself. That what you are is an open front and open back. The next moment comes. Welcome, wel-go. There is no advantage in keeping anything, or disadvantage. Sometimes something stays for a bit longer. But even that goes sooner or later. So the front door and back door are always open. And in the middle there is a collector functioning, collecting something he likes or doesn't like. And there is a collection of a his-story. But this will be gone sooner or later. When this body dies it will just go through the open back door, as everything. In German we say 'The last shirt has no pockets'. So you cannot take anything away from this collection of whatever deep insights, deep realizations. It will all be gone with this.

Q: So this collection is...

K: It's an analogy of a soul who collects little pearls of events and calls it my story. It's a relative soul of a collector, collecting relative events like pearls hanging around his neck, and calling it 'my story'. And it begins with my birth, and ends with my death. And in between there are bigger and smaller events and maybe a very big one would be enlightenment. And then he puts all the other ones into his back, that no one sees them, and only the enlightenment stone is in front. And then he shows it: 'Look how enlightened I am! This event on September 9, 1993, look at it, since then I am sharing that'.

Q: But event, after death, it goes out the back door.

K: Whatever enlightenment creates an enlightened one is bullshit. In one instant it's gone.

Q: But the energy cannot be destroyed.

K: Energy cannot be destroyed. But the phenomenal expressions of energy will be destroyed anyway, just by the next moment. So whatever comes is already gone. So what now comes as the next moment is already gone. By coming it's already gone. But what is the absolute Experiencer is not coming in these experiences of coming and not going in these experiences of going. So in going nothing is going and in coming nothing is coming. So an 'I am' came, and an 'I am' will be gone. And you still will be what you are, as you are now what you are. And to be that is Effortlessness. Efforts are only in dream. Making or not making an effort belongs to the dream phantom. Doing or not doing belongs to the dream doer. But that non-doership of Doerlessness, which is what you are, what all the doers and not-doers spring from, is always that what it is. Never has done anything. It's like the laziest of the laziest. The shyest of the shyest. It never shows up. And whatever shows up is a show of it, but not it. It's not different. This is the whole circus of a show of what is. But that what is the show is not that what is showing itself. What a show! Then it became Osho even. O-show! Once there was Osho, now there is No-show. Hello, good-bye. Teachers come, teachers go. Welcome, wel-go. Like Karl comes, Karl goes. It's already a ghost. That's why it's called 'goes-t'.

Yes, what else can I not do?

Q: The bottom of every thought is fear and time?

K: Where there is time there is fear. Where there is two there is fear. Even when there is just God and God. God knowing himself, there are two Gods. Already one God wants to be bigger than the other one. That's like the snake: the snake looks at its own tale and there is another snake suddenly. And then he brings his armor out, then fights this other snake. He wants to even bite that other snake. So it's a fairy tale. That's why it's called a fairy-tail: consciousness looking at its own tail and thinking there is another consciousness. And then he wants to build up a defense system. Then it becomes a diffi-cult. He wants to cultivate a harmony or disharmony with this other snake. There is a difference between the head and the tail. And then the head wants to tame the tail. And the tail is just moving. The whole movement of the universe is the tail of consciousness. The creator having a tail and the tail is moving. The Gnostic sign is like that – the Gnostic, the one who knows, is like the recognition of consciousness realizing that the tail is not different from what is the head. And then there is the peace of a Gnostic. And the Agnostic is ignorance, there is no knowledge. When you are the snake, who can be bitten by the snake? You cannot kill yourself. But if there is another snake then there is a poisonous other one who may kill you, and then you fight the other one, instantly. There is fear. So you wake up being a seer and the seeing what you see is different from what you are, so you want to control what is. Very suspicious: there is something else than you. Look at it! The whole world...

Q: You see something as separate.

K: It can only happen in separation. There is an experience of separation. But I can only say: by the experience no one is separated. There was never anyone who was separated. It's like the snake looking at it's own tail. It's still the snake. The ignorance is that you take this tail as a different snake. As the world is different from what you are. But now trying to overcome that, you make it more and more real. That's why you better don't know yourself at all, not even as a snake or anything. Just be the snake not knowing a snake. That what is the snake, what is there to fear?

That is what you cannot not be, your natural state is to be that what is Kundalini. But there is no one who has Kundalini. You are energy. But there is no one who has energy. Who is the owner of energy? Show me anyone who has energy. It's the other way around. Energy has you. Energy plays you. Who claims to have energy? A phantom!

You Have No Business With Yourself

Q: In that state of 'I am', the awareness, if I understood Ramesh right, he said the best thing that could happen is being connected to the Source. That's the best one could expect.

K: Connection is already...

Q: Yes. From what I heard you say is that in enlightened living, even that is saying too much, there is just the I, not even the 'I am'. Is that right?

K: I would not say connection. Just being what you cannot not be in that 'I'. Being the 'I' of the 'I'.

Q: That's the part which I was not very clear about, 'being connected to the Source'.

K: From the 'I am'.

Q: Yes. From the 'I am' point of view.

K: The 'I am' connected to the 'I', the I-awareness. The I-awareness is already prior to the 'I am'. So even being connected to the 'I am' awareness, already that might be the best you can get in the relative sense.

Q: So enlightened living is even prior to that, not living in the 'I am'.

K: Yes.

Q: So it is just the 'I'.

K: Not even that. Life itself, which is what you are, doesn't know any I, doesn't know 'I am', doesn't know any world. But the best you can get in this relative dream, that you are aware of what you are. And that 'I am' is aware of awareness. It is like the awareness of awareness, you can maybe get. That there is no one left who is aware, that you can get. But the absence of one is still a presence, is like a condition, it cannot be for what you are. Because for what you are, you are in the presence and in the absence of whatever. But the best you can get in the dream is the absence of one who is suffering or not. But even the absence of one who is suffering or not suffering is relative. Because for the absence it needs someone who is absent. It has to be in the dream. Whatever we can talk about, advantages and the best and whatever, has to be in the dream. It never applies to your nature. But that's not bad to get in the dream. So I don't mind it. But if you ask me what the absolute advantage is - there was never any dream and there is nothing to attain and there is no differentiation. There is no defining of any better or less or anything. So yes, in the dream you can reach whatever, the best, the highest and lowest, you can have. But for what you are it makes no difference. It's all a phantom getting better or worse. Because for what you are there is no better and good. The Ease you are was never never. And that ease of a phantom is the ease of a dream phantom. So, if it happens it will happen. But the question is: who cares?

Q: It may not happen?

K: It may not happen. It may or may not. But you cannot avoid it. The shift from the 'I am the body' to the 'I am' happens automatically and then the shift from the 'I am' to the pure 'I' may happen. And then even the shift to that what is the absence may happen. And then even the shift to the presence presence, and then to the I am of the I am, all of these seven states. But none of these shifts can get you closer to what you are. So in none of these states you can know yourself more or less. All of that is there because you dream it. And the absolute Dreamer cannot be found in one of these seven ways of dreaming. But again, in the relative way, that would be the best.

Q: So enlightened living is not really living in the dream, but just the awareness that the living is a dream?

K: That would be enlightened dreaming. Not enlightened living.

Q: So there is no enlightened living?

K: That's what I say. It is enlightened dreaming. In the dream there is enlightenment and unenlightenment. And there is better and worse. Only in the dream.

Q: Anything in time, space, any sound, is essentially dream stuff?

K: Yes. Even no time is time and dream. Even what is prior to that is dream. Or whatever you can point to is dream. Whatever you can talk about is dream. Whatever the intellect, the logos, can come up with is dream. But that there can be a dream, a dreamer, an intellect, a mind, that can then produce something in that dream, you have to be what you are. Without the absolute Dreamer none of that could be. And I can just point to: you have to be, and that is in that relative now, here, not different as in whatever closer or enlightened dream or unenlightenment dream. That doesn't know any enlightened dream or unenlightend dream.

Q: All these discussions can only happen in the dream. And all realizations happen in the dream.

K: Every discussion, whatever can be talked about, it's all dream time. The Aborigines call it dream time. But what to do? You cannot get rid of it. And you don't need to get rid of it. That's the problem. The one who needs to get rid of it has no power. And that what is Power, has no need. And that cannot be mixed. There is no bridge. That what is Energy never needs any change, and that what is already an expression of Energy has no energy, it cannot change anything. So there is no winning. That one you are doesn't need to win anything, and that what you think you are, whatever it's winning, it's already losing. So winning and losing is dream. Closer and higher and whatever you can come up with, even enlightened living, all of that is dream. But if we talk in the dream about a dream advantage, we can.

Q: Anything you can talk about is only in the dream.

K: Yes, but that's quite relaxing.

Q: Yes, not bad.

K: It's neither bad nor good. That's good. It's bad, even worse. This is the good news for what you are, but the absolute bad news for what you think you are. 'Poor me! Whatever I gain I have to lose again! Enlightened living is again a dream living. Huuuh!'

Q: In this dream you say you are what you are, you already are.

K: I just say you can not not be what you are. And that is what you are.

Q: That's the message?

K: That's the message. And being that what you can not not be, you can never not be anyway, there is no question about good and bad, there is no question about enlightenment or enlightened living or anything. All of that is dream. But if you want to talk about the dream and what can happen in the dream, we can talk about it. I have no problem with it. But still I have to say, whatever you reach in the dream will be a dream goal and you have to lose it again. And for me, to be what I am - incomparable with anything. Because there is no one who compares anything. There is no comparison, there is no discrimination, there is just being what you are. And the rest doesn't give you the rest of that just being what you can not not be. Because that is peace already. And can never be attained by any dream peace. So let the dream peace be peaceful or not peaceful, alive or not alive. The dead are in the dream and the one who is alive is in the dream, but both are dead for what you are. Because both can not touch what you are or alter or change that what is your Nature, which is Life itself. Even to call it Life itself is too much.

Q: At the time of death, death of the body, you are what you are. Is this consciousness...

K: ...it goes on and goes on and goes on. This consciousness will incarnate again and again and again. The only way to stop the wheel of reincarnation is just being what you are. The easiest way out is just being what you are. Nothing is easier than to be what you cannot not be. Anything else, any effort, you wanting to stop the wheel of reincarnation – you are already reincarnated again. Even wishing not to be incarnated, already you are back again in business. Because that confirms one who is incarnated now, who doesn't want to be reincarnated. So that incarnated consciousness will automatically reincarnate into something else, the next. In form. Information will happen again. But everyone wants to stop the wheel of reincarnation. Even the Dalai Lama wants to stop it. And no one ever made it! It cannot be stopped, because it was never running. That's the problem. There was never any movement. How can you stop what is never moving? Only in the dream there is movement and in the dream there is something going on. In the dream you may think there is a merry-go-round and you want to stop the marry-go-round. So maybe in the dream it stops one day. And then it starts again. But for me it's not even moving.

Q: Karl, you say there is no bridge. Yet what happens is the words are going in both directions. In one way it helps in creating the external world, 'I am', I am so and so. And then you point with the words...

K: No, I don't point to anything. You cannot say I point to something.

Q: It must be there before...

K: No, I don't say it must be before. I say it's in spite. It is with and without. It is not before and it is not after.

Q: But you say for that to happen you have to be...

K: No, you have to be in spite of. But not before. There is no time in that. There is no before in that.

Q: So you are pointing and we are using words.

K: I am pointing to that what is with and without. You are with the dream and you are without the dream. That's all. There is no before and after.

Q: The mechanism, the functioning...

K: What functioning? There is no functioning for what you are! Now you want to control the dream again!

Q: I am just pointing to the deceptive nature that is frustrating, the use of words.

K: I hope you are frustrated!

Q: The vibration of energy that manifests as words in the dream...

K: No, there is no manifestation of words. You want to control it again! You want to show the duality of words. But who sees the duality of words?

Q: The phantom.

K: So what is the problem with it?

Q: The words in themselves have a double edged sword.

K: There is no double in it. You just want to play clever, that's all. Play clever and be frustrated. I don't mind. The understanding is frustrating, because it is a misunderstanding.

Q: But this phantom sitting here...

K: You really think there is someone sitting here, after all these years I talk to you?

Q: But the phantom...

K: I should be the frustrated one! Thirteen years of talking to her! Still claiming to be the phantom! You have learned nothing! You are stupid as I met you. Born stupid and you will never learn anything! That my mother always said.

Q: And you believe it?

K: No, I know it. I am born ignorant. That what I am never knows anything. And I never learned anything. My Nature never learned anything. So she was right. The ignorance was there and now the ignorance is there.

Q: In all these years you had no modification, changes in your wisdom?

K: Not at all! Thank God there is no 'my wisdom'!

Q: No change in perspective?

K: Yes, but that is all stupidity!

Q: Ok. But there is a change in the perspective?

K: There is change of stupidity. But I haven't learned anything.

Q: It's all in the realm of stupidity.

K: It's all in the realm if stupidity. All the scientists are stupid. Everyone is science fiction. And science fiction is stupidity, is ignorance. So you are born stupid, and you never learned anything, and you will die stupid. Who cares about the stupidity you earned? More stupidity is still stupidity. There is more or less stupidity, that's all.

Q: So whenever one goes through the experiences - some of them call them calamities, changes, transformations -even to say all that is imaginary?

K: Bogus!

Q: You haven't undergone any change?

K: No.

Q: No experience of change?

K: There are experiences of change, but no one is changed.

Q: The one is never changed.

K: There is no one. That unchangeable, you make it different again to that which is changing. You want to make a difference. That what can be changed and that what can not be changed. Even that what can not be changed is stupid. The same stupid as that what is not Self.

Q: But the Self is unchangeable.

K: But the unchangeable is another concept only. You make it different from that what is a change. That what is unchanged is still part of the dream. Already the spirit is unchanged. So you think the spirit is different from what is this? Who makes a difference?

Q: So there is not something that you call Absolute?

K: I call it Absolute but I don't call it unchanged.

Q: Ok. So the Absolute is not unchanged.

K: It is neither unchanged nor changed.

Q: So what are the characteristics of the Absolute?

K: There is no characteristics!

Q: So that's why you call it Absolute then.

K: Just because it is called that. I don't have to invent a new name. I am just too lazy.

Q: Is there any evidence...

K: It doesn't need any evidence! Only you stupid need an evidence.

Q: Yes, I am certainly a stupid person wanting to know if there is something beyond stupidity.

K: Yes, but that's stupid!

Q: So calling it Absolute is also stupidity.

K: It doesn't know any stupidity, but I would call it absolute Ignorance.

Q: And absolute Knowledge.

K: Yes, but absolute Ignorance is absolute Knowledge. There is no difference. It will never know itself. And that one who knows himself is already more than stupid. You wake up as someone who is dumb. Waking up is dumb. And then you get dumber, become I-amness. And then you are the dumbest when you have a body. Dumb, dumber, dumbest. That's your so-called life. This relative life really starts dumb, to wake up in the morning. Then you get dumber when you have a spirit, and then it is dumbest when you have a body. That's all. Whatever you can experience is dumb, dumber, dumbest. So you are damned in dumbness. Any moment you are stupid enough to fall in love with one of this I, I am, or this body, you are dumb. And only love can make you so stupid to fall in love with an image of yourself. Then you are in this passion of love, and then you want to get out of this passion. Passionate love. That makes you stupid. And no other energy can make you so stupid as loving yourself. You cannot avoid it.

Q: So, one cannot talk about the non-stupid Absolute?

K: We can talk about it.

Q: In the realm of stupidity, in relative life, like mind, body, consciousness, whatever, in this there is a transformation taking place?

K: Every day. Every moment is different.

Q: And this transformation, can it go in one particular direction by investigating the experiences?

K: Yes.

Q: Is it an advantage to go in that right direction?

K: For the relative stupid one, yes.

Q: There is no approach to the Absolute?

K: No. No one ever attained himself.

Q: Not attained. But approaching?

K: There is no closer to That. There is no closer.

Q: There is some secret hidden desire that by investigating, analyzing, using your so-called intellect, there may be a possibility to understand...

K: Yes, maybe. But who wants to be a maybe? Whatever comes out of maybe-me will only gain a maybe whatever! Maybe, maybe, maybe. That's science fiction. Just imagining there is maybe a possibility. And there has to be already a maybe-me which is now dreaming that by maybe maybe maybe...

Q: Yes, but that's why we are here, for this stupid maybe!

K: Yes, that you became a baby, now you are a maybe.

Q: Absolutely!

Q: Karl, are you saying that essentially it is the source itself, which is playing out these 7 billion people and experiences...

K: It doesn't play it! Consciousness plays that. Don't mix that up.

Q: And so this is just for a game?

K: No one needs to know for what. It's just there. Call it play, call it entertainment, call it whatever. It makes no sense, thank God. And no one needs any sense out of anything.

Q: So it doesn't matter if anybody is a murderer...

K: Of course it matters in the dream! Do it, and you will be killed too. You cannot mix it. In the dream there are all the consequences you have to bear. Whatever is done, you have to bear the consequences. But for what you are it makes no difference. In the dream a person has to fulfill his role. It will be played. And there will be consequences for actions. And sometimes not for that one who has done it, someone gets punished not even having done it. Who cares? Consciousness plays all these things. Consciousness plays the doer and the victim, and the judge and whatever.

Q: So just because it is a game we cannot say that in life there is justice.

K: There is justice. Because consciousness gets always punished for that what consciousness has done. It's always a perfect justice and fairness. Consciousness, who is the absolute Doer, always gets punished for what the doer has done.

Q: Yes, it does get punished. But not the same body-mind.

K: Doesn't matter. It's all consciousness. Who cares what body-mind consciousness gets the lottery winning? It's a punishment to win in the lottery, because then you lose all your friends. You are totally alone, because suddenly everyone wants something from you. You know they don't just want to be your friend. It's all punishment. And consciousness is always the punisher, the punishing, and what is punished. Moment by moment. Consciousness is punishing itself in the misery of missing itself. It's a permanent punishment. And no one else can punish itself so very well as consciousness is punishing itself. Missing what is consciousness. Fantastic! What a punishment! That's why it is called U-punish-ads! Any moment you are missing yourself you punish yourself by missing yourself and being in the misery of not being what you are. And consciousness is stupid enough to miss itself. What to do with it? And this punishment is instantly. God punishing God that God is not what God is. God knowing himself, God punishing himself, by missing that what is God in its Nature. Just knowing himself, the purest knowledge to exist, already punishment happens. Instantly. How stupid can you be? And then you pray to that stupid God? What is what you are, and you cannot avoid it. I just can present the helplessness. You cannot avoid knowing yourself. So what? What to do? And by knowing yourself you miss yourself. So whatever you experience is misery. But happiness can not be experienced, thank God.

Q: Karl, a little clarification on this. Ramesh used to get very pissed off when anyone would come up with this 'there is nobody home'. He could not accept this concept of 'nobody home'. Yesterday I heard you saying - and I am just clarifying if I got this right: 'Enlightenment is despite there being somebody there or not being there. Presence or absence'. So it is not dependent on the absence, or it is not dependent on there being nobody home. It is independent of that?

K: Absolutely. I always have this with Tony Parsons people in Holland: 'Nobody home'. And I say: Who is not home? Who is the nobody who is not home, and who is realizing it? Who is there who sees there is no one? Who claims to be no one? I have no idea. But it happens. Shit happens. In the absolute I don't care if there is someone or not, claiming it or not. But if somebody asks me, I have to say 'bullshit!' Nobody at home is still one too many.

Q: Karl, I am looking at your story, and of course I am always looking at what happened to this guy and my mind immediately starts setting up a series of goals to be achieved in imitation of this or that. Whether I like it or not.

K: Automatic!

Q: And when you were talking about seven ways of realizing yourself, this also immediately sets up a series of goals to be achieved.

K: Yes, and I don't mind.

Q: It's all part of the same ignorant idea that you have to do this this and this in order to get that, it's all the same horseshit, bullshit, cowshit.

K: But as we talk about anything I can talk about it and point to it that in none of this you can attain what you are.

Q: What happens to me is that I immediately say 'before and after', this has to happen before that happens, it's another idea I have about what could happen or will happen.

K: And that will never end. And I say again you have to be in spite of this bla bla bla and that one who wants to achieve something. Because that inquiry of consciousness is a function of consciousness and will never end. And that is part of inquiry, making it before and after. And inquiry can only happen in before and after.

Q: That's the only thing that's going on here.

K: That's the dream.

Q: That's the essence of it, that it's continually creating a goal to be achieved.

K: Yes, there will always be a different trap. Now I present you the seven traps. And before there were maybe infinite traps in the first trap, like girls, mother, love, whatever, to achieve. And now there is a second trap like I-amness, then the more subtle trap is the pure I-awareness, that's really a subtle trap, and then the trap of the beyond. And then even the trap of the I of the I, and the trap of the I-am if the I-am, and then the trap of being that what is the world. These seven traps I can point to, I can show you, they may happen.

Q: The only thing I am left with at the end of all this is: anything I can think of, anything I think I understand coming from you, anything that's going on in my head that I recognize, means I am still caught up in this dream thing and there is nothing I can do about it. But it doesn't mean it's going to stop going on and on and on like this.

K: And even that understanding is another trap. Understanding happens and then it will be gone again and then there will be another trap. No end of that. And you will be trapped by what you are infinitely. And I can sit here and say: who cares about being trapped by what one is? This is the way you realize yourself. Being a trapper, trapping what can be trapped, and you are always the absolute trapper trapping that what is trapped.

Q: When you say 'realize yourself'...

K: No, I don't say that! I say 'what you are has to realize itself'.

Q: This is what I mean, I am paraphrasing.

K: And there will be no end to it. There was no beginning and there will be no end of it. The next sip of coffee is the realization of what you are. I don't say you have to realize yourself. It is the realization.

Q: Any functioning at any level is realization?

K: Absolutely.

Q: So what happens is, the mystical states, the mystical experiences, the siddhis, all these are like the candy in the window.

K: They are all just different realizations of what you are. All of this is self-experiencing, but they are not better or worse than a sip of coffee for what you are. So for what you are it doesn't make any difference, there are no levels in it. There is no higher or lower experience. You are experiencing yourself moment by moment in whatever state, and all the seven states are there. You cannot deny them. So not talking about them would not help. I can just point to them, and you have to transcend them all by being what is that what is dreaming them all.

Q: That which is dreaming, when it hears that, it assumes immediately that it needs to transcend...

K: Yes, you have to transcend the transcender.

Q: Which is another idea.

K: No, it is not an idea! You absolutely transcend the transcender by being that what is in spite of the transcender transcending or not transcending. That is transcending the transcender. It's the easiest you can not do. What's the problem? Renouncing the renouncer just by being what you are you do every night.

Q: But that in any way is not in our hands.

K: It's only in your bloody hands! It's only in that hand what has no hands.

Q: But how so?

K: How so! How can you not be what you are? Every night you do it naturally. So just be it here and now, that's all. How can you not be it? Just be lazy. You have no business! There is no business for you here!

Q: Ja. ('Yes' in German)

K: Ja.

Q: Ja. I mean no.

K: Who makes you so busy? You are only busy because you think you can make a bargain.

Q: I have a lot of ideas.

K: Yes, I know. You bargain with yourself. You become a little bargainer, buying low and selling high, like a little businessman. And you think when you have more then you are more. And that makes you frustrated, because having more doesn't make you more happy. Having more spiritual experiences doesn't make you more happy. Having more blissful bullshit moments doesn't make you more happy. Because you already know when they are happening they will be gone again, and then you have a hangover. And all of that makes you busy, like a businessman, like a dealer. And I just offer you: end of the business. Close the business. Because you have no business with yourself. This is closing down the business. Because you have no business, you are the business. But the business is not busy.

Q: It's very busy!

K: No!

Q: Yes!

K: No! There is no busy-ness in it.

Q: I have a lot of busy-ness!

K: Yes, you! A dream businessman in a dream business of buying and selling bullshit.

Q: Yes!

K: Yes. That's your business.

Q: I have got a steady business!

K: Whatever you can own and you can get busy by is what? Shit! It's a shitty business. It stinks, from the beginning.

Q: Now, let's not be negative!

K: You better declare total bankruptcy because you have nothing to lose anymore.

Q: I don't even need a lawyer for that.

K: No lawyer. No divorce. I can just give pointers. You cannot divorce from what you are.

Q: So the other thing I was thinking about, this business of sitting with someone, apparently the Upanishads means 'to sit with'.

K: Yes, that's the holy business.

Q: Yes, but here we are sitting with you, allegedly. I know for you we are not sitting with you, but for us...

K: I am sitting with myself.

Q: Ok, yes. But is that you or is That?

K: I have no idea. I don't have to know That.

Q: Ah, ok.

K: That's the beauty of what I am, it doesn't have to know what it is. I absolutely don't know what I am and what I am not. I call myself whatever.

Q: But for some people for instance they come in here, sit five minutes and they say 'no thanks'.

K: Thank God!

Q: But for some other people like myself it's like oxygen, it feels good, whatever.

K: Yes, because there is a comfort beyond your imagination. What I am doing here, I am the absolute dealer. I make you the absolute addict for what you are. And only by that absolute addiction you give up all the other addictions. And then in the absolute addiction there is not even an addict anymore. And that you enjoy to the max. Just by being what you are there is an absolute addiction as you cannot leave what you are, but there is no addict, and so there is no sufferer. And everyone comes for that only. Not because of understanding. That's good company. The absolute addiction, the helplessness, the no-way-out. That. And then for sure you go out and then become a businessman again. Because That, you want to keep it. You cannot help it, you want to have it for yourself. And then you lost it already, because it can not be owned by anyone.

Q: In the relative sense this whatever needs to eat and sleep and pay for the flights and all the rest of it. So we are functioning.

K: You better work!

Q: Yes, you better work. Yes. Well, trust me with that. I am busy with that! But the implication is kind of like: screw it, drop it all, forget about it – just hang out with whatever it is that's not hanging out with you.

K: That's why Ramana said: Do you have enough money to seek?

Q: I really don't, Karl. The way I am booking tickets, no.

K: You cannot help it anyway. But if you have money, inheritage, then it's maybe easier to hang out.

Q: But it seems like it is going to go on whether you like it or not.

K: Just to make it more or less painful.

Q: Right.

K: But it never cares about it, if you have something or not. If you have to do it you have to do it. You have to sit for ages, you have to sit for lifetimes somewhere in spite of getting anything.

Q: If what you are saying is true, then there is no time, then sitting isn't really happening, then we don't really have to worry about the lifetimes.

K: The experience of sitting will be there, I tell you that!

Q: Very depressing!

K: But that's the Yoga Vashista – 'see you next time!' And see you again and again. This moment of sitting as it never comes it never goes, will happen again and again, and you sit forever. And talk about yourself forever, on whatever level you talk about yourself. It's all self-talk. You talk about yourself buying a piece of meat at the butcher, you talk in the second about spirit, and then awareness. All different subjects, but you always talk about yourself. But by all that talking nothing happens.

Q: See, that's the other strange experience, listening to you is very familiar. It's very familiar, and yet I walk out of here and somebody asks me 'what did Karl say?' 'He says 'be what you cannot not be'. 'What does that mean?' 'If I know! Ask him!'

K: That's what I can only point to, that there is no advantage in sitting here. You don't learn anything. You don't even unlearn anything. Because that's just another trap. For me there is no learning or even unlearning. Because what you are never learned anything so it does never need to unlearn anything. And that one who has to unlearn something, uncondition himself, is still a dealer, a businessman who thinks by having less he has more. Let him do that. I like Rishikesh, they have got Rishis for cash. I like existence, it makes jokes over jokes over jokes. And it is so joyful in its jokes! Sometimes it looks a bit rough, but even that is a joke for existence. So in that sense these are all crash-test dummies for what you are. It will be crashed sooner or later anyway. And crash-test dummies are used for experiences, but not that there is one who can be killed by that, or gain something. It always looks for some dummy who is able to talk about that what no one can talk about. And if that will happen it will happen. But it's not a special dummy. It's still a dummy So this whatever you see here is still a crash-test dummy for that what is. Nothing special about it. Just a loudspeaker that can speak out what normally kills the loudspeaker. Because all the other loudspeakers that tried end up in a madhouse. There the loudspeaker was not ready for that, so 'bye bye, next one'. Consciousness really doesn't care. Fantastic. Never ending story.

Q: But enormous appetite also.

K: It is never satisfied. It can never get enough of itself. But it's beautiful. You can never get enough of what you are. There is not enough. There is never enough. It's always new and fresh. And there is never any experience of satisfaction. Because there is no satisfaction in any experience. So you are always hungry. And there will never be any end to it. So you will never get enough of yourself. There is not enough for what you are. Enough is only that what you are. But you can never get enough from your experience. There is no satisfaction in anything. Thank God. Satisfaction is your Nature. But this is satis-fiction. This now, is fiction. But That, the Nature of sat, is Satisfaction. And That, what is the Nature of Sat, doesn't know any Sat. But when the Sat knows the Sat, there is satis-fiction. And in fiction you can not be satisfied. This fiction can not satisfy you. So only that what is not satis-fiction, what is Sat, not even knows Sat or doesn't know Sat, in that there is satisfaction. It's a fact. That you are. So it's satisfaction. But here it's all fiction. Whatever you experience is fiction. And I like it. It's the best. You cannot know yourself, in whatever. Thank God. But any little imagination that you can be known, you become a sufferer. Already imagining that you can be known you make yourself an object of time, an object that can be known. Already that is hell. All of that imagination. But how can you stop it? You even have to be what you are in spite of that dumb idea or imagination of what you are.

Q: You laugh at yourself, calling it a dream.

K: This love happens. If you could stop it you would stop it right away. Because you started hating love. That makes you a seeker. So first, by loving yourself, you go out and want to discover everything. And now you started to hate yourself for loving yourself. And now by that hating that you have to love yourself, you meditate, you try everything to find a way out of this love affair. So first there is a loving, and now the hating. And if you would catch yourself, you would not embrace yourself. You would kill yourself right away for what you have done to yourself. Amazing. Not for love you are looking for yourself.

Q: I want to come back to something which you keep saying. I could not get what you meant by 'just be what you are'.

K: I didn't say that. Be what you cannot not be.

Q: So how do you be?

K: There is no 'how' in it. 'How do you do' is not in there.

Q: But also you said that happens when you go to the deep sleep state.

K: It doesn't happen. Everything drops and you still are what you are. You are in spite of the world.

Q: In deep sleep...

K: In deep deep sleep. Deep sleep is not it. Deep deep sleep is even the absence of the presence of anyone who is or who is sleeping or not sleeping. That what is the deep sleep. In deep sleep there is still an awareness there. And the deep deep sleep is even in spite of that awareness. And every night you are that.

Q: Is that the only way to be in that state?

K: No. Here now you are that.

Q: But I may be still dreaming.

K: So what?

Q: So in the so-called wakeful state, is one always what one is?

K: You are always what you are.

Q: In spite of all the dreaming?

K: It just means that you have to know yourself as that what never needs to know itself to be itself. And that is the deep deep sleep. It's not like you have to stay in the deep deep sleep. That would be too much. That would be one too many again.

Q: So you can be in the deep deep sleep while being awake?

K: No. Again, I have to just repeat: you cannot not be what you are. Now! And as you are now, you are in deep deep sleep. You are in the presence and in the absence, that's all. You are with and without. It's not that you are more or better off in the deep deep sleep. You are just with and without. And when you are without, no one complains when he is without. Complaining only happens in the with.

Q: And what you mentioned about something which is always satisfied.

K: That is what you are. Which is not satis-fiction. That what is a scientist is what he is. But the scientist who is looking for the scientist, that is science fiction. That what is the seeker is what you are. But the seeker looking for that what is the seeker, that is seeker-fiction.

Q: So whatever it is that sees, satisfies. It sees everything but doesn't see.

K: It doesn't see. Ok, I come back to my famous fist (makes fist): Heart. If you call this Heart, Life, Para-Brahman. If this wakes up, starts to realize itself, it may wake up as a realizer (extends thumb), experiencing itself as a realizer. Then experiencing itself as realizing (extends index finger). Then experiencing itself as what can be realized (extends middle finger). But all these three are what in Nature? The Nature of all three is that what is (makes fist again). So in the presence of realization and in the absence of realization, you are Heart itself, which doesn't know any Heart. That's all. That's the most simple thing. So you are here in the presence of realization, you are that what is the presence of the presence of the seer, the presence of the presence of seeing, and the presence of the presence of what can be seen. You are that what is the scenery. But you are not in the scenery. That's all. You are That what is That. You are Advaita where there is no second, and you are that what is Vedanta, the realization of it. Vedanta and Advaita is not different in Nature. But in none of this realization you can find yourself. In none of this trinity you have lost yourself. As you have not lost yourself in one of them, you cannot find yourself. As that what you are was never lost, it can never be found in one of these three. All of that is a manifestation of what you are. You are manifested and unmanifested what you are. And none of them are better or worse. The moment you become a realizer you are ignorant of what you are. But you are that what is ignorance. So that what is ignorance is what you are, as Knowledge. As there is only Knowledge. And no one can know that. But everyone is it. Very simple. Much too simple for your busy business.

Q: What is the first and last hindrance to find out?

K: There is no hindrance, that's the problem. What can hinder you to be what you are? There are no others. There is no second who can hinder you to be what you are. There was never any hindrance. Hindrances are only in the dream, when you are one of these three. And only God as a creator wants to change his creation. In this (fist) – there is silence. Peace creates peace. So harmony can never be in disharmony. There is no disharmony for harmony. Disharmony can only be in those differences when you landed in one of those landing places. And then you are already in a disharmony of separation. But it is a dream separation. It's a dream disharmony. Any moment you want to change this dream disharmony - you cannot kill it, you cannot get rid of it. Because how can you get rid of a dream? How can you get rid of an illusion? It is not even there. It has no substance. How can you kill it? How can you get rid of something what is not even there? So the main problem is, there is no problem!

Q: So this manifestation of the seer, the seeing and the seen, is a play of consciousness?

K: It's not a play. It is just the manifestation of what you are.

Q: Manifestation of consciousness?

K: Don't have to call it anything! Just be that what is manifesting itself. Just be that what is realizing itself, as a realizer, realizing what can be realized. But you are not different as the realizer from what you are realizing. You are That. And That you can not not be. Because there can only be the dream of a seer, seeing what can be seen because you are. And that, you don't have to know to be that. And calling it whatever it doesn't mind, it never minds. You can call it underwear. But just be that what you can not not be, and there is no second to it. Because it doesn't even know itself. That what doesn't even know itself, how can it know others? But any moment you know yourself you create others. Because you are lonely. Lonely God. And then creating lonely other Gods. Oh God oh God. Instantly. And then he maybe gets this state of being all one, and then he feels a little more in unconditioned love. But what is that unconditioned love? Another conditioning. Who needs this bloody unconditioned love? Only a lonely God who wants to be in unconditioned love with himself.

Isn't it fun? The Almighty, that what is Energy itself, playing stupid. And then being in self-pity. 'Poor me! No one loves me as I am. I need a soul mate who takes me as I am.' Isn't it fantastic?

Q: No!

K: Yes, if you are in that business you are in a hell of a business. Because you are a little devil who wants to be loved, even because he is a little devil.

Q: So the seer doesn't have the sense that he is creating himself?

K: Seer? There is no seer!

Q: The seer behind the seer.

K: There is no seer behind the seer! What seer would that be?

Q: That which makes the seer...

K: There is no that!

Q: Something that...

K: There is no something! Science fiction again! The scientist can not be killed. And the scientist wants to find out. And consciousness is like a scientist. He always wants to go deeper and deeper, he wants to go behind the scene. What is behind it? Enjoy it!

Q: Maybe...

K: You just want to survive as a little scientist who says maybe. You want to stay in business. But it's not my business. Stay in business and suffer. I have no business with that sufferer who wants to stay a sufferer because the sufferer suffers because he thinks then I can not be anymore. Because you fear that what you are, and I am not in that business. You fear that you can not exist when you would be what you are and there would be no fun anymore. So you would rather be in the passionate suffering fun than that what you are because you fear that would be the end of your little fun you have now. So you are in that business 'I have this little fun and I want to keep it, even if it means suffering. Because that I know, the other one I don't know. And I don't want to know maybe, because if I know I would not be there'.

But if grace is after you you will be dropped like a hot potato, sooner or later.

Q: But if there is grace...

K: If there would be grace, it would drop you right away, because who wants to have you? But even grace is a fiction. If there would be grace, none of you would be here. What kind of grace would allow you to happen? If there would be an almighty God, what would he do? You really think he would play with you?

Q: So you mean there is no grace, that's why we are here?

K: Because there is no grace there is grace. Because that what is grace doesn't know any grace and doesn't need any grace. And that's the grace of grace. But if there would be grace, that grace would drop you right away. If there would be a God he would just kill you at first sight. Because you would be too much, as everyone would be too much. If he could help himself, he would kill the whole universe in one shot. If he could avoid to wake up in the morning he would just shoot everything. If there would be a button you could press in the morning and the world would be gone you would never leave that button alone. Be honest! Whoever wakes up in the morning you would never leave that button alone! Every meditator wants to find that button, if you push here the whole thing is off. The off button. The killing button. There is a death intention in everything. You want to kill everything, because you are fed up with it. So if God could help himself, killing whatever, he would kill it right away. It can only be a relative God who knows this world and wants to get rid of it. That what is God doesn't even know a world, he doesn't even know himself. But only that is Energy, only that is the absolute Dreamer, and only that could whatever. But that has no interest. And that God who has an interest, has no energy for it. So there is no mixing, no bridge between it. The dream goes on and that what is dreaming everything has no interest in changing anything, because it doesn't even know a dream. It doesn't know a dreamer, dreaming and what can be dreamed. And that what knows the dream is already part of the dream. And only in the dream you want to avoid the dream, there it is a nightmare, in a good dream and in a bad dream. But for that what is the dream there is not even a dream. Sorry.

Q: Who is sorry?

K: I am lying. You should know me by now. I am lying when I open my mouth. When I say I am sorry, that is one of the biggest lies. I never regret anything. There is no regretting – for what? What is there to regret?

Q: Another way for not regretting is accepting.

K: Forget acceptance and just be what you are.

Q: That's a cliche, be what you are...

K: No. It's a cliche to accept. It's another cliche. It doesn't help anyone. I like Ramesh, I think in '95 he said: 'The closest you can get to acceptance is that you can never accept'. That is already a peace of mind, a personal peace of mind. Do that. If you can do that, be happy. But by none of that you can attain what you are, which is Acceptance. And Acceptance itself never needs to accept anything. It doesn't even know Acceptance, it is Acceptance. That is what is Heart, but Heart doesn't know any Heart. And Heart doesn't need to whatever, there is no need in anything. And that what needs to accept anything, let him accept or not. Who bloody cares if the phantom is accepting or not? But if you are interested in a phantom happiness, ok, a phantom is maybe less disappointed, in less discomfort, when there is an acceptance. Wonderful. I don't mind. But it's temporary, for sure. Because the tolerance limits are always there. And there will always be a tolerance limit that will be crossed, again and again. There was never anyone who was tolerant enough that he has no limits of tolerance. And only for that what you are there is no limit of anything, not even of tolerance. And whatever peace you can gain by tolerance or acceptance, it's a temporary peace. Enjoy it as long as it lasts. But know it will be gone one day.

Q: Hopefully it lasts for a lifetime.

K: Keep hoping! Hope is hell. Because only the devil hopes that one day the hell will be gone. When there is a devil there is hell. Instantly. When God knows himself he creates his own hell. Instantly. And no way out of hell. Hallelujah. And you can not get out of it, because this imaginary knower is already an imagined knower. And then that imaginary knower creating his own hell is an imaginary hell. Who needs to get rid of that phantom? Only another phantom. Only the phantom that knows a phantom needs the phantom to go. Let the phantom have fun. What to do with the phantom?

Q: So the phantom is dreaming it's having fun.

K: No. The phantom is not dreaming. The phantom is already something that is dreamed. How can what is dreamed dream something? You cannot even blame the phantom.

Q: The phantom doesn't live in a dream world?

K: The phantom is the dream. No one lives in any world. The phantom is the whole world, the whole universe. It's not only your little dream character! The whole world is a phantom, and little phantoms in the world, little puppets in the puppet house, all of that is phantom. It's not like this little character is a phantom. That would maybe be easy to get rid of. You just shoot it or something. But how to get rid of the whole manifestation? Everyone is only thinking of himself. 'If I get rid of my little ego I will be better off', says the ego. But how to get rid of everything here? Try harder! So everyone tries to get rid of the little personal story. And then: 'I have no personal story anymore. I am never born'. Says who? But the calamity of just being what you are destroys the whole story. There is not even a story of a universe, there is not even a universe. Just by being what you are. Instantly.

Q: Otherwise the others make you real.

K: Yes, you have no story, but the others, they know you. I always tell people who claim 'I have no story anymore. There is no one at home'. 'Live with your mother! She will tell you who is not born! And if you can live with her for 1 year, you come back. If you are still awakened then and you think you are enlightened, we can talk again. But try to live with your mother first'! Like a test-run.

Q: Is that how you tested your state, Karl?

K: My state?

Q: Your mother is dead now I understand?

K: Thank God! But now I have thousand mothers around me!

Q: You got one down and ten pop up!

K: Yes, at least! Now I have mothers all around the world who tell me what is good for me, what I should do.

Q: It's very opposite to meditation what you describe! Trying to do meditation or living with your mother.

K: Yes, try meditate with your mother! Or with your father. Even worse. No way out.

Q: So the way you look at the spiritual...

K: Business?

Q: Business. The people who are so-called enlightened, all the scriptures, all the philosophers...

K: I like it all! I love it!

Q: Yes, but you have an approach to that, like a destructive one, or deconstructive.

K: Yes, I kill it by loving it.

Q: What the Western philosophers call deconstruction.

K: No, I even go so far to destruct the destructor.

Q: It looks like you have a postmodern approach.

K: Post-mortem!

Q: Like demolishing everything there is.

K: Yes, but what I am really doing is demolishing the demolisher. It is like this is Shiva destroying Shiva. Because even in the destruction there is a hope that one day everything is destroyed and then you will be better off. No! I destroy the destroyer. That's your worst nightmare. I am sitting here destroying even the destroyer for you.

Demolishing the demolisher. Because nothing can be demolished at all. And who needs to demolish something? No, I am not demolishing anything. And telling the phantom: 'No one needs you to go!' That's the worst scenario the phantom can be not in. Because if no one cares if there is one or not, that kills the phantom right away! Only that there is no one who ever cared about the presence or absence of a phantom, that really kills the phantom. 'I am too much! Existence cannot be existence without me! Ha ha! I am too much!'. He always takes himself so fucking important that he thinks he has to go that Existence can be happy? Ha ha! What a joke! What a self-important bullshitter he is! He can be there or not, who cares? He can be there forever as a guest. That what is the house itself never has any guest. It doesn't even know the guest. Only the guest knows the guest. And so he is guessing all the time: 'Am I too much or am I not too much'? Guessing, guessing, guessing. A guest who is guessing what to eat next. Always hungry for the next. Always thinking 'who gives me attention? Maybe I have a party, have another guest in the house. And then at least the other guests know me'. And then you are a host. Hosting some phantoms. A phantom host hosting phantom guests. That is what this consciousness is. A phantom host creating guests because it cannot be alone.

Q: What you are doing is destroying the mirror in which you see yourself.

K: I am destroying even that what could be seen in the mirror. The only way to destroy the phantom is to be that what you are, which never knew any phantom. But any moment you want to get rid of the phantom, you yourself are a phantom. Only a phantom needs to get rid of a phantom. What you are doesn't even know a phantom. That's the pointer 'who cares?' That existence who cares about your presence or absence is a fake one. That what is Existence doesn't even know existence. There is no question of one who is or is not. But that's the worst scenario for the phantom, that not even he himself cares about himself.

Q: So existence is an assumption of the phantom?

K: The idea of existence is there only because there is a phantom existence. A phantom consciousness producing a phantom existence. Both comes together. A fiction creates fiction. A fictional consciousness playing all the roles. But already consciousness is fiction. That's too much for consciousness. You have to be what you are and you are already what you are in spite of consciousness. What you are doesn't need any consciousness. And that what needs consciousness to be conscious is false.

Q: You are not consciousness, you are despite of consciousness?

K: Absolutely! Who claims to be consciousness? Only consciousness claims to be consciousness. There are two consciousnesses. And consciousness is all there is. But whatever is, is not what is. Because that what has to be to be is fiction. That what you are doesn't even have to be to be.

Q: It seems like you can almost grab it.

K: It's more than grabbing it. You are it! That's more than knowing it.

Q: I am hearing it!

K: You are not hearing it!

Q: I am not hearing it. I am it.

K: After 13 years again!

Q: After 13 years, right. And I am still sitting here!

K: Imagine I would care about anyone's progress. And if someone listens to me. Or anyone's understanding. Imagine I would care about it. I really would be the most frustrated guy on earth.

Q: That's not such a problem!

K: I don't mind. I enjoy the impossibility of understanding what you are, moment by moment. Here and there. This is enjoying that, what can never be understood. And I cannot blame anyone that he didn't understand it. Because there is no way of understanding it anyway. And no need for it.

Q: That's the trap, the need for it.

K: Yes, you are a needy bastard because you need to know yourself. That makes you a needy phantom. So what? Still you are what you are!

Q: It's a co-dependency.

K: You are a company of co-dependencies. So any company is co-dependency.

Q: I wanted to understand what you mean by 'what I am is prior to consciousness'?

K: In spite. It is not before. You can call it prior or beyond. But it's even beyond the beyond and prior to the prior. The idea of prior. That what is prior to the idea of prior. That what is beyond the idea of beyond. That is what you are. Because that what is prior doesn't know any prior and that what is beyond doesn't know any beyond. So it's beyond the beyond and it's prior to the prior. It's that what is prior but doesn't know to be prior. And that what is the beyond of the beyond is that what is beyond but doesn't know any beyond. And that you cannot grab. Thank God. Imagine someone could understand that!

Q: Prior and beyond contain time, no?

K: You make it that! Because you want to make it personal. You want to survive in being prior. But in the prior you cannot survive, that's the trick. If you are just prior there is no one who can survive. So be prior. And in the prior there is no story, and without a story there is no me. That's the calamity that UG (Krishnamurti) talked about, of being that what is prior, there is a calamity of all stories of the whole universe. It's not only about your personal or impersonal. All you have learned and known gets burned down in that being prior. Because there is no one who cares. In this carelessness there is just a natural ceasing away of whatever you are and what you are not. Naturally. So it's a trick.

Q: Is that what he meant when he said with the calamity everything was washed out of his system.

K: Yes, because he is the system. Because the system doesn't know any system. That is the Absolute that is prior, and just being that there is a washing out of whatever can be washed. Even the washing gets washed out. Even the idea of a system gets washed out. Even the idea of purification gets purified. By that just being that what you are. Which never needs any purification. So that calamity is a calamity of whatever you can know. The knower, the knowing, what can be known, gets 'wisched weg' (German for: wiped away). If That is wishing you away, you will be wished away instantly. And if That is not involved, you can do whatever here, nothing will happen anyway.

Q: So we are running all the time from one thing to the next...

K: You are hamsters. Hamstering what can be hamstered.

Q: And if the wheel stops – wish-whack!

K: No, the wheel stops and then you go: 'For me the wheel stopped!'

Q: And then you give talks from the wheel.

K: Yes. Then you are Mr. Wheeler. He stopped his wheel.

Q: When you say that Arunachala is the source of the universe...

K: And even that source is an imagination.

Q: I was a little wondering about that...

K: By that what I am seeing that even the most superior awareness, which is pure light, is still imagination, and you are still prior or in spite of it - that takes the last hope of home away. And then so what? If that cannot even deliver the home you are looking for, so what? If even the divine light of Shiva is just an imaginary light. So what? What else can happen? What else can be taken away? What else can drop away, as that divine light of Shiva? So you have to be what you are even in spite, as you are already in spite. This in spite, this split second, this last home, gets dropped. But no one knows by what. But it drops away. What to do? And claiming that since then you are coming out of the absolute Darkness of your absolute Existence and the first experience is light, and the second is space and then this – it's a natural experiencing of what you are. But it's not something special. It's just as everyone is experiencing it. You are just fixed on this bloody me-steak. And you really imagine that something is at stake, if this steak is gone. And then the next thing you think, if there is spirit, then you are fixed on that. So you are a fixer. You are always fixing. You want to fix something which never needs to be fixed. So I don't have to be a hero to be what I am. I don't need hero-in. I am the Drug itself. I am the Ecstasy itself. And that Ecstasy is silence, which never can be disturbed. Nothing else can give me that ecstasy of what I am.

Q: You should be careful Karl, this is how cannibalism started!

K: You think when they eat this body...?

Q: Maybe, you know...

K: I know what you mean! But I can shoot. And 20 years Karate! But I know everyone wants to eat that what can not be eaten. Everyone runs around an enlightened sausage in the Ramana Ashram and thinks he can gain something by that. A mummified body, radiation of light, and everyone is running around and falling down in front of a sausage, on top of a lingam. I like it! How stupid can it get? Look at it! Just look at the divine stupidity! Running around Kailash, prostrating. Yet all of that has to happen. And all of that is unavoidable. In spite of no one needing it it has to happen. In spite of the universe being as it is already, and God being absolute, and all being complete, all little aspects of meditation, of whatever, have to be done, will be done, are already done. No way out! I still call it stupid. But you can not avoid to be dumb enough to believe in yourself. You will always again believe in what you are, and in believing what you are you left yourself. But by that believing in what you are, even in the experience of having left yourself, you haven't left yourself. It's an experience of the believer having left what is the believer. But even by that you haven't left. And then you maybe remember your religion, you come back. But by going back and by remembering no one goes back. But still it happens. So you cannot avoid all these experiences. What to do? I can only point out none of that can deliver what you are looking for. You rather be here now what you are and don't postpone that what never needs to look anyway. But even that is too much. Who needs that? But still I have to say it. This paradox you cannot break. In spite of everything you are, but still this happens. You have to realize yourself. You cannot not realize yourself. And if you realize yourself as this Karl talking about what doesn't need to be talked about, or you are butcher butchering a pig, or you are a householder. If you are a householder be a householder. If you are a good one you are a good one, if you are a bad one you are a bad one. If you are a lover you are a lover. If you are a good one or a bad one. It doesn't matter. You are absolute in your Nature anyway. You are an absolute good lover and you are an absolute bad lover. And you are an absolute whatever. An absolute stupid – does it take your absolute Nature away? No. No danger in anything.

Q: So you mentioned these people prostrating being some sort of a stupidity, right?

K: It's part of ignorance.

Q: They get what they want...

K: No, I don't see anyone there. It's just consciousness playing someone.

Q: But they are imagining they are happy in that.

K: No, there is no one who is imagining anything there. There is no one who is stupid, there is only stupidity. But there is no one who is stupid. And I only say you can only realize what you are in stupidity. But in that no one becomes stupid. There is no one who is stupid. Or dumb. But still there is ignorance. But in that ignorance no one becomes ignorant. Try to find one who is ignorant. You can not find anyone. That's the ultimate medicine of Nisargadatta: try to find the sick one. You cannot find anyone, wherever you look, it's gone. So what to do? It doesn't help. Thank God. You cannot get rid of what you are, and you are That. Whatever you try, there will not be any success in it.

Q: This word 'prior' was used by Nisargadatta also. You are prior to what you think you are.

K: You are prior to that what you imagine to be.

Q: You are using prior in the same sense?

K: Yes, I could use it like that. You are prior, you are in spite of the presence or absence of any imagination. You have to be in spite of the imagined to be. That there can be an imaginary existence, Existence has to be there, which is not an imagination. Existence itself, which has to be prior, during, and beyond. That presence and absence of any idea of existence. So it is already there when the idea is there, and it still will be there when the idea is already gone. So it is always in spite of the presence or absence. It's uninterrupted. It's never never. And only that is the Nature of life. That what is never never. And that what is an imaginary idea of never, or infinite, or finite, is all - pfffff.

Q: So that which is prior to existence or non existence.

K: That what is in spite of existence or not existence. In spite of whatever.

Q: It is not nothingness?

K: In spite of the nothingness. Whatever you say, it's in spite of. Never because of that.

Q: So you cannot say anything about it.

K: You can say a lot, but it doesn't make it that. You can call it whatever, but 'Absolute' comes closest. Absolute simply means there is no second. It is absolute.

Q: So whether you call it Absolute, the Self, Reality, Truth, it's the same?

K: If you call it something – use these words.

Q: So nothing special about 'Absolute'.

K: It's not special. I like Absolute the best. It's the most neutral one. Self always implies there is a personal or impersonal, you wonder about personal or impersonal. The Absolute is absolute personal when it is personal and the Absolute is absolute impersonal when it is impersonal. It is never losing its nature. It cannot lose its nature. In absolute personal experiences it doesn't become personal, and in absolute impersonal experiences it doesn't become impersonal. It is neither personal nor impersonal. It is experiencing itself in absolute being finite, and in absolute being infinite There is no difference for the Absolute. It is the absolute finite, as this moment, and the absolute infinite as that what is eternity. It is that what is eternity and it is that what is the finite moment, the temporary one. It is that what is the temporary and it is that what is the not temporary.

Q: You can call it Reality or Energy also?

K: I call it underwear. Because underwear you may drop easier as a concept than Self or anything. Because you cannot deal with underwear. If you go to your friends and tell them 'we talked about underwear'...

Q: Not if you are living in a civilized society, you can't drop it.

K: You can talk about it. Look, I am going everywhere and I call it underwear. And still people are coming. You will be surprised what you can say, and still people have to come.

Q: And get away with it.

K: You can hammer them, you can call them names, and they still have to come. No one can avoid sitting where one sits. And if I say beautiful words no one would sit there more than he has to sit there. This talking bullshit is so much fun.

Q: Truth is always unpalatable.

K: Truth cannot be swallowed. You cannot swallow Truth. Truth will swallow you. And if Truth is after you, you better watch out. It's already after everyone. That's the meaning of 'you are already in the tiger's mouth'. You are already eaten, you don't know it now.

Q: You and the tiger are the same.

K: That's bullshit. Both are phantoms. Who says 'me and the tiger is one'?

Q: The phantom.

K: Yes, so let the phantom be one with another phantom. Who bloody cares? Even grace is a phantom. If you are chasing grace you cannot find it. But if grace is after you, you better watch out. It knows you more than you know yourself. It is your very Self. And if that what is the very Self is after that fake self, it will just drop it like nothing. It doesn't even have to drop it, it will drop you just by being in spite of your presence or absence. It has already dropped you. Nothing has to be dropped. That's the absolute dropping. For the Absolute nothing has to be dropped to be the Absolute. So that is the dropping of the dropper. That is forgetting grace and being what you are. And that what is Grace doesn't know any grace and never needs any grace. But being someone who knows grace - oh my goodness!

Q: So it is comforting to know you can be what you are without knowing what you are.

K: You can not not be what you are. It is comfort without one who needs to be comforted. That is comfort. But there is no one left who needs to be comforted. There was never anyone who needed to be comforted by anything. You don't need any pamperer who pampers you, or comforts you. For what you are there was never any discomfort, there is not even any idea of discomfort. So if there is no idea of discomfort, where is the idea of comfort? Or when there is no idea of comfort, where is the idea of discomfort? Both come only together. Happiness and unhappiness come together. When you have the idea of happiness, you are unhappy. Instantly. Instant unhappiness.

Q: So there is nothing called bliss which doesn't have an opposite?

K: There is something you call bliss. Yes, there is. But because it is, it is not. I don't deny it. I don't deny anything. I don't have to deny anything to be that. There is bliss, there is ecstasy, there is enlightenment. All of that is. But because it is, it is not. Because it is, it has to be. As it has to be, it can only be a phantom. So there is bliss, there is grace, there is God. But because there is a God who is, he is not. Because a God who is, is not. And even the God who is not, is not.

Q: Because he is something which is beyond ease...

K: The Ease which is beyond the ease doesn't know any ease.

Q: There is a regression.

K: There is no regression. He wants to make it a piece of cake. If I eat the piece of cake, maybe that what is left is that what is cake. That's the old tradition of reducing, abstracting, substrating whatever can be substrated. So the piece of cake you eat away, and then what is left...

Q: It's called a denying technique.

K: The neti-neti. I like neti-neti. But I only like it because it doesn't help. Because there was no one in the first place who needed to be helped. So the neti-neti I like as nothing else, because no one needs it. It's amazing. I like it all. Money. I think money I like even more than neti-neti.

Q: Who is this who likes it?

K: This body. The phantom likes money. As much as possible.

Q: The phantom likes phantom money.

K: Because with money you can buy something for the phantom. Enlightenment you can just drop in the next rubbish bin. You only want to be enlightened because you want to make a business out of it. That's a phantom business. A holy business. And then you are one enlightened one who talks to other unenlightend ones. Then you are in the holy business. So it's all about money. There is nothing without that, money.

Q: So even this Ramana business was for money?

K: Ramana? Ramana had no business. That he always said, I have no business here.

Q: So there is something which is not for money or business?

K: No, everything is for money. Even bhakti is business. Jnani is business. You only want to understand because by understanding you want to buy yourself. Because then you think you have enough spiritual money inside that you can pride yourself.

Q: You are an absolute neti-neti, demolishing everything, but not asserting anything. Is there something you can say with certainty?

K: There is only the absolute certainty that you are, and out of that absolute certainty that you are, every word is pronounced by that. There is an absolute yes and an absolute no and an absolute maybe. There is only the Absolute. So it is an absolute Certainty. You have to be absolutely certain to be uncertain. You have to be absolute Knowledge to even claim you don't know. You have to be absolutely certain that you don't know.

Q: You wouldn't be looking for knowledge unless you knew you are ignorant.

K: You make it cause and effect again. You are a scientist and you will always be a scientist. And a scientist will never get what he is. You will always be science-fiction. You always want to cut it, particles and strings. That's hell for a scientist. You want to stay in hell. Because when there is no hell anymore there is no scientist. And you want to survive as a scientist. So you want to cut it down into pieces. You think when you cut it down into pieces you have peace. Ha ha ha ha. Then you want to put the pieces together again. Then you are puzzled by the pieces. So you become a puzzler. And the puzzler will always be puzzled because he is always missing in the puzzle. Because the puzzler cannot be found in the puzzle. So he will always miss himself in the puzzle. There is always one piece missing. So peace is missing. Thank God. Peace is missing in the puzzle, because peace is not part of the puzzle. Can you follow? That's called a follower. It's amazing – that what is peace in nature, the nature which is peace, that peace is puzzled that it cannot be found in the puzzle. And I talk to that what is peace, be happy that peace cannot be found in that what is the puzzle! You cannot be found in any puzzle of phenomenal experiences. Be happy that you always will be puzzled by how and why. It's like a wonder-bar. Amazement! Totally puzzled by your manifestation. What a wonder! There is no boredom in it. It only gets boring when you know how it works, when you imagine how it works.

Q: You will never get to that point of knowing how it works.

K: Thank God not! I am absolutely amazed that I can even see something, that there is something at all. Absolute amazement. How can that what I am even dream?

Q: You will never know that.

K: Why should I know it? It happens. I can only say: shit happens. So what to do? In spite of not needing anything, look, it happens. In spite of no demand of anything, look, it happens. The dream is dreamed. In spite of no one there who needs or doesn't need to get out or in, or anything, look, it happens. Even that happening is in spite of whatever. Whatever is, is in spite. Because there is no cause. There is not even a cause for that what is off course. So I do my best, which is for sure not good enough. Again and again. Again and again there is nothing to gain in whatever I say or don't say. Again and again in the gain there is no gainer. Again and again there is an attempt of gaining in gaining, but there was never any gainer in gaining and no loser in losing. Inexhaustible again. The next will happen. The next, the next, the next. And then, and then, and then. That's called Then-Buddhism. Then and then and then.

A never ending then. Then-sation, then-sation, then-sation. Next, next, next. And still there is no one who gains or loses anything in it. Existence doesn't get more in the next sensation and the next sensation and the sensation before. It is sensational. What a circus of sensational sensations, and no one gets anything out of it. Wonderful! No glorious gainer or loser in all of that. Because already the gainer is a sensation. And the loser is a sensation. What a fun!

Q: Maybe.

K: From the sensational position maybe sometimes it's a roller coaster. It costs too much.

Q: It's a real puzzle.

K: Yes, and you will never get out of work.

Q: You can never say anything with certainty.

K: But that you say with certainty!

The Game Is Never Over

Q: You say we have not decided to get into this dream. What if we want to get out of the dream?

K: Because by the experience of going in no one went in, trying to get out is impossible. Because you never went in. There was never anybody in the movie, that's the problem. The movie is just like a projection on the screen you are. And what you are never went into the movie, but now trying to get out of the movie is impossible. If there really would be somebody, there would be a way out.

Q: But we think we are in the movie.

K: It's an imagination. But how can you get rid of that? Who needs to get rid of an imagination? Even that is trying to get out. To control an imagination. You just have to be what you are. The rest is total nonsense. Trying something or not.

Q: Yesterday you said that even self-inquiry is not leading to anything.

K: Yes, I am just repeating Nisargadatta or Ramana, they all said it.

Q: But as far as I read in the books, Ramana is advising everybody to do self-inquiry.

K: I would advise too.

Q: But if it doesn't bring you closer to yourself, why do anything?

K: If you want to stop suffering, because that is in the dream, then self-inquiry maybe kills the sufferer. But you won't become that what you are by that. So yes, if you want to end suffering, then self-inquiry can maybe end the suffering by ending the sufferer. Because in self-inquiry you just give your attention to that what is attention. There is no time anymore, there is no coming, no going, there is no past, no future, there is no place for a me, for a sufferer. So you may end suffering. Or the sufferer. But you cannot attain what you are. Yes, you can maybe end the suffering by self-inquiry. But by self-inquiry you can never attain what you are. So it's still psychotherapy.

Q: But as far as I read, Ramana said you will attain your Self by doing self-inquiry. Did I misunderstand?

K: Sooner or later all ideas drop anyway. And in the meantime you can self-inquire and maybe there is not so much suffering. That's all. But the idea of me came by itself and will be dropped by itself. It's not because of something. But until then, as Ramesh said, the non-doership, the total understanding, is maybe ending the suffering. Then there is a kind of peace, and that you can do. But by that you cannot attain what you are. Because you cannot become what you are. So you can do something, but by that doing you will not become what you are. You can maybe make the dream a better dream.

Q: I am trying to figure out what you are telling us. I am what I am, that's clear, but don't see it.

K: You will never see it.

Q: So if I do nothing, then maybe nothing happens?

K: Yes, and that would be fine enough for what you are.

Q: That maybe, but not...

K: But not for me! Ha! But the me is like a fleeting shadow. A fleeting shadow which came and will be gone one day. It's like a ghost. And the ghost always needs something.

Q: But what is the difference between you – I mean you are sitting there and I am sitting here?

K: Yes, that's all. That's the only difference.

Q: No, you must know or realize something we don't.

K: Yes, I am realizing myself, moment by moment.

Q: What does that mean?

K: Moment by moment, the next sip of water, the next breathing in, is the realization of what I am. It's never special. It's just the next.

Q: So that Self doesn't mean much?

K: No. There is nothing special in it. You are looking for something special. You find something and from then on you will be happy forever. No, that doesn't happen. You are already the Self which is realizing itself moment by moment. There is no way out. And it will always be different. But by all the differences you don't become different. That's all. You have to realize yourself.

Q: I have the feeling that something is standing in the way.

K: What is standing in the way is that you believe in your imagination that you have to know yourself to be yourself. And I tell you you will never know yourself. If you could know yourself there would be a second one.

Q: But that doesn't mean it is better to stop the self-inquiry.

K: I didn't say that. No, it started by itself it will stop by itself. It's not in your hand anyway. Whatever comes next will happen anyway. It's already finished.

Q: But I am coming here or going to satsang teachers because I want something.

K: I know. And everyone sitting there and telling you 'I cannot give you anything'. And you think, 'hm, what am I doing here'? But that's the best anyone can point to – that you are already absolutely that what you are, and you cannot get more or less as that. And no one can ever make you that, and no one can transmit it or give you any understanding of that. Because what you are never needs to understand itself. But still I have to tell you, as Ramana said, you have to realize yourself. But you take it personal. I am talking to that what you are in Nature. And that what is your Nature is already realizing itself moment by moment since you were born, every moment you have an experience of yourself. Even sitting here, listening, is self-realization. Talking is self-realization. Whatever happens is self-realization, moment for moment. But there is no special thing in it. Every experience is a self-experience. The Self experiencing itself. Realizing itself in whatever is and is not. That's all. And you are that. And you cannot not realize yourself. So you are already Reality realizing itself moment by moment. And what is your imaginary idea of what you can call suffering is that you believe that you have to know yourself to be yourself. This little tendency, this little imagination, makes you suffer. It's amazing, how stupid one can be. Suffering about something that never needs to happen.

Q: But most of the Satsang teachers say that suffering can be ended.

K: Yes, by being what you are.

Q: So we want to know what to do to end it.

K: You cannot do anything. Whatever you do is maybe contra-productive.

Q: But you have done something.

K: Yes, but in spite of that I was what I am.

Q: How do you know that? You have done it. How can you know it would have happened otherwise?

K: Because it never added anything to my nature. That what I am was uninterrupted what I am. There is no more or less to it. And it never needed anything to do. And all the stories are fleeting shadows that no one needs.

Q: So there was no use in that whole search?

K: No. Totally useless. But that's the joy of it. That's the entertainment. I cannot claim that I did something and by that I realized something. No. I was always already what I am, and was always realizing myself in whatever happened. And that is not something I can claim.

Q: So you think if you would have not done the whole thing you would still sit here?

K: I have no idea. It would be different, but I would still be what I am. Because you believe Ramana did something. Did Ramana do something? Or did it just happen, 15 years old, going down on the ground and then the death experience came?

Q: But after he told everyone who came to him to do it.

K: Yes, but if everyone comes and asks you 'can I do something?' And you say: 'No, you cannot'. And after a while 'maybe I tell them and then they leave me alone. Because then they go home and they are in their room and just do self-inquiry so that they don't bother me anymore'.

Q: You think so?

K: Who knows? I don't know. But if I say that, it is as true as someone saying there must be something. No one knows. So maybe he was just trying to keep everyone busy so that they don't bother him. Who knows?

Q: So in his case it has happened at the age of 16.

K: Even Nisargadatta said it – in spite of all I have done, even in spite of the 'I am', in spite of the inquiry, in spite of believing in my master, I was always what I was.

Q: But all these people say that only after they have done all that, no?

K: But before they could not say it because there was no tool to say it. They are just learning the tools to say it. The words for it.

Q: So for that you have to do it?

K: No, nothing has to happen. As I said the other day, the loudspeaker can be prepared to pronounce things which normally cannot be pronounced. That's all.

Q: So if one feels attracted to that self-inquiry, it's ok to do it?

K: It's like the next sip of coffee. If you drink coffee it's good to have coffee. If you drink tea, it's good to drink tea. If you do self-inquiry, it's fine. No, I like it. In the dream it's the best you can do.

Q: For some reason we sit here and not in the swimming pool.

K: But this is self-inquiry.

Q: That's what I mean. For some reason we do this.

K: Yes, but I would maybe like to sit...

Q: ...in the swimming pool?

K: It's like after 60 years or so Ramana dead now, there are so many books and so many interpretations, and I know in the Ashram is only that what glorifies him. But he was totally different too. Sometimes he was making many jokes, and then someone wrote them down, and now they become like a wisdom thing. I have no idea.

Q: Yes, we don't know what he really said. And he spoke Tamil. But I really want to stop that sufferer.

K: Yes, and I can only point to - it's the easiest you can do just by being what you are. That's the only thing you can do to stop everything.

Q: Yes, I understand...

K: It's not an understanding, it's just being what you are in deep deep sleep. In spite of everything. In the absolute absence of any presence of anyone who knows or doesn't know, you exist. And that existence is without suffering, as in deep deep sleep. That's all.

Q: But how can I be...

K: There is no 'how' in it! To know yourself as that, to know yourself now as that what doesn't need to know itself to be itself. It's more than easy.

Q: Why do we not understand it?

K: Because it doesn't need to understand. If it would need to understand it would be relative. But because it is absolute it never needs to understand. It's already complete, absolute, nothing has to be different. And it's actually absolute Helplessness in itself. It cannot even understand. There is no way of understanding. And thank God no need for understanding.

Q: That means then I just have to wait until it happens?

K: Nothing ever happened anyway. It will never happen. You will never know yourself.

Q: But now I am not the same than in deep sleep.

K: Of course you are! Your Nature is not different now than in deep deep sleep. Your Essence, what you are in Nature, your Self, is now what it is in deep deep sleep. And in deep deep sleep there is no question about suffering, sufferer, knowing, not knowing. And just to be that what you are in deep deep sleep here now is just being what you cannot not be because you are in the presence and in the absence of this dream what you are. So you don't depend on the presence of this dream to be what you are. Whatever happens in this dream, you are in spite of it already. Never because of what happens in this dream you are what you are. So it's more than easy to be what you are, because you cannot not be that. Which is in spite of all you can imagine. But now in this dream there is a phantom who doesn't believe what one says, because he wants to own it. There is this ownership tendency. Controlling, owning.

Q: No, I don't want to control. I want to be out of it.

K: Yes, that's controlling You want to be out of yourself. Because this is your very Self. This is what you are. How can you leave what you are? What a bullshit idea that you try to get out of what you are! This is what you are. Not more and not less.

Q: This phantom is also what I am.

K: Of course! Whatever is, you are. You are the presence of whatever is. And now you are trying to get out of it, you suffer about that. You want to avoid yourself. You want to kill something that you are. What an idea! How can you leave what you are? Even trying is suffering. 'Everything is wrong. I don't feel so well. I hope it would be different. I would not even be born'. You always have a death wish. You want to escape. For that you meditate. The self-inquiry is a death wish. You have to be a Dervish, not a death wish. You have to dance around yourself, not have a death wish. It's amazing, that you try to avoid yourself. It's fantastic. You think you have to go out of something where you are not even in, because you are that.

Q: But why is it that we are trying to leave ourselves all the time?

K: Because you experience discomfort.

Q: But why...

K: There is no why! Every moment there is a discomfort of existence. You only can experience yourself in discomfort. You cannot experience yourself otherwise. Every experience is a discomfort experience.

Q: So it's natural we want to get out.

K: No, it's not natural, it's just because you want to escape the discomfort and you are looking for comfort. But that is part of the dream.

Q: Not every experience is discomfort.

K: Of course! Everyone is in discomfort. Even comfort is relative to the other one, it's still uncomfortable. You will never get comfort anywhere. Any experience will be suffering, will be relative.

Q: So we want to end it.

K: Yes, but ending it is impossible. How can you end what you are? You can only realize yourself in relativity. How else can you realize yourself? There is always an experiencer different from what he is experiencing. And in that way you are realizing yourself. You experience yourself. You cannot end it. You will never experience happiness. Never! You will always experience unhappiness in the experience of relative experiences of being different from something else.

Q: That will never end?

K: There is no ending to it. This is the way you realize yourself.

Q: Suffering.

K: It's not suffering. The moment you are what you are you cannot suffer about what you are. What is there to suffer about?

Q: Experiences?

K: No, you only suffer because you don't want to suffer. There is a sufferer who doesn't want to suffer. Because he wants to avoid the discomfort. And you trying to avoid yourself you suffer. Trying to avoid yourself is suffering. Trying to avoid the relative experience by believing it has to be different. Then you suffer about how you realize yourself. But not because of the experience. Only because you think it has to be different. Your bloody imagination that you think it has to be different, it has to be always blissful, enlightenment, pure light. You have an idea of truth. You have an idea of freedom. Your bloody ideas of how it has to be, that's your way of suffering! And you cannot blame anyone else. It's all your bloody ideas. Imagining some truth, and beauty, and blissful states, and the grace of tralala. And then you complain that you suffer, that it's not right, that something has to change. If you want to blame someone - you are so stupid! No one else. And you can only experience yourself in stupidity and ignorance. You can never experience Knowledge. Whatever you experience is stupidity. It's stupid to wake up in the morning, and stupid to experience yourself. It's stupid to realize yourself. But this divine accident you cannot stop.

Q: What do you mean when you say there can be suffering but no sufferer?

K: There is an experience of pain or suffering or mind. But there is no one who owns it.

Q: But normally there seems to be one who owns it.

K: For you! And? You keep suffering. But it's not my problem! 'Normally!' What is normal? To be Dutch? When you have a nationality and when you have a mother you are already fucked. Instantly. The moment you are born you are fucked. That's the nature of you coming out of fucking - you are fucked.

Q: So now what?

K: Yes, now what? Then you believed your bloody mother.

Q: Now you keep fucking.

K: Now you have sex to get out of it. Tantra or something. They all try to have a little orgasm. And in the orgasm there is an absence of a me, and then you want to have it again and again. Even by meditation you want to reach this absence of a me. And you believe that the me has to go for you to be what you are. That makes you depending on the me, that the me has to go that you can be better off. Because that's the idea of the me: a me without a me would be better off, says the me. Permanently trying to get rid of the me. And then complaining that it hurts. No way out! That's what I can only point to.

Q: Can't be!

K: Ha ha! I tell you!

Q: That's bad news.

K: That's the good news. You cannot go out where you are not in.

That's the best news you can get. Imagine there would really be a way out, that would be the really bad news. Because then there would really be somebody in it who needs go get out. That's like the so-called senior disciples of someone. They went to everyone, and they even claim 'I went to Ramana, I visited everyone', and then it seems like they are backed up by someone. Like someone sitting there who has all that lineage on top of him, all these pimps. All the Papajis and Ramanas, and then being a whore for existence, and all the pimps backing him up.

Q: But as long as we believe we are in it we have to do something.

K: You still are what you are. Do it. Don't ask me. If you ask me what you can do, I can only tell you be what you cannot not be. Then you will be fine. If you just could drop the mind you would be fine.

Q: Are you serious now?

K: I am absolute serious. Just this little mind, this little ownership.

Q: But how you drop this?

K: You cannot drop it. Because trying to drop it you want to make it your dropping. Impossible. I said 'if you could'. But you can not. You have to be with and without that me, mind, ownership, what you are. You have to be in spite of that. So you have to devote the devotion. As Ramana's 'renunciation of renunciation'. You renounce the renunciation. You see that you can never leave what you are. Everyone goes to him and everyone reads him. And only reads what he wants to read. But the more they think he says, they just doesn't see it. What is this renunciation of renunciation? What is this devotion of devotion? Being what you are! Because what you are has nothing to devote. And there is no need for devotion, for anything. How can you devote something that you don't have? Renouncing? What is there to renounce? You cannot renounce what you are. This is just being what you are. Renouncing the renouncing. And not trying to renounce something and then being an untouchable somewhere. Total detachment is just being what you are because in the total detachment there is no second. That's all. Your Nature is total detachment. But you cannot gain it because you are it. But everyone who needs to be detached is like a little me who wants to have an advantage, that's all. A greedy bastard me who wants to have an advantage of being detached from something.

Q: You still experience being uncomfortable?

K: You can only experience dis-ease. The Ease you are you cannot experience because in the Ease you are there is no experiencer. And whenever there is an experiencer there is an experiencer in the dis-ease of separation. All the experiences are experiences of dis-ease. So it's like a total disease. But you cannot get rid of the dis-ease. So what to do? You have to be in spite of the dis-ease what you are. Not because of the absence of the dis-ease. If you wait that this dis-ease will go you will wait forever. Never ending story of that what is the realization, and the realization is always relative experiences.

Q: But is there a difference in your experience of life from mine now?

K: No, I think the experiences are not different. But that what I am is neither the experiencer nor what is experienced. I am always that what I am, in spite of the presence or absence of anything.

Q: So it is different.

K: It's different, but it doesn't make us different. You take it personal. And I am neither taking it personal nor impersonal. I don't take anything. I am That. I don't have to take anything, because I am already that what is. And that is what you are too. There is no two. So you are the absolute Owner but you can't get enough. You even want to have nothing. You are already nothing and you want to own nothing. It's impossible. You are nothing. When there is nothing you are nothing when there is everything you are everything. But you cannot own it in any relative way. There is no one who can claim it. Your Nature is already that, so what? And you cannot escape. So this 'no way out' is good news. And you will never be happy. It's another good news. He he he. The good news is there was never anyone who was happy on earth. Never. There was never any happy one.

Q: You are sure?

K: Show me one! You can not even show me one who is unhappy. That's the good news. So that there cannot be anyone who is happy, the news is like there is no one who is unhappy. Because it is just an experience of an experiencer who is happy or unhappy. There is an experience of a phantom who is sometimes comfortable and sometimes uncomfortable. It's a phantom life. So what? The whole consciousness is a phantom. But what you are is absolutely in spite of it. The Ease you are you never left. And what you are is always absolute Ease.

Q: But how did that all come to you what you are talking about?

K: It doesn't come. I was always that.

Q: No, but that you are talking about that.

K: I don't know.

Q: I can not talk like that.

K: I could not talk like that either.

Q: It suddenly came?

K: It comes. Right now. I never said it before. I never thought about what I say. If I had to think about what I say I would sit here and be totally exhausted. If I would say that what I say I would be totally fucked. And very loaded. No, I am like a loudspeaker who doesn't mind what comes through.

Q: But was there some sudden change in you or something?

K: Even you are a loudspeaker, but you are a personal loudspeaker. But it doesn't make you different.

Q: That's what I mean. You were a personal loudspeaker also.

K: Sometimes I am a personal loudspeaker. Talk to me about stock market or something else. Suddenly I become a personal one.

Q: But when did you get impersonal?

K: It was always there. Your attention just goes only to the personal one now. The impersonal is still there. You just don't give it attention. Self-inquiry is actually putting attention to that what is attention. There is no two. Being attention, that is self-inquiry. Putting awareness to awareness is not becoming aware of awareness. Being awareness, that's self-inquiry. I know it's always done personally, because everyone is asking himself 'who am I?'. And then comes this so-called answer as absence, or nothing. But that's not the right thing. The self-inquiry of Ramana is not 'who am I?' but 'am I?' It's always 'am I?'. 'Am I' and out of 'am I' comes 'I am'. We don't even know where it starts and where it ends. Is it first the I or first the am? 'Am I, I am, I am, am I...' - it becomes like a stream of sound. Like a stream of whatever you are, of that uninterrupted Presence. So it's not the question 'who am I?' and then the answer is this Presence. No! The self-inquiry is 'am I', staying in the 'am I', and staying in the 'am I', it becomes naturally impersonal.

Q: 'Am I' as a question?

K: Just stay in the 'am I'. Just sit down and make 'am I, am I, am I...', and suddenly it becomes 'I am'. You don't know what is first anymore. There is no questioner anymore after a while. It just becomes like a sound, and then you cannot take it personal. There is no answer to it, and then the questioner naturally gets annihilated, if it works. But I know this personal self-inquiry always leads to the answer of awareness. Of that what is the 'I am the presence'. And then all the teachers say 'I am the presence'. Because that is the answer to that 'Who am I?' There is this presence. That is one answer. But every answer is questionable. So, it cannot be it. Every answer can be questioned again. But this 'Am I, I am', there is an uninterrupted Presence of that, but without anyone who is present. There is no answer. This was always there. When I was in the mid '90s in Tiruvannamalai there was this big discussion between Ramana scholars between 'Am I' and 'Who am I'. And it was always like a big fight. For me 'Am I' is more accurate. All the interpreters take it personal and they want to make an understanding out of it. It's natural. I was sitting ten years and talking in Tiruvannamalai, every year for a few months. And had to make this Ramana banana different. Because everyone has these ideas, how it has to be. I do my best, wherever I am, but I don't know. For me it was good to read not only Ramana but to read Sadhu Om or some other disciples from Ramana, their stories out of their perspective. And then Ramana becomes a total different story. He was not this holy man or something. He was so simple, and full of jokes. Never serious. These stories that he was sitting down and there were many ants and he was sitting down and killing ants by sitting down. And then the disciples: 'Oh, you killed all the ants!' 'Yes, i asked them to go, they didn't listen'. These stories you don't find in the Ramana Ashram. Because Ramana has to be this glorified whatever. No, he was quite funny. What I don't like right now is that it becomes Ramana-ism. Becomes a religion now. It's like Buddha always was against religion and cultivating anything. And Ramana the same. What you are never needs to be cultivated or never needs any religion. There is no lineage of the Self, there is nothing to do, the Self is ever realized, and whoever claims to be realized for sure is a bogus fraud. Forget it. But now it becomes like 'self-inquiry leads to self-realization'. Impossible! So it becomes a religion. The 'self-inquiry religion'. 'Advaita-ism'. So Vedanta now embraces Advaita. Normally it's Advaita Vedanta. Now it becomes Vedanta Advaita. So now by realization you can realize your true Nature. Ha ha ha. Totally opposite. They turn everything around. But why not? No one cares. That's religion. That's how religions are made. Now there is even popes of Advaita somewhere, and Advaita unions. The jokes are infinite. Even in Advaita-land.

Q: Karl, why do you say there is no way to escape the traps?

K: Because you are the trap. You are the trapper, the trapping and the trapped. And the trap of love is always there. You cannot escape this love trap. You always step into that falling in love again. No way out.

Q: But this is the way you realize yourself, what's wrong with it?

K: What way? Everything is wrong! It's all wrong.

Q: Why the trap?

K: Why not? There is an experience of the trapper and and an experience of someone who is trapped. Always. And being trapped by oneself, who cares? Being enslaved by oneself. You are the master and the slave. You play both roles. It's always SM.

Q: So actually this is the good news?

K: The good news is that first you cannot escape what you are and you will always be a slave for what you are, a slave of love. You will always be a slave of being in love with what you are. Small or big. A slave of love of your body, of your little me, of whatever you put your attention to, there is love running. You cannot escape love, and you cannot not love yourself. No way out. Even trying not to love yourself is out of love. Because you have the idea not loving yourself would be better. So out of love for yourself you try stop loving yourself. It's all love. So in spite of not needing that bloody love, you cannot escape it. Because any moment you exist, you are awake, love is running your whole existence. And always good intention, the intention is always love.

Q: Even in the absence?

K: In the absence there is the absence of love. It is still love. No love is still love. That's why they say your Nature is love. But I would not agree. That would be too much love.

Q: So the bondage is really the freedom. Because the bondage is the evidence of freedom.

K: Yes, but freedom is just an idea. Freedom is bondage. You will never be free.

Q: As long...

K: There is no as long!

Q: The moment you believe there is a way out, you are already in.

K: In what? Even that doesn't matter. Believing or not believing, does it make you different? It is a joke. It seems like I just remind you that you made a joke and now you have to start to laugh about it. This is your joke! The joke that you believe that you have to know yourself to be yourself. And now to suffer about the joke is quite a drama.

Q: Seven billion must not be wrong if they suffer.

K: If there is two it's already wrong, so whatever one says is wrong. Seven billion wrong or one wrong - whatever can be said is wrong. That's the beauty, that's the entertainment, everything is empty. Whatever you do or don't do is empty. But wonderful. You don't have to be clever, you don't have to be scholared, you don't have to know or not to know. Nothing is needed for you to be what you are. You are in any circumstance what you are. Any given or not given circumstance you are that. And your Nature never demands anything. There is no demand from what you are. That's why they call it Acceptance. But Acceptance cannot be owned. It will never be your Acceptance. You are Acceptance. And your Acceptance is running permanently. Without that Acceptance there would be no dream, there would be nothing. Acceptance is the Nature of existence. But it will never be your acceptance. But what you try is you make it your acceptance. And then you are suffering about not having it. The same with Knowledge. Your nature is Knowledge. But Knowledge cannot be owned. But you want to have it. And by you trying to have it you are suffering. What a joke! Knowledge wants to have Knowledge. It's already absolute Knowledge, trying to make it relative. And you trying to make Knowledge relative you suffer. And you are punished by yourself by that. And I totally like it. Ignorance is instantly punished.

Q: But it is not our fault.

K: Who else's fault? Who is so stupid to believe that he has to know himself to be himself? Say it!

Q: God!

K: God? So it's God's fault? So God is stupid?

Q: Yes.

K: I agree. When God knows himself he is the most stupid guy on earth ever known. God not knowing himself he is Knowledge himself. But God knowing himself he is total ignorance, but still what he is. So he is absolute Ignorance as he is absolute Knowledge. So his absolute Nature is in absolute Knowledge no different than in absolute Ignorance. It never is changing his absolute Nature. But in the absence of knowing he is absolute Knowledge. In the presence of knowing, he is absolute Ignorance. You can even say the nature of ignorance is Knowledge. So what has there to happen? The only little suffering part is: you want to have it! You are greedy. And even people who do self-inquiry they want to earn it, they want to gain it. There is something personal on their agenda. They want to escape from something with it. But it is never meant like that. I am not here to end suffering. I have no interest in ending suffering.

Q: So what are you here for?

K: I have no idea.

Q: To see us!

K: To see ass! Yes.

Q: You said everything is business in the dream.

K: Business? What business? What do I get here?

Q: An advantage.

K: For me it is an advantage here? To see you?

Q: Don't say no!

K: If you ask me, it is neither advantage nor disadvantage. For what you are there is no such thing. But for the one who is in the dream, everything that one is doing is business, for sure. Always wanting an advantage.

Q: And for you?

K: I am just Helplessness who cannot avoid this bloody meeting. If I could, I would! I am honest! I would just sit somewhere and watch television, for the rest of my life.

Q: But it is the same for us!

K: What?

Q: Do we have a choice?

K: You have a choice!

Q: No.

K: No? But that one who has no choice has one choice too many! Bloody trap.

Q: Some teachers will say: 'Come to Satsang. Be in Satsang'. And you say: 'Try not to come'. But it's exactly the same.

K: Yes, go away! Go now! If you have to go you will go anyway, in spite of anything. Going will happen or staying will happen. But who cares about if you are staying or going?

Q: So what is this absolute Knowing?

K: In Reality there is no knower and nothing is known. In Reality. But in this realization there are infinite knowers who know something. So yes, there are knowers in realization, but in Reality not. It's always yes and no, it's always a paradox. In the dream all of that is there. In the realization whatever you can imagine is there. And there is choice, there is no choice, there are all these experiences. But in Reality there is not.

Q: And all the dream, all the greed, all the business, all trying to get what one wants, is there absolutely no care about that?

K: Reality never cares about anything because it doesn't even know if there is something or not. And that what is already unreal always cares. There is a permanent care-business. So there is loving-caring in the realization, but in Reality there is no loving and caring.

Q: So there is a use to be sitting here for the apparent dreamer, and there isn't.

K: Maybe, maybe not. Here everyone cares why he is here or not and now you want to know how it is. But Reality doesn't care if you want to know or not. So there is a Carelessness already there which is Reality, and it really absolutely doesn't care if you care or don't care.

Q: But in consciousness looking for itself there is...

K: Actually it never looked for itself. It is just a dream of looking. She is a business lady, she wants to make it a business now. Even consciousness is a business.

Q: When attention is on attention there is no problem. But I can't control that either.

K: No? But who can not? Now you are coming to the non-doer. 'I can not and tralala'. You are just shifting positions, going to a safer place.

Q: There is more comfort when attention is on attention.

K: So you make it a business again.

Q: I want to be in there all the time. That's why I say I am totally addicted to the absence.

K: So you want to make a business for absence now?

Q: Yes. Absence business. That's what's happening with you. That's why I come.

K: For the absence? 'My business is the absence'. How many absinthes do I have to drink for the absence?

Q: I see your point of cutting down everything and saying like the presence and the absence is the same. You have to be in spite of the presence and the absence.

K: I always say you are not different in the presence and you are not different in the absence. So presence absence makes no difference.

Q: There is a dream advantage of the absence.

K: Yes, stay in the absence if you can!

Q: But I can't. That's why I come to satsang so much.

K: I am always pointing to the helplessness.

Q: But I come to satsang for that.

K: For the absence. How can there be a meeting in the absence?

Q: There is no meeting then, that's the point.

K: There is no meat anymore.

Q: Yes, there is meat, but no...

K: Satsang normally means you forget your meat and you become the space. And in the space there is already oneness and then you come for that oneness experience of not being limited to this body, being more in the so-called presence of the space. That's normally the satsang idea.

Q: Many do that. They give experiences to people.

K: That's why they are singing, they create all these oneness experiences.

Q: So what are you doing?

K: I am not singing.

Q: So it's like this neti-neti.

K: For me it's more the presence of Carelessness. If you are in the personal or in the impersonal or whatever, I really give a shit about it.

Q: And yet even at the end Nisargadatta said 'who even cares about the I-amness...

K: Even consciousness, who needs that fucking consciousness? I don't need it, but still it's there.

Q: Yes, but it was always in the end...

K: It doesn't matter when they say it! Should they say it first and then say that what they said before? Listen to that!

Q: Yes, I see it. It' still to get something...

K: There is still always a personal thing running. I am totally impatient for going into the levels of something.

Q: Have you always been like that, cutting everything?

K: Yes, with cows you have to tell them where to go. When you are a farmer, if you want to milk a cow. If you want to go from A to B you cannot make a maybe. 'Maybe you go this way'. What I am doing here, I can say the most bullshit whatever, I give a direction, but I say it as if it was absolutely true. And I don't care. This Carelessness, if it's true or not, that's what you are coming for. And not that it's true or not. That there is no one who cares about if it is right or not. Because it never needs to be right what you say. And will never be right. So whoever comes here comes for that so-called carelessness of speech. No one wants to have the final solution here or anything. No one expects to get some final understanding here or something. Just for that experience, for that mood, that there is no one who cares about what comes out of this. That carelessness everyone is interested in. And I agree, that is like self-inquiry. You are interested in that carelessness. And that ruthlessness. And this totally untouchable what you are. Which can never be changed by anything. That you are coming for. But I cannot do it by talking softly. Sometimes I do.

Q: How can you say that even if consciousness is not there, we are what we are? How can you know it?

K: It's not a knowing. But before consciousness wakes up, you are already what you are. And then waking up happens. Otherwise there cannot be waking up. It is not a logic. It's your daily experience. Before waking up, before the first purest notion of awareness can be there, you are already there. And then awareness happens.

Q: That's not my experience.

K: That will never be your experience. But still you are prior to that first experience.

Q: How do we know that?

K: There is no 'how'! You are that! You have to be what you are that even awareness can be. And you will never know that as a person. You cannot put it in your personal pocket, saying 'I know now that I am before'.

Q: But that consciousness comes and goes uncontrollably it seems.

K: Yes. That's your helplessness. You cannot interfere into the dream, because you are the absolute Dreamer. Because what you are is never in the dream. So you cannot do anything in the dream. The dream actually is already dreamed. You cannot change something which is unchangeable. The next is the next. Never ending story of next in that so-called following up of experiences. The next reaction is the next reaction. The next is the realization of what you are as the one before was. Never ending story of you realizing yourself. Because that what is prior to the first experience of awareness, which is never born and never dies, you cannot get rid of. And because you are That, there will always be the next. And the first is awareness, and then comes I-amness, and then comes whatever comes then. Who cares what? Right now maybe this thing here has a 'prefe-Renz' that I wake up in Renz. After the I comes I-am and then Renz. I am Renz. But one day it will be over. The Renz came, and the Renz will go. 'Renzed out'. Rinsed out.

Q: But that which is prior to consciousness, does that have any control?

K: It is absolute the Almighty, the absolute Dreamer, Brahman himself. But he cannot control himself, because for control it needs two. There is no two. We are talking about non-duality here. There is no two. And if there is no two, there is that what is Brahman, there is that what is Heart, and Heart cannot control Heart. Reality cannot control reality. And that Reality is realizing itself as a realizer realizing what can be realized. The father, the spirit and the son. The seer, the seeing and what can be seen. The whole scenery is a realization of that what is That. The Heart of what is Heart. And that what is Heart has no Heart, it is Heart. So Heart, Reality, realizing itself in whatever way. As the lover, the loving and the beloved. That is the normal thing. The lover is God, the spirit is loving, and then the beloved is this body, or Jesus, or the man, or all the experiences. So that what is Heart realizing itself as lover, loving and the beloved. But the nature of the lover is Heart, the nature of loving is Heart, the nature of the beloved is Heart. So in nature there is no difference in anything. And that what is the nature of the lover, the loving and the beloved has nothing to gain and nothing to lose in how this love affair is running. But when you are the lover who is different from the beloved, then you suffer about the difference. That you are different from something else, then you suffer about not being what you are. That is called suffering. But whatever you try to become what you are, you want to make it a personal heart. 'My heart'. Impossible! This will drop as every night it drops, and you are Heart without experiencing of anything. So Heart experiencing itself in the morning as something, as a seer, seeing what can be seen. But not by whatever this seer is seeing and doing and inquiring it will become Heart. Because it already is that what it is. No way! So whatever happens in the dream, in this so-called love affair, cannot affect what you are. So you cannot become what you are by whatever way you experience yourself. As you already are that what is experiencing itself. Reality realizing itself as whatever. So you have to realize yourself. And as you never started, realization never started and will never end. So what? The next is the next. The next sip of coffee, the next word, the next presence, the next absence, the next whatever you can experience. Always the next. Never ending next. And then and then and then and then. And it is always different. Sometimes it is very uncomfortable, then it is more comfortable. But it needs one who discriminates between comfort and discomfort. And already that one is one you can experience, but not what you are. The discriminator who discriminates between comfort and discomfort already is a phantom. And if he is starting not to discriminate anymore, who cares? Who cares if he discriminates or not? Who cares if he is suffering or not suffering? The main question is: Who cares?

Q: The sufferer...

K: Yes. One sufferer and the other sufferer. Because when there is one there is two. Because without a second there would not even be one. Imagine you would be enlightened and you could not tell anybody! Many people want to be enlightened. But for whom? Imagine no one cares if you are enlightened or not, not even yourself. Imagine no one cares if you suffer or not, not even yourself.

Q: That would be nice.

K: You see. That is your Nature! Because that's the same. Enlightenment means being happy ever after. But if there is no one who cares if you are happy or not, not even yourself, and your Self never cares if you are happy or not happy. I always ask people: for whom do you want to wake up? Imagine you wake up and no one cares! Not even yourself. And you cannot tell anybody. What to do with all of that enlightenment, realization and deep insights?

Q: Enjoy it?

K: Yes, but if no one cares, who has the joy? It just becomes the next sip of coffee, your bloody realization, your bloody insight. Not more and not less. And in Nature it is like that. The deepest of your fucking realization, you can dip into your total tralala, will be dipping into ignorance. And it doesn't matter how deep you dip into ignorance, it will be ignorance. Because only ignorance has depths and heights.

Q: It's nice what you say that samadhi and when you have a cup of coffee is not different.

K: No difference. Yes, a few guys said that, like Nisargadatta or Ramana: all the seven states are different states of realizing yourself, samadhi or not samadhi, relative or not relative, they are all in nature not different. They are all just different ways of realizing yourself. So the quality is always Reality, which is what you are in all circumstances. There is no difference in quality. So the next sip of coffee, the next breathing in and breathing out, is as good as samadhi or not samadhi. Or whatever highest experience you can have. And in nature the Highest doesn't know any Highest. And the Lowest doesn't know any Lowest. So in the Highest there is no Highest and in the Lowest there is no Lowest.

Q: So Samadhi doesn't know about Samadhi.

K: Otherwise it would be a personal samadhi. And what kind of personal samadhi would it be? I always was suspicious of people saying 'Oh, the Master is in Samadhi now. We should be quiet'. 'He cannot talk right now, he is in samadhi'. Everyone: 'Oh! Very important! And our Master, he can go into samadhi! It's our Master! And my Master is better than any other Master. Because he can go into samadhi whenever he likes'. But that is whatever Zen means. Zen means the next sip of coffee is the realization of what you are. And the next sip of coffee is in quality not different than the deepest absence experience of any kind, experience of light, or anything you can experience. So in all that the only quality is that what you are. But not the way you experience yourself. The ways are infinite. But there is no way to become that what is the quality you are. That's Buddha. So if you meet Buddha on the way: Peng!

Q: I had a dream: you were trying to kill me.

K: And?

Q: Nothing happened.

K: Yes. That's all I do. That's what I am doing permanently. I am shooting and shooting and shooting at the duck you imagine to be, and maybe the duck even gets shot, but what you are is unaffected, all the time.

Q: And then there were more teachers trying to kill me and then the dogs were eating my body...

K: That sounds good. This is a good sign. I like these dreams and visions of killing and being killed. The worst you can imagine happens, and nothing happens. Fantastic! All your fear was for nothing! Still you are what you are and nothing happened. It's like you die and no one dies. All the psychological drama about it, all for nothing! Like you win the lottery, a few million dollars, and you don't feel different. But you expected to really be happy, and nothing happens. Or you marry, the dream comes true, and you think 'Shit, I don't feel anything!'

Q: So you are saying that you realize yourself in discomfort?

K: You always have to realize yourself in all opposites. Because you want to only realize yourself in comfort you suffer about discomfort. The idea of awakening, the idea of enlightenment, means that you get enlightened and then you are always happy. That's enlightenment. But it will not happen.

Q: So is this discomfort because of the presence of the body?

K: No. Even when you are already spirit it is uncomfortable. Maybe it feels like comfort. But it is still discomfort because it may end again. There is no comfort in anything. So take comfort in being that what you are. Because that never needs any comfort. And that is comfort itself. And that what needs comfort is a phantom. So whatever, even the comfort of I-amness, of oneness, is a discomfort, because there is one who needs comfort. It's a fake one. As fake as that me you imagine to be, is that comfort you can experience. It's all false. And that's Ramana again: from the beginning there is falsity. It starts false, and whatever comes out of false, false happens. False, false, false, false. So the root thought 'I', the root thing starts very early with the awareness-I. There is this most subtle I, the awareness notion of I, the purest what you can get. But even the purest is already false. Because the purest is only pure compared to something else. So it's false. So out of the purest comes false, not pure, and all you can imagine coming out of the first imaginary I, all the other images following this image, this I-maze.

Q: So when we leave the body...

K: Who is leaving the body?

Q: Spirit maybe?

K: Spirit?

Q: Yes, what happens when we leave the body?

K: I don't know. Is there anybody home? Who is now in the body? And who is leaving the body?

Do you leave your body every night? Because in deep sleep there is no body. So it is like death.

In German we call the deep sleep the brother of death. Because the experience is the same. Would you mind not waking up again? Is there somebody when you are in deep sleep who would mind waking up again or not wake up? So no one cares. And that is what you are. But waking up happens anyway. And then the drama continues. But in that deep deep sleep there is no one who would care about waking up or not waking up. So who cares now? One image caring about another image? One idea caring about another idea? Because that what is your nature is in the absolute absence of all the ideas absolute not caring if it wakes up or not, or if something happens again or not. It would be absolutely fine if nothing would happen again. But out of that helplessness it happens again. And then out of that first false waking up, all the other false starts to unfold. Unfolding – unfalsing.

Q: So waking up happens to whom? Waking up happens to the body, isn't it?

K: No! Waking up happens to what you are. Your Nature is in the absence. This is what you are. In every deep sleep you are experiencing the absence of any presence. And then in the morning you wake up, this Energy you are wakes up in this body or all the other bodies or not bodies. The Energy is not different that wakes up, it's never asleep. Just, you are just not experienced by what you are. You take it personal as you think you are the only one. The Energy is living everything. That is never asleep or awake, that what is Energy, that what is Reality, that what is Brahman. Maybe half of the humanity is asleep, then Brahman is experiencing himself as asleep. And in the other half of humanity Brahman is experiencing himself as something else, eating a piece of cake or something. Brahman is never asleep. So your Nature is never asleep. Just not experiencing this whatever you think you are. It only knows you when you appear like an image. Otherwise it doesn't know you and it doesn't mind if you would never come back. So your Nature would never mind if you never wake up again. Because it would not miss you. And now every night it drops you, because it doesn't even need you now, to be what it is. It never needs you. And it really doesn't care if you get enlightened or not. I tell you. It couldn't care less. If you wake up or not wake up is really like a sack of rice falling down in Beijing. So much Existence cares about your presence or absence. And then everyone thinks Existence takes care! About what? 'About me'. 'Please, take care of me! Help me!' Ha ha. It doesn't even know you! The dogs could get you and maybe it cares more about the dogs getting something to eat than about you. Or not less or not more. Maybe it cares more about the dogs. Because God becomes a dog and maybe cares about dogs more.

Q: So what about the grace that places us here?

K: Grace never places you anywhere! Why should grace place you? You think grace needs you?

Q: No I don't.

K: You see. Why should it place you somewhere? Just an accident.

Q: How do I get to be here?

K: Who is here? Look who he thinks he is here!

Q: So when there is nobody...

K: Where? When? Now! There is no body! What is this body? A piece of cake! Or many cakes.

Q: So when the body dies, do we wake up and sleep again in that state also?

K: The Self never sleeps, the Self is never awake. As I just tried to tell you. If Energy wakes up in you or not, it doesn't really care. If there is seven billion or 70 billion or no humans running this earth and being or not, Existence doesn't care. It can be 150 billion pieces of cake. It's like a big celebration, but birthday without you. It's always a birthday, there are many cakes, many candles.

Q: So one can say: forget grace now. Gratitude is also an image.

K: Gratitude is still arrogance. I am in gratitude because something happened to me that I liked. You can do whatever, doesn't matter. There is no judging. That existence is never judging what you do or don't do. It's only you judging your bloody doing or not doing. There is this little judge inside and you are always in a court case and you always try to punish yourself for something you have not done. Because that is your game. You feel very important when you have a judge, like a moralistic ethic system running, and then you tell yourself what you have done right and wrong and you compare yourself with others. That's the game of phantoms. Just trying to survive and being important.

Q: That game is over with you?

K: The game is never over. I am the game. How can I be over with the game? I am the bloody circus! And sometimes I experience a clown. This is the clown. Or clone. But the circus doesn't mind how many clowns are in the circus, and sensations. The circus is still the circus. You cannot not be the circus. You are the circus. And when the circus wakes up, it is never asleep. The sensations are always acting. You always think because you fall asleep that you are the most important whatever and that Existence goes asleep. What will happen if I have no body anymore? What will happen if I leave this body? Or the body is leaving me?

Q: Do this kind of realizations still happen after the body is gone?

K: What kind?

Q: The comfort and discomfort.

K: There is a different experience of discomfort. It is not the end of discomfort. Maybe then the next is the next. But that problem will be gone, for sure.

Q: Which problem?

K: That problem. That what now is asking something. That one is gone. But for that one there will be maybe ten others. Look, it never stops. Yoga Vashista, King Rama, so many books, the Mahabharata, and Arjuna, and Yudhisthira going to hell and accepting and bla bla bla. And look - the story continues, as if nothing ever happened. All these fantastic stories of realization. In spite of Ramana, in spite of Buddha, in spite of Jesus, in spite of all of that holy holy bogus, nothing happens. And I tell you, Ramana would like that when I talk like that more than anything else. And that one who would try to defend Ramana, ha ha ha. If you defend someone you don't believe in him really. Then you really make him something weak. Whatever you defend, you make weak. Ramana would never need to be defended by anyone. Or Nisargadatta. And that is a sign of what you are, Reality, never needs anyone to defend it. 'Ramana never said that'. Who cares if he said it or not? Everyone is counting every word.

Q: So this love story continues, because love is loving itself?

K: Self-love never stops. Look: seven billion coming out of the Self loving the Self. It's like Self trying to penetrate the Self. That's why I like this Indian symbols, like the penis, the lingam, and then the yoni, the cosmic vagina, and then the vibration creating all these possible vibration and information systems, out of energy.

Q: So that's even before Adam and Eve?

K: No. Adam is the lingam.

Q: It became personified.

K: It's not personified. It's just for kindergarten, religion. Normally it's just the male principle and the female principle. And Adam is the original man, the original nature, the gestalt. And then comes Eve, it's like space, the mother. And then Adam starts to vibrate in that what is Eve. The male principle starts to vibrate in the female principle. And that is creating everything.

Q: So Eve really is holding a lot more than the man?

K: What?

Q: You say she is space, so she holds a lot more...

K: She is not doing anything! She is just bloody space. Not holding anything. She is nothing, there is only space.

Q: It seems so tiny...

K: It's a cosmic vagina. But if you believe you have one, it becomes a comic one. The same for men. You are the lingam, you are the light, but you think you have one, and then you become a comic. It's like a comic strip. No, it's a symbol. First there is awareness, the light of Shiva. And then comes space, and the lingam starts to vibrate, and then in that absolute vibration creates all that can be created as information of vibration. This is all vibration of energy. Even the scientists would say you can't find any matter. It's just vibration of light, that's the closest you can get. But that what is light you still don't know. And that is Para-Brahman. And knowing him as Brahma he knows himself as light, as creator, starting to know himself. And the love affair comes later. It's just innocent vibration, in an innocent space. And then out of that innocent penetration, comes all that – look at it! And then that what came out of it wants to know why. 'Why did this bloody vibrator start to vibrate?' 'If he wouldn't have started to vibrate I would not have this problem!' 'How can I stop this bloody vibrator?' 'So now I meditate and try to stop this bloody vibrator!' 'And I go deeper and deeper and if it doesn't stop I try everything'. That's called self-inquiry or meditation. You try to stop the vibration of light. Amazing!

But then you cannot stop being horny. You maybe become a celibate. You celibate forever. That's what is called the Brahmacharya, because you are keeping it quiet.

Q: So when people say: 'The energy here is nice. This person has a nice energy, or this temple, or this home'.

K: You are resonating with that space. There is a harmonic resonance.

Q: And if there is a negative energy...

K: Then you don't resonate as you like it.

Q: So in that moment...

K: Next day you can go to bed with that guy right away. It's amazing. One day you marry one and the next day you could kill him. That really often happens.

Q: Always.

K: Actually always. People marry when they take the anti-baby pill. And then they want to have a baby, so she doesn't take the pill. And suddenly the whole energy is different and they cannot fuck anymore. The attraction is totally gone. The smell is different, they don't resonate anymore, and they have to divorce again. So many things one has to think about before getting married or says 'forever'. So it's nobody's fault. It's just energy resonating in comfort or in discomfort. And it can all change the next day. Nothing is for certain or forever. It's all unpredictable. Some days you like yourself and you say this guy I could be forever. And the next day you could kill him right away. Heaven and hell. And when you call it heaven, in oneness with yourself, then you think 'this could go on forever, I would not mind'. And the next day it becomes hell and then you could kill it right away. Fantastic! Unpredictable love. Uncontrollable, unpredictable. Always different. But the father you could always kill!

Q: The shift of perception of awareness to awareness. But I am not sure, awareness being aware of awareness, it's not something being aware of awareness?

K: Huh?

Q: Awareness being aware of itself.

K: Huh?

Q: Because there can't be two awarenesses.

K: Huh? So it's a false awareness. A false awareness becoming aware of a false awareness. False, false, false. The false becomes aware of the false. Does it make a difference if the false becomes aware of the false?

Q: So what can see that there is two awarenesses? Awareness being the witness? Putting awareness to awareness?

K: The meaning of putting awareness to awareness is being awareness not knowing awareness. But the moment you know awareness there are two false awarenesses. So your natural state is being awareness, not knowing awareness. But the moment you have awareness, it's artificial. An artificial owner owning an artificial awareness. Because there is two. There is separation. And separation cannot be real. Because that what is awareness doesn't know awareness. How can it be owned?

Q: So what is it then? Is it a recognition that recognizes that or sees that?

K: Sees that?

Q: You mean that would be a Jnani state?

K: What Jnani state?

Q: Awareness recognizing false awareness.

K: No. When a Jnani knows a Jnani, then the Jnani is still an ignorant Jnani. When a Jnani is a Jnani, Jnani doesn't know any Jnani anymore. It is Jnani. It is Bhakta. But there is no one who is Bhakta. Or Jnani. When a Jnani knows to be a Jnani, for sure it's a false one. If a Jnani makes himself different to something else and he takes himself as a Jnani, and you become an Ajnani, whenever there is one who makes a discrimination, that's ignorance. In Nature there is only Nature. For a Jnani there is no Jnani.

Q: So it's not a recognition?

K: No. It's just being what you cannot not be. When there is awareness, you are awareness, but not knowing awareness. When there is I-amness there is I-amness, but you don't know I-amness. When there is the world there is the world, but you don't know any world. When there is the absence there is the absence and then you are absence. You are always that what is. But there is no one who is that. Never was. So no one can claim that. There is no before and after in it.

Q: This is where I am still trying to survive.

K: You survive in artificial. Because the artificial needs an artificial experience to stay in the artificial existence. It is a survival system of the artificial. The false needs false experiences to stay in the false. Because in Reality it cannot survive. So whatever the me is doing, even self-inquiry, is trying to stay as a me. Because in that expectation it confirms that there is one who needs to do something and can get something. And that's his nature. The phantom will always try to survive. Consciousness will always try to make a concept out of how it has to be. Even the idea of knowledge or Jnani can only happen in the unreal. Reality doesn't know any Reality or difference. There is no difference in anything. So even the idea of Jnani, Jnana, or Bhakti, Bhakta, is only in the dream. For what you are there is no such thing. Only in the dream there are names and concepts and whatever you can come up with. Reality would never pronounce itself as anything. And that what is pronouncing itself as something is an artificial pronouncer pronouncing an artificial statement. And Heart never pronounces itself. This is living itself as an artificial creator, an artificial creating, an artificial what can be created, as in differences. But this doesn't become artificial by that. So it is That by being That. But it doesn't know to be That.

Q: This is the 'Am I' you are talking about?

K: No, this is the Heart. The 'Am I' is being the 'I am'. That's already quite comfortable. We talked about self-inquiry ending the suffering and staying in the 'I am' or I-amness. The I-am or oneness is already quite comfortable. So if you ask me what you can do in the dream to be in more comfort, you can do self-inquiry, you can stay in the 'I am'. And then maybe in the awareness. It's better than here. But whatever is better than something else has to be in the dream. So yes, if you ask me personally 'what can I do to have a better life and peace of mind and feeling good?' Ok, do self-inquiry and stay in the I-amness. And to stay in the I-amness you just go 'I am, am I', and then naturally you enter that flow of I-amness. If you do it 24/7/365. And not only a few hours a day. It has to be an uninterrupted flow. That already is grace if that happens. That you even can lift your eyebrow is grace. So by that grace which puts you in this misery, the same grace puts you into the non-misery. But the more comfortable is still not comfortable enough. There is still that what discriminates between comfort and discomfort. And that is always like hell. Only in hell there is heaven and hell. Only in separation. And separation means time, hell, discrimination. There is something good and something bad. That's called hell. So God himself being the devil creating his own hell. Hell-elulja. God not knowing himself there is neither hell, nor heaven or anything. Then God is that what is God not knowing God. But the moment God knows God, there is bi-God. Two Gods. God and God. And then comes the whole story of the love affair with himself. And the lover and the beloved are different and then he fights with himself. The whole story as we know it. The whole

Mahabharata, all the wars. The moment God knows God, God is involved with himself. But one can call it love.

Q: Tainted love.

K: Tainted or not. It's never fulfilling that love. This relative love of God loving God is never fulfilling and never ending and there is never a happy end in it. No happy end. And if you see that there is never any happy end in that relative love affair, in that relative story, the idea that you can get what you may be longing for in that – I would call it shit - maybe ends, and then you are that what is in spite. And that's already fulfillment itself, being in spite of all that dream, in spite of all that oneness, separation, samadhi.

Q: That's great. Great for what? For whom?

K: In the dream I would say if you can enter the I-amness and you can stay there, why not? Why should you suffer? But if you ask me if that would be the end of whatever, no. All ends just by being what you are. Because for what you are never anything started and never anything ends. So the absolute end of the story is just being what you are. As you don't know any start you don't know any end. But that what knows a start will always look for the end. And always look for a happy end. But, no way!

Q: If you are in the I-am, is it still in consciousness?

K: Yes.

Q: And if you are what you are, is it still in consciousness?

K: There is neither awareness nor consciousness or anything. Then you absolutely don't know what you are and what you are not. There is a total absolute absence of any presence of any idea of what you are and what you are not. There is absolutely no discrimination of anything.

Q: Like deep sleep?

K: I's deep deep sleep. Deep sleep they always say is awareness still. Awareness which is different from I-amness, and then whatever is this dream. So the deep deep sleep is the nature of deep sleep. And then from there you become the nature of I-amness, and then the nature of the world, by being what you are. But that is never different in nature. It doesn't know any difference. It's never different in anything.

Q: But can you be what you are now, when you are talking?

K: I talk? Do I talk? Of course I am what I am. Talking or not talking. You think when I am talking I am not what I am?

Q: No, but you are now conscious.

K: I don't need to be conscious.

Q: You are not conscious?

K: No.

Q: Not aware?

K: No. If I would be aware I would be different from something else. What I am is never aware or conscious or not conscious. What I am has no idea about consciousness.

Q: But how can you talk then?

K: Talking happens. It's a miracle. It's fantastic.

Q: But you are conscious of the talking, no?

K: No. Something comes out but if you ask me a bit later 'Did you say something', if you ask that what I am, I would say I have never said anything.

Q: You are not conscious of the words?

K: No. And as I said, I absolutely don't care if they are right or wrong.

Q: But you see us?

K: I see asses.

Q: But you see some people here?

K: No, I just see information of something, I don't know. I see differences, but the differences don't make any difference.

Q: Don't you have to be aware to see something?

K: No.

Q: What does it mean then awareness?

K: Awareness? Awakeness. Something has to be awake. But there is no I in it. I would go as far to say 'I am awareness, when there is awareness. And I am I-amness when there is I-amness. And I am this when this is there.' But it's not that I have to know that. Just by being what I am, what I can not not be, I am that. I am always that what is. And that you can not not be. But it never demands it. There is no that I now have to be present or I have to be aware or something has to be conscious to do something. The words are just coming out as they come. I could not think what I say before. I am much too lazy to be aware about what I do. It's inexhaustible. The whole thing happens by itself. The dream is already dreamed, things already happened. Moment by moment it is just another frame of the movie, which is already finished.

This is like a discussion which is never ending. Consciousness always sitting somewhere and talking about how it is. Never ending story. Since whenever. So there will never be any end to this because there will never be any final talk, or final understanding anybody. Consciousness will never understand consciousness, in any relative way. But just by being what it is, it doesn't know any consciousness anymore, by not knowing consciousness. And that is the nature of understanding itself, of knowledge itself. And there is no need of understanding or knowing anything. Just by being what you are. But any moment you want to know, you separate yourself from yourself, even in an imaginary separation, and then you want to know your beloved, and that's impossible. No way. But by just being what you are you are your beloved and you don't have to know that. And by that you own your beloved absolutely. The absolute Ownership is just being what you cannot not be. That's an absolute Ownership, just by being what is. But trying to own it relativity, being the owner of your beloved by knowing your beloved and controlling your beloved, that's called suffering. That's this relative love affair you suffer about. You control everything already. You cannot control anything anymore, because you are that what is. You are the absolute dreamer who dreamed the whole dream. But now it's too late. Now you cannot change it anymore.

Q: But now I think I am this phantom.

K: Yes, and that's part of this dream. That's the way you realize yourself now in a personal way. But it doesn't make you less, or more. The Energy you are, the Life you are, doesn't get less if it's realizing itself in this relative little me. The experience of being small doesn't make you small. The experience of a little me doesn't make you little. That's the beauty of that what is the absolute Experiencer, it doesn't become what is experienced. It still remains as the Nature it is. So there is no danger in anything. But you want to know that! Personally. Everyone I know wants to know it personally. They want to put it in their pocket of knowledge and it always has to be available for me. 'Whenever I don't feel so good I take it out and present it to myself and then I have a tool for being happy'. Fantastic! So everyone is like a disciple, which means you want to learn how to be happy. You want to have tools and concepts how to do it. And understanding, and little sayings, that you just repeat something like a mantra. 'If I repeat that mantra I will be in harmony with everything'. Wonderful mantras. Sometimes it works for some time, sometimes not.

It would really be something if I would sit here and try to end someone's suffering!

Q: You can try on me!

K: Then there would be pity here.

Q: No, you can do it without pity.

K: No, I need pity, otherwise I have no interest. Pity needs one who pities himself, and then seeing other ones who suffer too. It needs one suffering who sees another sufferer. So I have to play that game and pretend there is a sufferer talking to another sufferer. 'What can we do? In my case I found this tool: I just accept everything that comes. Maybe you try it too'.

Q: You suffer?

K: What I am never suffered.

Q: Before you suffered?

K: There was no before for what I am.

Q: You have no memory of suffering?

K: What I am has no memory of anything. What I am is Memory. What I am is That. That's why sometimes I talk about things I have never heard about. It cannot come out of this little whatever. I don't know. You have to tell me whom you ask? You ask the phantom Karl or what I am?

Q: The phantom. That phantom is still suffering or not?

K: Sometimes it is uncomfortable and sometimes comfortable. And sometimes there is back pain.

Q: But do you care about it?

K: I absolutely care. I take pills, sometimes I even go to Ayurveda clinics. Sometimes I go to the dentist if I have tooth pain.

Q: Do you suffer about that?

K: If it takes too long. If it goes for a few days I think 'Shit, maybe I take them all out'!

Q: So it's a careless caring.

K: Nothing changed. Nothing has to change. The story continues. Until the last breath of this tralala. That I like about these guys like Nisargadatta and Ramana: It is a disease that will go by itself. It came by itself, it will go by itself. So what?

Q: But he seemed very detached, Ramana.

K: No. He was like a fury in the kitchen! That's the beauty of your Nature. Nothing has to be changed. You can be the asshole you were before and it doesn't matter. And I would not try not to be one. Maybe you even become the absolute Asshole. Maybe you don't care anymore if you are an asshole or not. For some it's not so nice around you. Some complain. Nothing has to be changed. You don't have to be a nice guy afterward. You don't have to be loving. Some give this impression, suddenly they hug everybody. I am happy that no one touches me. Who makes the standards? That's the best answer of Ramana and Nisargadatta. Both gave the same answer. 'Who makes the standards?'

Such An Absolute Perfect Trap

Q: We have been searching and searching and now we get the answer that you cannot know yourself.

K: No, you cannot know yourself, but you cannot not know yourself.

Q: And all this is for comfort?

K: You are looking for a comfort which you never lost.

Q: But still the seeking is because there is discomfort?

K: No, you experience discomfort, and the comfort you are you will never experience. So you never lost your comfort, but you will always experience discomfort.

Q: What can be done in relative life to make it more comfortable, maybe we can talk about that?

K: We always talk about it. 'How do you do?'.

Q: Maybe we would like to know from you what we can do to make relative life more comfortable. If we cannot know what we are.

K: Next time if you want to go into two liquids meeting, and something happens, you don't enter that.

Q: I don't enter that?

K: Yes. That would be the Tibetan Book of the Dead.

Q: Yes, but that will be next time.

K: But that would be my advice. If you can do that. Because whatever you do now, it's too late anyway. Now you have this body and something is born, whatever you do now is trying to heal something what is unhealable. You can just make it less painful maybe.

Q: What can we do in relative life to make it less painful?

K: Go to a doctor.

Q: I thought maybe you could give us some nice advice? Apart from the doctor.

K: The best dentist would be: being what you are is out-rooting all the ideas what has to be healed or not healed. That's the absolute doctor, being what you are. That would be the absolute treatment. Just being what you can not not be is being the doctor himself. Not needing any doctor. So being that what you are would be the end of all ideas that something has to be different or healed, or that you need to be healthy or purified, or you need comfort. All of that will in an instant be gone. In a split second all the ideas of health and disease and comfort and discomfort are just – bye bye. So if you ask me, that's for me the absolute treatment. Out-rooting the root-thought 'I'. It's like a root treatment. But it hurts sometimes, without narcotics. It's a root treatment without narcotics. And I think it hurts. So what I am doing here is giving a little laughing gas, making a lot of jokes so that the root treatment doesn't hurt so much. Because otherwise it quite hurts. And you don't sit still.

So, what else?

Q: Maybe one question I can ask again because I haven't understood really.

K: I think we will talk about that the next 20 years.

Q: What do you mean by 'false evidence appearing real'?

K: Yes, false evidence – because you take the evidence that you have a body as real. So an appearance of a body, an appearance of energy, you take as real. That there is a body. That's a false evidence appearing real. So this appearance, this phenomenal experience of a body, you take as real. It's a false evidence, that you think 'but I can touch it, I feel it'.

Q: But it is appearing real to the Reality?

K: No, it's appearing real to a phantom. Because even the phantom is a false appearance. So it needs first a false appearance of a phantom. And then the phantom is a care-taker and taking something as real or unreal. So the first root I-thought, the phantom-I, the awareness-I, already is false. And that appearance of light and sound you take as real. From there on this is a false I. And from there the falsity happens. Whatever you take as yourself is false. So if you take yourself as awareness: false. If you take yourself as consciousness: false. If you take yourself as the body: false. Whatever you take yourself as being, is false. Even you taking yourself as being is false. Whatever you claim to be is false. From the beginning. False, false, false. And that's the nature of neti-neti-neti. Whatever you can experience, even the experiencer, is false. Is not it.

Q: But who makes the experience?

K: There is no who.

Q: Then how do we get that spirit?

K: Yes, how can that what is energy experience itself? Maybe you can say that what is Para Brahman, not knowing himself, first knows himself as an experiencer. But that what he knows himself as first, as an experiencer, already is an experience, not what is the Para Brahman. You will never know if it is personal or impersonal. If there is one or not. But that what is Para Brahman doesn't have to know that, if there is one or not. Because there is a total absence of any presence of anyone who needs to know anything. So now it's too late. Because now there is someone who needs to know if there is one or not. And that's too late. For some people, for some teachers, there is one. And for some people, for some teachers, there is none. But both are concepts. The main thing is, your Nature never needs to know if there is one or not to be what it is. That what needs to know what it is, is already too late.

Q: What is the right time then?

K: There is no time at all. There cannot be any right or wrong time. Because time is the idea of separation. Time is the idea that there is a second edition of existence. But there is not. So that's a false evidence, that now you experience moment by moment, you think there is time. You experience yourself as an experiencer being different from what you experience. That's like an evidence. 'I am here and the experience is there'. But it's a false evidence. If that would be real, it should be always like that. So all the evidences are giving you a wrong picture. It's all wrong. All empty. So whoever claims to know what one is, for sure is wrong. Wherever you land, is wrong. Wrong, wrong, wrong. So landing is wrong, not landing is wrong. Whatever you do or don't do is wrong. But that's fun! Isn't it fun? If everything you do or don't do is wrong? And that what is right never needs to be right. And whatever needs something to do will always be wrong. The right is always right and that what is not right is always not right. And that what is right doesn't need to become right and that what is the unreal never becomes real. So to be right is very easy. But to become right, to make it right, is impossible. To know yourself as what you are, is absolute easy. Because just to be what you are, what you cannot not be, is absolutely easy. But to become it is impossible.

Q: But all of us want to become, become, become...

K: Yes, what an idea! And that no one can explain. All the big guys, Ramana, Nisargadatta, always said: How can that happen that the seeker is seeking that what is the seeker? Because without the seeker being there would not be a seeker, seeking the seeker. But how can that happen? It happens. Why not? Everyone asking 'Why? Why?'

Why not? So if you ask me, this is the way you realize yourself. In looking for yourself. Like you inquire into your nature. Moment by moment experiencing what you are. Realizing what you are. But the word realizing means 'real lies'. It's not truth. Whatever you experience is lies. Aspects of what you are, but not what you are. So the truth, if you call it truth, can never be experienced. And what kind of truth would it be you could experience, and you would be different from it? A relative one.

Q: Truth is a concept again?

K: Everything is a concept. But that there can be a concept, you have to be. So 'to be or not to be' is not the question. It's a concept. Ramakrishna's basic teaching, pointer, was, that you even can question to exist you have to exist first, prior to that questioner who is questioning if he is or is not. That what is the questioner has to be what the questioner is that there can even be a question or an answer or whatever you come up with. That there can even be a realization, a realizer realizing what can be realized, prior to that, in spite of that, is that what is Reality. The Reality of the realizer. So you can even deny to exist, but that you can deny to exist, you have to exist. So it's very easy. But impossible to get. So no way of owning it. That's the beauty of your nature, you cannot own yourself. That's the beauty, maybe you call yourself that what is Heart. But that what is called Heart can never be owned by anyone. And cannot be broken by anyone or anything. And that relative heart you have, will always be broken sooner or later. And so it is like a heart ache.

Q: But it breaks and again breaks and again breaks.

K: It breaks and breaks and breaks. And then it heals again and breaks again. It heals again and breaks again. It's like a bone. You can break a bone infinite times and it will heal again and then you break it again.

Q: Sometimes we feel maybe it's the last time...

K: Ha ha ha! And then you recover...

Q: Then you recover but then...

K: Then you break again. Then you have hope again, 'maybe the next one is better than the last one'. And the next one is even worse than the last one, always. Then it breaks again. And the love story doesn't end. Your heart is infinitely broken already, but it always heals again because you forget how it was the last time. And you hope the next time will be better. It's crazy. How stupid can one be? But as absolute Knowledge you are, as stupid you are in your realization. Absolute Nature, absolute in it's knowledge and absolute in it's stupidity. Always falling in love again with images, with false evidence. And you cannot avoid it. Again and again. Every morning you fall in love with this whatever it is, and then you start caring about it. Brushing your teeth and thinking it gets better.

Q: Unless this vehicle is there...

K: No, even as spirit you experience yourself. Even without this vehicle you experience yourself as space. You don't need the body as a little vehicle to experience yourself. You have even the big vehicle, the spirit, to experience yourself. And then even awareness. You experience yourself as awareness. And the awareness doesn't need any body.

Q: We will not know the spirit, we know this vehicle only.

K: If you want to talk about your awareness, where there is no two, because now you create someone you can talk with. Because you want to talk with yourself. Because having that experience and you cannot share it, means nothing. So if you want to share it you need to be a member of humanity, one talking to someone else. And then even when you get enlightened, you want to share it. It's amazing. I always say: Imagine you would be enlightened and no one cares. No one wants to know it. It becomes a joke! It is a joke. And if you can make someone laugh, it's the best you can do. 'Are you enlightened? Ha ha ha!' What a fun.

Q: So Karl, you are saying that in spirit also you realize yourself. There is a oneness feeling?

K: Spirit is part of realization. It's one room of your house. Awareness is a room. Spirit is a room. And this is like a crowded room. Overcrowded actually. And then you go to the absence, to the cellar, where there is no room. Then you don't experience any room. And then you go to the roof-top and then there is an open room. Then you have an open heart, an open house. And then downstairs there is a closed house. You have all the different parts of the house you can experience.

Q: But even existence as a spirit is discomfort?

K: No. But the opposite of discomfort cannot be the absolute Comfort which has no opposite. So even the comfort is a discomfort. Because when there is comfort there is discomfort. Both comes together. So even the comfort is discomfort because it creates discomfort, because there is one who discriminates between comfort and discomfort. So even the comfort of oneness, creating two-ness, is a discomfort. It's amazing. But I am happy to destroy it. This famous oneness: 'And I had this blissful experience, and that blissful experience'. How many blisters does one need?

Q: We were watching UG (Krishnamurti) this morning...

K: No!

Q: Yes, we did. It was good.

K: The barking dog.

Q: Absolutely. And he said, if I am not wrong, even neti-neti has a goal. So he barks about it. And he kept on and on about neti-neti. He said even there there is a goal. Just leave it.

K: So you have to make neti-neti about neti-neti. Because that's neti-neti. Because he didn't go far enough. I don't agree with him. The neti-neti is even the neti about the neti-neti. He liked to bark, that's all. He was so angry.

Q: Angry about?

K: He went to Ramana and asked Ramana 'can you give me what

I am? Because it seems you have something that no one else has'. And Ramana said 'yes, but can you take it?' That pissed him off. Because he thought he was the most ready guy on earth. He did everything. But then the little guy sitting in front of him: 'but can you take it'? That's the main question. You can never take it.

Q: Actually when I was watching him I felt there was a lot of similarity to you. You don't bark as much, but it is very similar.

K: I have to work on that. Woof woof woof. Yes, he was ok. I like his lies mostly. He said every morning the Prime Minister of India calls me and wants to ask what he should do. Of course he was lying, but everything you say is a lie. Why not tell that lie. Why not really lie?

Q: You have been saying that the moment you start speaking everything is a lie.

K: The Nature of every word is true. But not the word you understand. But the Essence of everything, whatever vibration is Energy, that what is. So they are real lies. So even the lies are real. To call that 'Lila', one wants to be detached from something. It's another goal. Then it's a personal advantage. 'I am detached now because I see everything as Lila'. No! You are that what is Reality and this is your realization. And there is no one who can escape it.

Q: So these are the real lies?

K: Yes, these are real lies, and you experience yourself in real lies. And the experiencer and what can be experienced are real lies in experiences. But not in their Nature. The Nature of the world is what you are, the Nature of the universe is what you are. You are the Nature itself. But there is no second nature. That's all. But that one who says 'this universe is all a lie', he wants to claim that he is real. Ha ha ha ha. So everyone who understands something wants to understand 'everything is false, but not me'. All a misunderstanding, from the beginning. Missed-understanding. Missed in action.

Q: You asked in the beginning if anybody lost something. I lost the clarity!

K: I am very happy for you!

Q: I thought you would.

K: Because who needs that anyway? 'I lost my clarity'! Ha ha ha ha.

Q: It was nice to have it for a while.

K: Where did you have it? Where did you keep it, that you could lose it?

Q: Every time I looked I understood something, and now I cannot find myself anymore.

K: You cannot find yourself?

Q: Or I can't find a resting place.

K: A resting place? Now you become like Jesus. He claimed even as a Son of God he cannot find any rest. Watch out, now when you go back to Israel, the nail and the hammer are waiting.

Q: Yes, my parents!

Q: Yesterday you were talking about the meditation, that 'am I, I am'. I didn't understand.

K: That would be self-inquiry. The answer to 'am I' is 'I am',

Q: 'Am I?' There is a question mark?

K: There is no question mark. You just pronounce 'Am I' and then out of 'am I' you don't know where it starts anymore, it just becomes 'I am'. So the question is the answer. But the question 'who am I?' - it's always like it becomes a special answer. But if the question becomes the answer, it becomes a stream of existence in the presence. So the 'am I' becomes the presence of 'I am'. And in that there is just what you are. If you want to do something, self-inquiry, that is the question which is the answer. So there is no questioner and no answerer in it. So in that question there is no questioner. In the answer there is no answerer. So the question is the answer. It becomes like a stream of presence. And that you have to do 24/7/365.

Q: Only 24/7/365? That's all?

K: If you do it uninterrupted, even silently, you don't even have to pronounce it. You just stay in the 'am I, I am, am I', it just becomes like a sound of Om, like a light and sound, permanent stream of existence. That is like when Ramana said that sound remained, the shruti in Indian music, this basic sound of a vibration of existence. And the rest of all the other sounds are just like notes on a screen of that. But the basic sound is uninterrupted. So all the other informations are varying, but this is uninterrupted that. And if you can just stay in that, I promise you after whatever time there will be no me anymore. Simply staying in that, being that, there is a total annihilation of any idea of any relative I. If you can do that. But you cannot do it. If it will happen it will happen by itself. Because your pressure will be so high or your so-called 'earnesty' – it's a false translation of Nisargadatta – it needs that unavoidable demand of existence which presses you into that sound, to give your attention only to that what is attention. A permanent stream of what you are. And that is like being depressed 10 meters under water, not getting any air anymore for the me. And then automatically by being what you are it becomes a total ease. But without that you will always try to get a personal comfort, more advantage. So all the other meditation, whatever you try otherwise, yoga and all of that, is all for a personal advantage. But this is like a total demand of existence itself which is pressing you into that concentration camp of that uninterrupted 'am I, I am'. It becomes like a holocaust for the I. You will be burned out by just that. But if that happens, it's in spite of what you have done or not done in your whole existence at all.

Q: So when you say it's an unavoidable demand of existence, is earnestness...

K: No, it's not earnestness. That's why it was a misunderstanding. It's not earnestness. Earnestness is bullshit. What was the translation of Nisargadatta?

Q: Unavoidable longing.

K: Yes, the unavoidable longing giving attention to that what is attention. Which is not an earnesty. Which is just giving attention to attention by just being what you are. And without that nothing will happen. And your personal earnesty, you can be earnest like hell, nothing will happen. You can call that is earnesty, but it doesn't need to be earnest.

Q: Even that what is coming out is the unavoidable pressure that is coming from existence.

K: You mean the absolute demand. It's not a pressure. It's an unavoidable demand of totality, by which this question even comes. And this answer. It's all part of realization and if realization becomes this unavoidable attention giving attention to attention by being attention, your natural state, then it will happen, in spite of all of that happened before. Never because.

Q: So you cannot not be who you are because that is that pressure which is...

K: But you can go astray with your senses and your attention. And by going astray with your attention, giving attention to a false evidence, you are missing yourself. It's like an accident.

Q: So missing yourself also is the unavoidable pressure...

K: Yes, but it still is misery. And I sit here and tell you the misery will never stop. But you cannot find anyone who is miserable in it. The misery is the experience of separation, and it will never stop. And you have to be what you are even in the presence of that misery of separate experiences. If you cannot be what you are in that, you will never become it in anything else. And that awareness, that this will always be there, this is like Yudhisthira being in hell, and there was an absolute absence of a tendency of avoidance. It cannot be done. It's just not there. And in the absolute absence of any tendency of avoidance, there is a total acceptance by nature. And then you are acceptance. But you don't even have to accept hell. There is just no tendency of avoidance, and then there may be hell or not hell, who cares? And that's your natural state. That's your very Nature, who is acceptance itself already. Always accepted everything. And that one who didn't, who cares?

Q: But all this, whatever we are talking about...

K: Whatever can be pronounced is false.

Q: No, but whatever we are talking about, this itself is a concept. And even if you experience it, is it possible for a person like you to make us see that?

K: What?

Q: 'I am, am I, I am, am I'.

K: No, I cannot make you do it. I cannot make you see it. I can ask you, as a pointer, try it. And if it is meant for you to happen, it will happen.

Q: Meant for me to happen, that doesn't mean that I am already programmed...

K: Then it is already in the program. But even that I give you the pointer, that I give you that hint, it's already in the program. And maybe by that hint you do it. So that I talk to you is a demand of Totality. And that maybe it fruits in you and you do something, is also a demand of Totality. And if it happens then, you cannot avoid it. So if by whatever I tell you now, you will sit down and this 'I am, am I' will just happen, it will happen. And if by that result this so-called relative me will burn out in that case, it will happen. But it's not because I talk to you. I already talk to you because everything that happened before made me now talk to you. So the total demand of all the moments before is creating this moment now, creating these words, and all that happens here. You call it concept. I just call it the uninterrupted infinite now which is an infinite realization of Reality. Maybe a concept too. But it sounds good. No, the main thing is, the only thing: you can even deny to exist, but that you can deny to exist you have to be. So you can not not be what you are. This is maybe a pointer to that what is not a concept. That there can be all these concepts and all these lies, you have to be what you are. But also to be what you are means you are in spite of these concepts. Because every night in every deep deep sleep you are in spite of all the presences of concepts and absences and whatever you can imagine. So your existence is not depending on any presence. And that is not a concept because everyone experiences it every night. But you are right, the rest is just fishing in the dark.

Q: But the rest is just this vehicle...

K: Yes, but in that rest you are experiencing the absence of the body. You cannot say that you don't experience something. The perception is still there. That what is what you are is not sleeping because the body is asleep. You just turn away from that body experience to that absence of this body. From the beingness to the non-beingness. From that manifestation to the non-manifestation. Every night in deep deep sleep you experience a non-manifestation. And then in that absence the body can rest. And in the morning you wake up and then the body has to work for you as a tool. And in the night the body is exhausted by your taking it as a tool, and then it goes to sleep. And you just experience the absence of it. But it doesn't mean that you sleep. Because your Nature never sleeps. And maybe it is never awake. It is experiencing awakeness, and it is experiencing non-awakeness. So awareness and unawareness. The underwear. Being aware and being underwear. So in that sense I am pointing to it that that what you are is never never. But you will never know what it is. But that is what you are. Because whatever you say about it, it's not it. Whatever you say about what you are has to be a concept.

Q: Is nature perfect?

K: Nature? Nature doesn't need to be perfect. And that what needs to be perfect cannot be perfect. That what is perfect doesn't need to be perfect. So it is imperfect as perfect as perfect. And that what needs to be perfect to be perfect is for sure artificial. It's like Knowledge. Knowledge never needs to know or not to know what it is to be Knowledge. And that knowledge which needs to know for sure is artificial knowledge. Or relative. So perfection that needs to be perfect is relative perfection. The absolute Perfection is - there is no need for any perfection to be what it is. But all ideas are that it has to be perfect. Everyone wants to be perfect.

Q: I just wanted to understand, what we call Nature, do we really require to take care of it?

K: It takes care anyway. But it doesn't know you. It takes care about everything. The absolute care-taker. But it doesn't even know to take care about anything by taking care, it's just taking care. So that what is realizing itself doesn't even know that it is realizing itself, it is that what is Realization. So it doesn't even know realization. But by being it, it takes absolute care. But it doesn't care about taking care or not.

Q: The whole change that is likely to happen in 2012...

K: Oh God oh God! It's a nice concept. Something will happen. I will celebrate for a long time because it will be one week after my 60th birthday. And something will happen, I am afraid, I left the fifties. Something always happens. But what they claim that there will be enough awakened ones on this earth and then there will be a transformation of consciousness into the next level. Oh my goodness! Imagine that there should be an evolution of consciousness. What kind of bullshit evolution would it be that needs to evolute?

Q: There will be more Indigo children and Indigo people...

K: 'Indi-go'. Go go go. What kind of idea becomes consciousness if you think consciousness needs to whatever. Imagine there would be personal consciousness. Imagine there is human consciousness. What kind of consciousness would that be? And then transforming or transmuting from personal consciousness to impersonal consciousness. Imagine every person becomes impersonal. The baker is not baking anymore. The waiter doesn't wait anymore. Everyone is awakened. I don't like it.

Q: There would be no drama then.

K: No, if everyone would really be awakened, it would mean there was unawakened ones before. Even the idea that there can be awakening is already hell. Even the possibility that people can wake up means there are people. And if there really would be people, that really would be hell. What a hell would it be, if there really would be unawakened people! And then these unawakened ones wake up. Help me God! Hallelujah and praise the Lord that this never will happen.

Q: You said you don't recommend to be born again, but my question is...

K: But I recommend it to you now that you are never born! Not even again. Be what you are which is never born now! Why wait until then?

Q: But my question was, if it is in your hand...

K: In what hand? Do you have hands if you dissolve? Can you handle it?

Q: Of course you have no hand, but how to say it? I don't know how to express it.

K: If you cannot even do something now, how can you do something then?

Q: But why did you say it?

K: What? I said you better be not born. And you are not born now. Why wait until that happens? Because then there will be nothing happening again. As now nothing happens. Because now no one is born. And then no one will be born. But now you believing in being born you committed suicide.

Now you are experiencing to be dead. Now you are longing to be alive again. And the easiest way is just being what you are, which is never born. So what are you waiting for?

Q: But do we have a free will, Sir? When you are programmed like that...

K: No, no one is programmed. Only consciousness is programmed, but not what you are. Your Nature is never programmed. Consciousness is a program. So forget consciousness and just be what you are. And don't excuse yourself as 'but I am programmed bla bla bla'. Consciousness always excuses itself, always justifying what it is not doing. That all happens in consciousness. But for what you are it makes no difference. You don't depend on what happens in consciousness.

Q: Whatever we are talking about now, it's the realm of mind...

K: No. I am not talking to bloody mind. I don't know any mind. There is no realm of anything. I am talking to what I am.

Q: Who is talking?

K: I. To I. 'Who is talking'!

Q: So when you are talking to what I am, it's not different to talking to...

K: I talk to my dog as I talk to you. I even talk to my shirt. 'How are we today?' 'Ok, one day more'.

Q: You, the observer, the observed...

K: It's all concepts. All there is, is Existence, or what you call Self. And Self talks and Self listens. There is no observer, observing, observed and all of that. It's all too late. It's intellectual sport. That's all. I sometimes do that too. But it's sport. If that's part of entertainment, why not? But thank God, no one needs it. But it's fun.

Q: It misleads you. The fun takes you away from the inquiry.

K: No, fun is inquiry. In fun you cannot be. Fun is the most dangerous for what you imagine to be. In fun you cannot be. There is no phantom in fun. In fun there is fun, and maybe tom, and maybe not. But fun for sure. So fun is there with and without tom.

Q: Fun is a serious matter.

K: I tell you: fun is more dangerous for your idea of what you are than anything else. You may laugh yourself to death. Easier than inquire yourself to death. That's why everyone likes comedians so much, because in the comedy you are not there. In the big jokes you are just laughing yourself away. So it's very dangerous. And if you really see the joke as the joke, understand the joke 'how could I ever look for what I am as I always was and am and will be what I am'. This joke is an uninterrupted joke. And then seeing oneself, looking for oneself, becomes a joke. The Almighty sitting somewhere and thinking 'I have to know myself to be myself' is a joke. So it's an uninterrupted comedy. You call it divine or not. It's a comedy.

Any other serious questions?

Q: So the moment you look inside...

K: Look inside?

Q: Yes, look inside.

K: You have an inside?

Q: That's what I was doing for many years. Looking inside. And there was something there.

K: No!

Q: I don't know now what it is.

K: What did you find there?

Q: I don't know, just nothingness. Like this thing where you don't name it..

K: You are like a black hole?

Q: Not a black hole. Because there was still somebody there who is saying there is nothing there.

K: So there was not nothing? There was something that you called nothing. Ah..

Q: But now why should I do it anymore? I agree with you, when you laugh about it, everything is ok. Nothing to do. But sometimes when attention goes inside now, I don't know what to do with it.

K: Why should you know what to do with it? Do you look at a piece of shit on the street and ask 'what should I do with it?'. And you look at a piece of shit inside and you ask yourself because you take it more personal. 'My bloody insight'. But it is like a piece of dog shit on the street. The dog looking at his own shit. Outside and inside shit. 'What to do with it?'

Q: It was a precious...

K: Precious shit. Precious is always under pressure. Because you have something you have to care of. So it becomes a treasure you have to care about. And then you fear to lose it again. And now you look at it and ask 'Why did I even look at it?' I always ask you, if you really want to treasure yourself, just be what you cannot not be. And that is treasuring what you are. And treasuring some whatever inside or outside bullshit experience is giving attention to shit.

Q: We are so used to doing something. Like watching it, letting it be...

K: 'Virgin Mary came to me, what she told me, let it be...'

Q: What's next?

K: What to do with all your time? Don't ask me! There is so much entertainment. Watch television. Or go to the cinema. Or look inside. But don't expect anything.

Q: It becomes second nature. Because you have done it for so many years, that searching.

K: But it doesn't make it more true.

Q: It's not about true. It's about what to do now!

K: You are so afraid that you get bored. You are so afraid of boredom. You fear boredom more than anything else. 'If I really wake up, what shall I do?' You are more afraid of waking up than anything else. 'What shall I do when I wake up? I cannot go to the cinema anymore, I can have no boyfriend, no television, I cannot read anymore, I cannot go to any guru. What shall I do with all my time? Nothing is important anymore. If I go here or there, both is not different. Maybe I have to sit down forever. Because doing is really wrong. But not doing is wrong too. It was so nice when I was still hoping that I get something out of something'.

Q: Yes, that is true!

K: 'I was flying around the world to meet a guy just for two hours. And now I can't even buy the ticket anymore because I have no money anymore after all that'.

Q: How to see boredom?

K: The moment you exist you are always bored anyway. Existence is boredom, moment for moment.

Q: Nature is not boredom.

K: Nature doesn't know Nature. In Nature there is no one who could be bored. But the moment there is one, one is bored. God knowing himself he becomes bored about himself. And by his own boredom, he creates all that. Look at it! All entertainment so that God it not bored. It's all about the boredom of God. And now he complains that it is not entertaining enough. 'Now I want to go home, I don't like the movie anymore'. Then he becomes a seeker. 'I am fed up now with my own movie. Now I meditate. Now I go inside. Because I am fed up with this movie, it doesn't entertain me anymore. I know everything. It's all pale. Now I go home. Now I become spiritual. Now I go to ashrams'.

In the beginning everything is like: 'Oh!' Like a kid: 'Wonderful!' And then there is a point where you get bored. And then you think there must be more to life than this. Then you may become spiritual.

Q: The ashram thing was wonderful. Everything. It was like a lovely circle. But later, all the curtains dropped.

K: After a while even that gets boring. And then comes the next one. Nothing holds. You can maybe go to bhajans and chant and sing holy songs for years. And there will be a moment where it drops. Where you think 'Not again. Shit. Another bhajan. Another holy song. I better go to Shakira'. Maybe there is more Shakti in Shakira than in Shiva-Shanti-tralala. Who knows?

Q: When I am in normal life...

K: What life?

Q: In daily life...

K: What daily life?

Q: Ok, when I am there...

K: When you are dead? What happens when you are dead? I would call it the daily death. So when I am in my daily death, coming out of bed, going to my daily death. Death happens.

Q: So in the middle of this...

K: In the middle of being dead. Sometimes I am feeling more or less dead.

Q: In the middle of this, everything is so impermanent.

K: That's called death.

Q: It is very intense.

K: It is very intense, impermanence.

Q: And I am also impermanent.

K: Imagine! Death is impermanent. So what do you want to say?

Q: I try to tell you something, but it's not easy...

K: No? When one is dead it's not easy.

Q: It is very paralyzing.

K: That's what I said, you get bored and then you are paralyzed. And you don't know what to do anymore.

Q: I get bored? You think it is out of boredom?

K: Death is boring.

Q: So what to do with it?

K: I don't know what to do with death. Just let be dead what can be dead. Death is dead. What you are never needs to be entertained. But if you want to be entertained by death, you are dead. Deadly death. How many times should I say that? You better enjoy to be that what never needs to enjoy anything. And that is your Nature. But the moment you are someone who needs to enjoy something in daily life, then daily life becomes a daily death. A zombie tries to entertain himself in a death experience. Dead, dead, dead. Go back to samadhi and then we talk again.

Q: Even after samadhi you are the same, so what is the use?

K: But if that is samadhi, if you don't know any samadhi which can give you a special experience, then that's called the natural state. And that's the Nature of samadhi. But that what knows samadhi is not samadhi.

Q: You know it by memory.

K: That samadhi you can know by memory is not samadhi. It's just a special death experience. Samadhi is a natural state of what you are, and Samadhi doesn't know any Nature of Samadhi. And that what one can call samadhi and knows as samadhi, is a fake one.

Q: Ok. So there I don't go.

K: Any other questions about samadhi or the daily death?

Q: Actually it is so much part of our daily talking, we say 'enjoy yourself'.

K: 'Be happy'. It's amazing, everyone who asks you to be happy makes you unhappy.

Q: That creates a lot of ideas that make you suffer.

K: You are right. The idea of happiness makes you unhappy, for sure. The idea of real makes you unreal. The idea of freedom makes you imprisoned by that idea. Everything you create as icons makes you a slave. And what kind of pressure is that that you have to be happy? And who bloody needs to be happy to be what one is? Who needs this bloody happiness anyway? And everyone is talking about it: 'Are you happy?'. And everyone wants to hear 'not really'. 'Me too'. It's always the question: 'How are you?' After a while you learn to say: 'Not really', then they are ok. If you say 'I am really happy' they try really hard to make you unhappy. Everyone around punches you and tries to prove that you cannot be happy. 'Around me you cannot be happy'.

Q: The phantom wanting to get out...

K: Out of the fun?

Q: Get out of the suffering. It has no power to get out. But it still tries to get out.

K: The 'fun-tom' became a 'sad-tom'. And as a 'sad-tom' he seeks a way out. First it starts like a 'fun-tom'. And then it's quite fun. But then it becomes sad because it becomes boring. And then it becomes a 'sad-tom'. And then he makes 'sad-ana'. Sadhana. Because he wants to go back to ananda.

Q: And then they are both sad. Tom and Ana.

K: Then they marry and then they will be unhappy forever. So I ask you to make happy-ana. I like happy-ana.

Q: You say there is no bridge between the phantom that cannot get out, and that what is the phantom but doesn't need to get out. Between these there is no bridge, is that right?

K: The phantom is in the permanent need to get out of something. But it's a phantom experience. So it's a phenomenal experience of one who does exist. And that is always under pressure or the longing to get out of that. Because any moment you exist you are relative existence and relative existence is always not good enough. So in that relative existence you always miss what you are. Any moment you exist, you miss that what is your nature.

Q: So is this like saying that is that what is anyway, that is that what cannot not be?

K: No, what you cannot not be is never missing itself. And that what you imagine to be will always miss itself. And there is no bridge. So the unreal will always miss the Real, and the Real cannot miss the Real because the Real doesn't even know the Real. So that what doesn't even know the Real will never miss the Real. And that what knows the real is already unreal, because only in the unreal there is one who has an idea of real. Only in the unreal there is a missing of the Real. Because the Real is always real never missing the Real because there is no idea of real or not real. And there is no bridge between that.

The unreal will always be unreal. And the Real will be Real. But the Real doesn't have to become Real, and the unreal always wants to become real. That's the nature of the unreal. Because to be unreal is unbearable. So consciousness tries to know consciousness because already consciousness is unreal. No way out.

It's very easy. That what is real is easy, because there is nothing more easy than to be what you are. But it's absolute impossible to become it. The moment you try to become it you are one who lost it. Because you just confirm that there is one who needs to be real. That one who needs to be real will never be real.

The doubtful existence will always out of the doubtful existence doubt itself and by doubting itself trying to get rid of the doubt. And trying to get rid of the doubt, trying to become real or knowing what it is. Because that what it would be would be not doubtful. But trying to become it will always be a doubtful attempt. It goes on and on and on. Never ending story.

It's like Shiva creates his own puppet house, and then playing with the puppets he becomes a puppet himself. And then trying not to be a puppet, he stays a puppet. And that's the nature of Shiva, becoming a Jiva. Playing around with himself. Creating images of himself, and after a while he believes in his own image. So he cannot even blame anyone else. He is stupid enough to play with himself. And then he becomes this real play. And then trying to get out of the play because he gets bored with the play, is impossible. Because he was never in the play.

This trap is so absolute. The trap is you falling in love with yourself. You are becoming a lover and you create your beloved. And then you play with your beloved, with your beloved me, with your beloved self. Then there is me, myself and I, and you play around with it. And after a while you forget it's only a play. That you created the play. That it is just an energetic dance with yourself. And then it becomes real. And then it becomes boring, because that is really a fake reality. Because you see it, it doesn't fulfill you. And then you want to get out of it, but the moment you want to get out of it, you confirm that there is someone in it. And then trying to get out of it, it never ends. Never ending story of consciousness trying to get rid of consciousness. Fantastic. The play tries to get rid of the play. Shiva tries to become Shiva. And that's impossible. The Self will never become the Self. In any relative experience. But it tries and tries and tries. So the inquiry will never stop. Because any moment you are not what you are, you are suffering about it. There is a me in a misery of missing what the me is. But the more the me wants to become that what is not the me it is confirming that there is a me who needs the me to go. It's such a perfect trap. Such an absolute perfect trap. And you cannot avoid stepping into that trap again and again. Because you are the trapper the trapping and the trapped. So you cannot avoid falling in love with yourself again, again and again. And in all that again and again there is nothing to gain, or to lose. And again and again and again, it doesn't make you more or less however it is. No more and no less you are That. And no way out. And you cannot escape what you are. And realizing yourself is falling in love with yourself again and again and again without any interruption. Every moment is another falling in love with the next. This love story with yourself is a never ending love story. Because in that love story you realize yourself. So you are fucked forever. That's called peace. And there is no hope in it that you ever can escape yourself. No way out. So peace off.

Q: We are living a life of concepts only.

K: You experience yourself in all possible concepts. But that what is experiencing itself in all the concepts can never be experienced. And you are right, you can only experience yourself in concepts. Because that what is experiencing itself in all possible concepts can never be experienced. But you cannot stop it.

Q: You cannot stop it, but that should not make you miserable.

K: How can you suffer about yourself? That's the question. Only the idea that there are others, that you and what you experience is different, that you are the lover who is different from the beloved, that's the suffering point. That's the misery. By being what you are, which is the sufferer, the suffering and what he can suffer about, the lover, the loving and the beloved, where is the suffering?

By just being what you cannot not be, that's the absolute end of any idea of two. And when there is no two, how can you suffer about yourself? Suffering is only there because you hope this whatever will end some day. That's suffering. That you can end yourself. By whatever you do. That you are finite. That you have a happy end. The special idea that there will be a happy end. Because of that you suffer. Even the idea of end is suffering. With the idea of beginning the sufferer begins. And the idea of end makes the beginning real. If there is the reality of a beginning, there is the reality of an end, and that's already suffering. So the idea of happy end confirms that there was a beginning. And where there is a beginning there is suffering. Fantastic. What a trap. This bloody enlightenment idea. Happy end. And that experience that you will be happy forever and ever. Ha ha ha ha.

It's unbelievable. The idea of happiness, especially of the happy end, creates all the unhappy beginnings. All that bloody suffering.

Whatever is bloody, whatever has blood in his whatever, is a bloody suffering. And for sure not life. Because life doesn't need any blood to be life. And that what needs blood to be alive is a bloody suffering. So now you got it. Your precious body. Eckhart Tolle calls it 'pain body'. You pay every day. It's a paying body.

Q: The pain body is a good chapter for the phantom. It does work. It's a nice chapter.

K: Yes, trying to escape the pain. Meditation is like a pain pill. You close your eyes and 'I am not here, I am not here'. 'I have no body, I have no body'. Or 'I go into the pain, I go into the pain'. 'There is no pain, there is no pain'. 'I don't pay attention, I don't pay attention'. 'No pain, no pain, no pain'. Everyone did it! I am talking with experts only. They are all experts here.

Q: Watching the pain.

K: Watching the pain. 'Let the pain go by'. 'Stay as a witness'. 'Be a screen and not the projections'. 'The screen cannot suffer about the projections'.' So be the witness and not what can be witnessed'. All these fantastic techniques and concepts. You tried them all. And look where you are! Listening to this guy! Ha ha ha ha. Look who I am talking to! All the experts!

Q: We are all in the club.

K: We are all meeting in the 'diffi-cult' club. It's very easy to join the 'diffi-cult' club. It's very easy to be difficult. The difficult is always there. You don't have to work for it. It's impossible to be easy. But it's difficult not to try.

Q: Now I don't believe in enlightenment anymore and I don't know what I should want? You just smashed it.

K: That's what you come here for, that you drop that bloody idea of enlightenment. Because who needs to be enlightened?

Q: But now I have nothing to do.

K: You see, now she has nothing to do. Now she complains! 'What shall I do now? Tell me'. Because enlightenment is always like a good entertainment show. You can sit down in Tiruvannamalai, have a Chai, and talk with your neighbor about enlightenment, about good gurus, bad gurus, and where you went to, and what is truth, and Ramana is like this, and Ramana said... . Only because you have this idea of enlightenment. And now you cannot even sit there you think? Maybe you can still sit there. Imagine!

Q: I have no interest.

K: But that's still too much interest, 'I have no interest'.

Q: You say there are some who meditate for years and look where it's got you, you are still here.

But people are listening to this for years, and they are still here. So what would be the difference?

K: It's not different. That's what I pointed to.

Q: So there is absolutely no difference?

K: Whatever you do or don't do, if you meditate or don't meditate, if you sit here for thousand years, it doesn't make any difference for what you are. You still have to sit here.

Q: So it makes no difference whether you sit here or at home?

K: No, you cannot. When you sit here you sit here. You cannot sit there.

Q: Or you sit there.

K: Then you go now. And try. Wherever you are you are. Then just be where you are.

Q: And there is no difference between the two?

K: There is a difference but it doesn't make one. So if you sit here or don't sit here, if you meditate or don't meditate, there is a difference. But it doesn't make a one. That's all. And if you have to sit here anyway, you better enjoy it, if it doesn't make any difference anyway. It's quite peaceful. You came here that maybe it makes a difference.

But then you sit here and maybe you see it doesn't make a difference. But even that doesn't make a difference. So what to do?

Q: All our scriptures say that all these words - one should go beyond the words. Words are only a tool to communicate.

K: You should be in spite of the words. As you already are in spite of the words. So you may enjoy the emptiness of the words because the words cannot give or take anything away from what you are. That's the entertainment or the joy of words. They are so empty because they cannot change you. They cannot give anything, they cannot take anything. They are just there for entertainment, or joy. Call it whatever. The emptiness of words, that they cannot do anything to you, that's the beauty of the words. And that's going beyond the words, because going beyond the words is not expecting anything out of the words. And that's why this is meditation of words, the talking itself is meditation. Because in this talking there is no expectation or any intention to get something out of it. So the whole presence of 'I am', I-amness, is all entertainment. There is no expectation and no intention that by whatever happens, whatever understanding or not understanding, you can get more or less as you are. And that is the nature of meditation. But any hours you sit down for special meditation, expecting to get something out of it, for sure that is not meditation. That is working. Working for an advantage. Trying to get a peaceful mind is working for a peaceful mind. And I don't call it meditation. It becomes a personal meditation with an intention. And then you are a hard-working me. And then you want to get something out of it.

Q: 'Medi-tension'!

K: Yes. Dr. med. Medicine.

Q: You said meditation is doing. It's not.

K: When there is someone expecting something out of meditation.

Q: Not expecting something out of it.

K: But I tell you, the one who sits down for two hours a day and trying to meditate, to calm down the mind, expects something from it.

Q: But that's wrong meditation then.

K: Whenever there is a meditator it's wrong.

Q: No, because then there is an ego...

K: No, there is no 'then'. Meditator means wrongness, false!

Q: So I am also false here.

K: If I would talk to someone sitting there and I would have an intention to teach you something, or that you learn something, that would be wrong. But I am just hammering you down with words and don't expect anything to happen.

Q: Lost.

K: You see. That's why I talk you to death. So I am not interested that you get something here. Or take something with you when you go.

Q: Because the getting would be at the level of the phantom.

K: What you can own is shit. You can only own shit. Understanding cannot be owned. Understanding is your Nature. Knowledge is your Nature. But it cannot be owned. So you cannot take it with you. You cannot have it. And you cannot repeat it. So I am talking to that one who is the owner, I may talk to death, and then understanding is by nature. But that is not an understanding you can claim, which is yours. It's just that what you are, which is Existence itself. So there is no need of taking it or owning it or keeping it. But the moment you go out you want to have it again. Because you try to remember 'what happened there?' And then you are back in that ownership thing. Unavoidable. So I try for whatever time to talk you to death. And then there is this famous absence. And then you go back, and then - back in business. Because the moment you want to tell somebody what happened here and you want to remember, then you are in trouble. Then you make it a concept. Then you make it a teaching. And then out of the living words become dead words.

Q: The one who is realizing 'I am a phantom' is ignorant?

K: If you realize yourself, if you experience yourself, you experience yourself in absolute ignorance. And if you don't experience yourself, you experience yourself in absolute Knowledge. Which is the absence of any presence of anyone who knows or doesn't know to exist or not to exist. But the moment you experience yourself as existence, you experience yourself in ignorance.

Q: But the one who thinks that 'I have understood the phantom'?

K: It's the Absolute becoming relative in a relative understanding. So you claiming to have understood you become a relative stupid. And being relative stupid that hurts, that's suffering. But being absolute stupid, who cares? Only being relative, relative knowledge or relative stupidity, relative ignorance, that hurts. Relative to someone else. But being absolute stupid, absolute ignorant, there is joy.

Q: Because there is no one?

K: There is no one who could suffer about anything. But in the relative there is always an owner who is different from something else. And that difference you suffer about, being relative to something else.

Q: You can't help being relative.

K: No, you cannot help experiencing yourself as being relative, but by experiencing yourself as being relative, you don't become relative. You are still absolute. But any moment you are relative and relative is your true reality, you become this little Jiva. And a Jiva is missing Shiva. And the me is a missing of what one is. It's 'me-sing'. The song of the me. The me singing: 'Poor me, poor me, poor me'. It's a me-sing. It's like when you are singing bhajans and chanting, the me is singing like as if you are walking though a dark forest. And then you are chanting and singing with people together because you fear to be alone. You sing together so you don't fear anymore. So you make yourself relative and small, because you have to overcome some fear by singing to God or praising the Lord or something. Makes you small.

Q: Is this Existence what they call God? What is God? The Existence itself?

K: God is an idea. The moment you pronounce God, God becomes an idea. The moment you pronounce Existence, Existence is an idea. The moment you pronounce Reality, Reality becomes an idea. Whatever you pronounce: Ideas. False. But try not to do it. Everything is wrong, pronouncing or not pronouncing. But that there can be pronouncing or not pronouncing, that what is unpronounceable, the absolute Pronouncer, which can never be pronounced as what it is, has to be there, has to be what you are. So pronouncing yourself is stupid. It is absolute stupid to talk about what you are or discuss what you are. It's really disgusting. But not to do it is as disgusting as discussing it. So pronouncing or not pronouncing, it doesn't make you more or less, that's all. Pronouncing is stupid. But you cannot help it. Not pronouncing would be better. But for whom? Only if it would make a difference. So why not pronounce what can be pronounced? Who cares? If anything cannot change anything anyway. What's the problem with the problems?

Q: Einstein's theory of relativity.

K: Einstein. He believed that God doesn't play with dices, that there was a plan. So he was thinking there is one who knows what he is doing. And that was really stupid. Imagine there would be a God who knows what he is doing! What stupid God would that be? If he would know what he is doing, and creating all that mess!

Q: God doesn't play random games.

K: For me it's all playing with dices. Let's see what comes out next. Like roulette. There is no intention in God. If there is a God. And there is no discrimination of good and bad. So how can he have a plan of something, or direction? There is no direction in God.

Or erection. That what can have an erection is already a relative lingam.

Q: Is there no intelligence?

K: Intelligence is already stupid. Intellect is stupid by nature. Intelligence! Even the word intelligence is stupid.

Q: I mean God is intelligent design.

K: No. How can he be intellect, look, creating this guy? Now you really have to doubt it. Every morning looking into the mirror you know God is stupid. How could he have created a guy like that? It's impossible. Not by intention. If he cannot help it, ok, excused. But if he would have an intellect, watch it.

Q: What is this 'me, myself and I'?

K: You are shifting always between these three levels. The whole day you are shifting between 'me, myself, and I'. When there is me there is like a disturbance. When there is myself there is just like space, spirit. And when there is I there is just the witness. Nothing happens. And you are shifting between these three reference points every, day more or less. And if you are more than 5% or 6% or 8% in the me, you already end up in the madhouse. The body cannot take it and you will collapse. You have to balance it in this psychological drama. So if you are not naturally shifting every day, going to the myself, to the I-amness, and then even most of the time to the I, just being there without even knowing to be there, you could not even take it. The body would just be totally sick. And if people are much more in this me and this disturbance, the body shows in diseases, naturally. Look at madhouses, there are all these crazy people who are just exploding 'me-s' for a while. They lost their me, they lost their personality. And then the doctors sitting there and trying to fix them again. Putting them back and talking and talking until the me is back. Fantastic. All the drugs.

Q: Then the doctor gets it.

K: The doctor gets the money, yes. The doctor needs a doctor himself, for sure. The doctor is part of the inmates. Absolutely.

Q: When something like what happened to Ramana happens in Western society ...

K: Something happened to Ramana?

Q: Yes.

K: Now you go too far.

Q: How can I say...

K: You mean a guy like Ramana, sitting 15 years in a cave, and the worms biting him, maybe they would just put him in a straightjacket and put him in the madhouse?

Q: Yes.

K: And in Tiruvannamalai they create an ashram around him.

Q: Yes. Like in Western society this cannot happen.

K: No, it can happen. Francis of Assisi was totally mad and then he became the holiest guy of Italy. It can happen in the West as well. But it's very thin the line between putting someone in the madhouse or making him a holy one. The books of the Vatican are full of people who went crazy for God. And got into that divine madness. It is a tradition of the Western world as in India. There is not much difference.

Q: But I think there is some difference between those who really went crazy and those who really understood.

K: Ramana went crazy. The crazy wisdom. That's knowledge. Knowledge is crazy wisdom, there is no structure in it.

Q: But there is a difference. I don't mean in him. Between Ramana and Francis of Assisi, and someone with psychotic experiences there is a difference.

K: Like you?

Q: No, not like me.

K: You talked about bliss events. That's all psychotic. All your samadhi experiences are psychotic. Even now sitting here is psychotic. Believing you have a body is psychotic. You are in a madhouse! Where else do you think you are? This is all psychotic. Believing to be born. What's more psychotic? That's a crazy idea that you believe that you are born! And that makes you part of this madhouse, an inmate of crazy ideas. So who do you talk to? Who do you think you are? You think you are sane?

Q: Yes. No.

K: You are in good company here.

Q: Really?

K: Insanity is your playground. It's all insane. Even waking up in the morning is insane. And having a body-experience is a psychotic experience. There has to be a psyche, a soul, an Atman, this basic soul, an experiencer experiencing himself as something, and already that is psychotic. When God knows himself he creates his own madhouse. The whole universe is a madhouse. The politicians are the worst cases. And the doctors are the most sick.

Q: Ramana was not psychotic.

K: Of course he was psychotic. He called it 'I experience a sickness'. This is a psychotic experience of having a body.

Q: But...

K: There is no but. Why do you repeat him not knowing what he said?

Q: I don't repeat him, I speak myself.

K: You don't speak yourself. You make bloody Ramana special, that's all. You make him a banana.

Q: Him?

K: Yes. You make Ramana a banana for a monkey mind who thinks that Ramana was better than someone else.

Q: I don't think that.

K: You just did it. You said in Ramana's case it was different.

Q: No. Because you are constantly cutting me off before I end the sentence.

K: Imagine I would not cut you off. We would sit here forever. From the first night on she was making speeches!

Q: What is in the West...

K: Why are you always making these differences between the West and the East and bla bla bla? Because you read it somewhere and now you repeat it. That's all.

Q: You think so?

K: Of course. Maybe I can even tell you what book and what page. Maybe I read it too. Everyone is reading it somewhere and then repeating it and someone writing it down again, the West is like this, and the East is like this, and bla bla bla. My goodness! And then: 'I better go to the East, because I don't feel like in the West...'Fantastic! Any other East and West question?

Q: You said thinking that you have a body is psychotic.

K: Yes.

Q: So you completely negate the body?

K: No. But I don't have a body.

Q: But if you got hit by a bus now...

K: I have an experience of a body. But it's not my body.

Q: Then who's is it?

K: I don't know. Consciousness or whatever. Why should I care who's body it is? It came to me and it will be gone one day. So what about this body? It doesn't belong to me.

Q: So you are not attaching yourself to the body, but you are not negating the body?

K: I am neither attaching or not attaching. It's just a fleeting experience. So it's not what I am. That's all. There is no ownership in it. It's like the sun is rising, the sun is setting, and I don't claim the sun is mine. It's not my sun.

Q: But you still take care of the body. You feed it...

K: I don't feed it. It takes care of itself. I want to stay in bed, and the body wants to go to the toilet, and he is always winning. It's not me. I want to stay in bed. So who rules? And who takes care? The body takes care. So let the body take care. He knows best what to do about this body. Why should I care about it?

Q: Suppose I have a heart problem, I need to walk.

K: You have a heart problem?

Q: No, not me. Suppose someone else had to walk for health reasons?

K: Why should I care about someone else?

Q: I am not saying you should care. I am asking a question.

K: You don't ask a question. You want to make a care-taker out of me. That I care if someone cares or doesn't care. Should I care if you care or don't care?

Q: No, because you say the body...

K: I just said it's a fleeting experience. It came, it will be gone one day. But it doesn't make you more or less. So while it's there it's there. Or not. No one cares.

Q: But you are not negating it?

K: No, for sure not. When it's there it's there. But it doesn't make me more or less. When it's there, ok, when it's not there, it's ok too. Why should I negate what's not there? First I have to find a body to say it's not there. And when I find a body it's already too late. And I don't negotiate with my body. Because I know the body wins.

Q: So you can't take care of the body?

K: The body takes care of itself. There is much more knowledge in the body than I could ever have.

If you just don't interfere, everything is fine. The moment you interfere, you are sick. Because then you always find something that is wrong. Because your ears are too long or your nose is too wide or this is too short – the moment you look at it you find something wrong. Then you need make-up, you have to shave, then you really have to work. But you can't help it. The moment you look in the mirror you do something. Naturally. Make faces. You play with it. It's like a puppet you play with for a while. And the puppet will be gone one day. So enjoy the play but don't expect that the absence of the body makes you absent. You are in the presence and you are in the absence of that body. You are in the presence and in the absence of the universe. So why do you care how this is? You play with it for a while and then the play is over and then the play continues in another way. So it's not so important the whole thing. That's why when Ramana had cancer: Ok. The body has cancer, so what? Do something or not. So he let the doctors do what they do or not do. But if that happens or not, if you care or don't care, you cannot decide.

Q: What happens when the body is gone?

K: As I said. First you have to find a body that the body can be gone. If you ask a physicist they say where is the body? It's just a cluster of energy showing itself as a body. But you cannot find a body. You just find an information system of energy that you call body. But how can that go? Did it ever come? Energy taking an information, and then the information becomes something else. But energy is not coming and not going. So what is coming, what is going? Energy always taking a different form. But that what is form is always fleeting. But that what is taking the form, showing itself, will never be known and will never show itself as what it is. It always shows itself in something else. But it will never show itself as what it is. So it will always be different, but does it make a difference? No. Body or no body. Anybody. Ok my dear bodies.

It's All Self-Love

Q: It was once said by you that the Self is the abyss. That the me fears the abyss. Could you say something more about that?

K: The abyss is just the absence. That you cannot find any hold anymore. You have no ground. This groundlessness you call abyss. And without ground the me cannot exist. So in this groundlessness there is no ground for any existence. That's the abyss.

Q: So the me is fearing the abyss?

K: The me knows without a ground it cannot exist. So it always makes a reference point, a ground, a base. Otherwise it cannot find its place. It always has to land somewhere. Landing somewhere is looking for a ground. Being grounded. Rooted somewhere. That's why being rooted, you are rooted in that idea of awareness. This root thought 'I', you are grounded in awareness. And without awareness, that would be too much. That's why many teachers land in awareness. Because it is still quite safe. But the abyss is like the absolute absence of any presence of any idea.

Q: So in the awareness there is still the me?

K: Yes, because for any experience, even the experience of awareness, it needs an experiencer. So there is a difference between you and awareness. Even if you claim to be awareness, there is one who claims to be awareness and makes himself different from something else. So having awareness or claiming to be awareness is not different, because it needs one who claims to have or to be that what is awareness. And it's always one too many. So whoever claims 'I am choiceless awareness' – ha ha ha! Even calling it 'choiceless awareness', one tries to make it better than something else. That is why the abyss is so feared.

Q: Many teachers use this analogy of the mirror and what is reflected in the mirror to represent Reality.

K: It's just another bullshit of awareness. Whatever you say, whatever you claim to be, is bullshit. Being the mirror, or being the diamond, whatever you come up with, is esoteric bullshit. And every teacher needs a technique and needs some bullshit teaching, otherwise there would not be any teacher. So being a teacher he needs to try to find something that some people listen to. And then he makes it very clever. So you are like in front of a fairy tale. And you believe whatever. 'Yes, me too. I want to be the mirror too. I want to be the canvas where all the projections are dancing on, and I am unaffected. I am totally detached from everything'. How often did we hear that? And how many books are written where this is claimed? I was even amazed that in the first book of Nisargadatta he was using this allegory. But later on he said who needs this? No one needs it. Even that is too much.

Q: Ramana used it also, the screen.

K: Yes, and then everyone repeats it. What he was using is like if you are just that screen, that canvas, and that is an impersonal one, then by that nature, that there is no one who fears the abyss, by that the abyss takes you just as it is. So it is like a trick for them. But I don't believe in tricks. I don't see anyone who needs to be tricked. That's my problem. So in that sense I even have to say Ramana still thought there had to be something that needs to be burned out. Annihilation of the me. What? What me? And what has to be annihilated. By what? And stirring with his stick of awareness into the fire until the stick is gone. Sounds good. You can sell it. You can write books about it. And everyone: 'I have to now inquire about it. I have to stir my stick into the fire'. Sounds good. So maybe it works, maybe not.

Q: This is another trick.

K: Everything is a trick! But in spite of all the tricks or not tricks you are what you are. And if this will drop that idea of what it is, it will drop it in spite of all that tricky tracky trucks. I don't have tricks or no tricks. Opening your mouth is a trick. But you expect - what?

Q: What about the analogy of the ocean and the waves?

K: That's the biggest bullshit! That's Osho. That's the ocean show on the shore. No, all that is futile. It's just like lullabies for one who needs to go to sleep. It's all like a lullaby: 'Sleep, my baby, sleep. It's not so bad. You just do self-inquiry and you will be happy.'

Q: What about self-improvement techniques?

K: Then something like you comes out of it! Everyone who is doing it or who has done it should look into the mirror.

Q: You make a distinction between awareness, attention and perception. And you seem to favor perception and attention over awareness.

K: No, I don't prefer anything. What I said is that perception is even without perceiving. But show me awareness which is without being aware.

Q: I don't understand. Perception is without perceiving?

K: That's why they call him 'the absolute Seer'. Para Brahman, the absolute Seer, which cannot be seen. But there is Perception. His Nature you can call Perception. Perception doesn't need to perceive something to be what it is. But awareness has to be aware to be.

Q: Isn't it just...

K: No, it is not semantics.

Q: ...words? I just see you favor perception.

K: No, it's not my favoring it, it's just the Upanishads, the whole tradition, whatever - the Seer is what you are. The absolute Seer which can never be seen by himself. Even Ramana calls it the absolute Seer. And whatever the Seer is seeing, the first he is seeing is seeing himself as awareness, becoming aware. The first experience is awareness. So prior to awareness is that what is. Whatever you call it. Para Brahman, Seer, some call it Perception. Perception with and without perceiving anything. Perception experiencing presence, perception experiencing absence. But Perception is uninterrupted. You will never know if there is a perceiver or not. Some call it the absolute Perceiver, the absolute Perception or whatever. But the main thing is, it's absolute. Because it is in the presence and in the absence of whatever you can imagine what it is.

Q: I suppose because awareness, there has to be an awareness 'of'.

K: No, it doesn't need awareness of, but it has to be. Awareness has to be to be. There has to be an experience of existence as awareness. But that what is whatever you call, doesn't have to exist to exist. It is in existence and in non-existence what it is. But everything else is fiction.

Q: I was reading Ramana's 'Forty Verses' the other day, and I think in number 7 it says 'Awareness and the world rise together'.

K: When that what is the nature becomes aware, with that awareness everything is already there.

Q: The commentary on it though completely messed it up. The commentary said it is the awareness that is the permanent...

K: The commentary is like a soccer game. What happens on the soccer field is one thing, but what the commentary makes out of is a totally different game. No, don't read commentaries.

It's always a pity that he never spoke English. So it is already translated into English. With Nisargadatta it's from Marathi. Then it always becomes a mess. But why not? It's messy anyway.

The main pointer is, to know yourself as you know yourself in the absolute absence, which means in deep deep sleep. In the absolute absence of any presence of anyone who is or is not, you are. And to know yourself as that, which is absolute in spite of whatever you can imagine, you cannot not be. Because you are even in the absolute absence of any presence what you are. And by being what you are there was never any problem and there will never be any problem in anything. That's all. The rest is semantics, or bla bla bla. This pointer always points to that what is your nature, which is independent of any presence or absence at all. So it is pointing to the Absolute you are. And the rest cannot make you that. Nothing can make you that. That's the main thing. None of this understanding, even to understand that, is not making it. You are already that. So nothing happens by that. You don't attain what you are by that. But understanding it is maybe not so bad.

Q: Yes, but when I see understanding or even the word knowing, it's...

K: Knowing not. Knowing is bad. Understanding is something else. Understanding is without anyone who understands. Because that what you are is in spite of one who understands or doesn't understand. It is already prior to that one who understands or doesn't understand. So in that understanding naturally, that understanding sinks automatically into that what never needs to understand. So it's like another trick. But it may or may not work. Nothing works. That's why you are the laziest bastard you cannot not be. Because you never worked anyway. And that what works will never work it out.

Q: So in spite of what you are...

K: No. You are in spite of what you think you are.

Q: So in spite of all that, this improvement stuff happens.

K: No, not in spite of that. That what needs to improve itself, what has to prove itself, is a phantom. And a phantom always needs to prove itself, its doubtful existence. And it always wants to improve in that proof. To make it more solid and grounded.

Q: To have an advantage.

K: Not an advantage. Just fear of the abyss. The fear of 'maybe I am, maybe I am not'. This doubtful existence that always needs to improve or prove itself. That's the nature of consciousness. Already consciousness is a phantom and always needs to prove itself, permanently.

Q: And so the body-work and this work and that work will continue. And it won't make a difference either.

K: It always makes a difference. But to whom? There is always a difference. Even if you go through all these states and ways of realizing yourself, it will always be different. But it doesn't make any difference.

Q: So it makes a difference to the me?

K: No, it is always a difference of experience. But by differences of experiences, you don't become different. So perception doesn't become different by the way it is experiencing itself. Or perceiving. Because before the perceiver is perceived, perception is there. But you always claim that the perceiver has to be there that perceiving can happen. No, perception is already there before the perceiver is even perceived. So already the perceiver is part of what is perceived. This little shift, that you are not the perceiver who is perceiving, you are already that what is perception perceiving the perceiver. And the perceiver, which is already perceived, whatever happens to him or not, which is always different, makes any difference to what you are. Nothing else.

Q: So you don't need a perceiver to perceive?

K; No. Because even in the absence of a perceiver, you perceive the absence of a perceiver. And in the absence of a perceiver is that what you call abyss. Absolute absence of any manifestation of any experience. The darkness itself. Like deep deep sleep. There is perception without perceiving anything. But still it's not asleep or awake. You cannot make perception awake or asleep. It never sleeps, it's never awake. It's always that what is. It's Nature itself. And Nature, Reality, starting to realize itself, it becomes a realizer, which is a perceiver. But the realizer is already part of realization, not real.

Q: So is it a thought?

K: It's not a thought. It's just you experiencing yourself as an experiencer. But that what is experiencing itself as an experiencer, is with and without that experience what it is. It doesn't need to be an experiencer to be what it is. That's all. To make it an idea or anything, you already make yourself one who thinks. That doesn't work. You are that what is experiencing itself first as a creator, or realizer, but prior and in spite of this first experience, you are what you are. In spite of it. With and without. Never because. The first experiencer is because you are. But you are not because of him, because of that experience.

Q: It is experiencing itself as the perceiver?

K: You cannot call it 'experiencing itself'. Just be that, don't call it anything. Before the slightest whatever you can perceive, which is the perceiver, you have to be as you are already what you are. But whatever you call it is wrong. Whatever you call it. Even to call it Para Brahman makes him an object. Whatever you say. Just be that what is in spite. But you will never know what that is. And if you name it and frame it you already put it into this dream. Then it's too late. That's why they call it 'be quiet and see'. But don't be something what can be seen. Because that what can be seen - the seer can be seen, the seeing can be seen, that whole scenery - is your manifestation. But you are with and without manifesting yourself what you are. Don't even try to imagine what it is. You can, because it doesn't matter anyway. You do anyway. You are anyway what you are. So imagine or not. Who cares? The thing is: if you imagine it, then you imagine it to be different to something. And then you are already in that dream of differences. But why not? Even to make that dangerous – for who? So for me it's always like you can or you cannot or you do or you don't, who cares? It will happen anyway if it has to happen. And you can not not imagine, because by imagining yourself you realize yourself. So what can you do? And then you even imagine to be that what is imagining itself. No way out. But for all of that you have to be what you are.

Q: For me it has been: just go back until the limit, which is supposed to be awareness for me. You go back and you find awareness, and you cannot...

K: Yes, in the presence you can only go to that.

Q: And then what? From there...

K: Then you even imagine yourself beyond that.

Q: Yes, imagine. That's the word.

K: Yes, of course. In that dream you can imagine anything. You can even imagine to be beyond. Imagine! Imagine you are John Lennon. Ken Wilber now has seventeen levels he goes back to. Seventeen! Next year there will be eighteen. And he is always one further than he writes about. Because you have to be beyond these seventeen to write about seventeen. So next year he will enter the twentieth maybe. He is the best. Imagining levels.

Q: So even peace is a part of the dream?

K: Yes. Even peace is part of the dream. Even calling it peace you make it an object. It doesn't need peace. Shanti! Who needs shanti?

Q: So what is this peace that everybody is seeking?

K: It's a peace of mind. 'Peace off' mind. That's what everyone is looking for.

Q: So the end of the thinking mind?

K: It's the end of me. Everyone is looking for the end of me. Because the me is imagining that the me is better off without the me. That's why it's called peace. 'If I would not be me, there would be peace'.

Q: Is that true?

K: Yes, every night you enter that peace. And the me knows 'without me I am better off'. And every morning the me comes back.

Q: The me can never go?

K: No. The moment you become aware the me is there. But the me knows 'without me I am better off'. Because where there is a me there is a discomfort. So you are looking for comfort. And every morning you wake up and there is that what you are, you know there was a place where there is no complaining. 'I cannot even know what it was, deep deep sleep, whatever you call it, but I cannot complain about it, so it must be quite good. I don't even know what it was'. So there is an absence of the me which is not so bad. So you know that. And from that moment on the me is there, you want to get rid of that me. Because there is one too many. Naturally. Because you know, by intuition, by whatever, that in the absence of the me you are better off. And then you want to be enlightened because the me would be gone.

Q: So does the me go when you are awake?

K: The me? Where can the me go? You have to make it an a-me-go?

Q: So is there no peace at all?

K: There is no peace. What kind of peace is that which needs the absence of a me?

Q: It's two.

K: It's a relative peace which can be entered. You really have to work your ass off to get rid of the me, and then you can rest in that absence of a me. But that what can rest in the absence of a me will always come back again. So what is this absence of the me? What kind of peace is that, that needs the absence of a me to be peace?

A depending one. A relative one. So are you really looking for that which is still depending? Needing some absence? Or needing the presence of being aware? That one who needs to be more aware and needs to be in the choiceless awareness? All of that is trying to land somewhere where you can be better off. So you are better 'off'. When you are 'on' you know it's bad. So you are better 'off'.

The nature of the me is like 'the other side of the shore is always greener than here'. Wherever you are is bad. Where you are is bad. So wherever you look you are not, you imagine that you are not there, on the other side. 'Beyond I cannot be, so when I go beyond, I leave the me here. So when I go there, I will get rid of me'. For that you make the journey, all the time. The whole thing keeps you going because you imagine 'when I reach that point I will get rid of my so-called me'. But the moment you get there, you will see the me is already there. 'Hello!'.

Q: So the Absolute is in spite of the me?

K: The Absolute doesn't even know any Absolute. How can it know any me if it doesn't even know itself? That's the beauty of the Absolute, it doesn't even know itself. The Absolute doesn't need to know if it is absolute or not. And that what needs to know if it is absolute or not, what is that? It can only be a relative me and a relative absolute. So you make it an idea. Me me.

I always come back to this absolute absence. As you are that. This presence doesn't make you more or less, as the absence will always be there. So your nature is uninterruptedly what it is. And nothing else counts. You are that what counts. But you are not something that can be counted. That's the beauty. You count everything, you experience everything. But you cannot experience That. This counter was always there. But you never count the counter. You only count what you can count. And the first you can count is the counter. But the counter is already something you can count. That's the tenth man. You count everything else but you never count that what is counting. Because without that what you are, there cannot even be awareness you can experience. Whatever you can name and frame cannot be there without your being That. But That you never count. And I can just point to That. You never lost yourself. How can you find yourself? How can you go home when you never went out? I can only make these pointers. But look, it never works!

Q: What is this allegory of the spider you were mentioning?

K: That was actually Ramana's allegory. Consciousness is like a spider. It's realizing once in a while that it cannot catch itself in its own net, and then it is withdrawing the whole spider web. The web is only there because it wants to catch itself. But then once in a while it is realizing it cannot catch itself in its own web, because it will always be uncatchable by its own intellect. So the intellect cannot catch the intellect because the web is made by itself. And then by that understanding it is withdrawing the whole web. But the moment it has withdrawn everything, it forgets that it cannot. Because there is no memory in that what is the spider, there is only memory when there is a web. Without the web there is no memory. So by having no memory, it forgot that it cannot realize itself in its own web, so the moment it wakes up again it starts to make its web again. Stupid!

Q: Passing time.

K: Not passing time. Just trying to catch itself. Because the moment there is a spider it's one spider too many. No way out. But once in a while the spider comes out of individual consciousness and then it becomes cosmic consciousness. But the comic in this cosmic consciousness is that as cosmic consciousness it cannot remember that it shouldn't start again. So what is it doing? Bloody starting again trying to catch itself. It cannot even remember that it doesn't work. Because there is no one to remember and there is no time in that cosmic consciousness. So cosmic consciousness again becomes comic consciousness. It's a comic strip of consciousness. It already forgot that it cannot catch itself. So it starts from the beginning, from scratch, to make a web to catch itself. Until in one instant it sees it cannot be caught by its own web, then it withdraws everything. But the instant it withdraws everything by just understanding or seeing it cannot be caught or realized, because it already is that what is realizing itself - no memory - so the moment it is aware again it falls in love again and trying to know itself and creating the whole web again. Like now the whole internet, all the websites, all that is part of the spider web consciousness. And now consciousness wants to be interacting with everybody, wants to know everyone. Facebook. All consciousness. Consciousness wants to know every face. Makes now a facebook. Or Twitter. Twitter, twitter, twitter, twitter. Wants to know every moment what everyone is doing. It's so curious, so greedy for information. That's consciousness, greedy consciousness, greedy for itself. Look, what it is all doing! All these information systems, television - information, information - like a hungry wolf. Vampire. Like a dog biting its own tail and now sucking its own blood. That's consciousness. Always news news news. How many died in that? Only two? No, it's not enough for news. Has to be hundreds! Always more, more, more. Tsunami, 200,000. Ok, that we can talk about a bit longer. When it is a German consciousness it says: 'Is there any German dead? No? Ok, we don't want to know it'. 50,000 Africans or Indians, but only one Westerner. Oh, one Westerner died! And they make it a very big thing. Otherwise it doesn't even enter the news. Very selective.

Q: Indians don't count.

K: Try to count Indians! It's quite too much. 1.2 billion now. You never reach the end. Because there are more born every moment than you can count.

Q: UG, when you said that he influenced you...

K: What did you say? Total bullshit! I never said I was influenced by bloody UG. Now you go too far. A new rumor is born. Never ever. When you asked 'did you ever meet anyone who was ok?', I said when I met UG he was ok. If I would have met Nisargadatta I would have said ok, Ramesh was ok, UG was even ok ok. But I never said I was influenced by that guy.

Q: Ok, wrong. I thought 'ok ok' meant there was an impact.

K: No, no impact at all. That's really the absolute impact, when there is no impact from that one, because there is no one who has any impact. That's that what is. Because if there is one who wants to make an impact and has an impact on you, that's for sure not ok! Bloody influence! It's like an influenza! You make me sick. I say a lot of things, but that not. I would really know that.

Q: Except grand-ma, nobody else has influenced him.

K: There comes the truth! Only my grand-ma is my master. There was no other influence. And she was 130 kg. And that was quite an influence.

Q: This me who is trying to get something out of it...

K: No, it's consciousness who tries to get the best out of itself.

Q: And it's not possible? I mean, it doesn't take you anywhere?

K: It cannot own itself, that's the main thing. But it's imagining that it can own itself. So whatever it is trying to do, it tries to own itself, to know itself. But it will never know itself. But it tries. So it will always inquire into that what it is, but it will never know it. But it tries.

Q: Because it's a phantom?

K: No, because it's in love with itself. This bloody love, that makes you so stupid. Only love makes you so crazy that you are after yourself. What else can make you so crazy and stupid? Only love! Tell me anything else that can make you so stupid to try to become what you are? Tell me? This bloody love is the only magic that can make you so stupid that you really believe that you can know yourself. Fantastic! You are crazy for yourself by love. So only love can make you so stupid that you suffer about yourself. You suffer about being in love with yourself. That's your suffering. That's the whole reason you suffer about yourself, because you are in love with yourself. And because you love yourself and you don't know yourself you suffer about not knowing yourself. This bloody love is like a high icon, that's really the reason of suffering. This bleeding heart for yourself. Bloody love. Valentine's Days and all of that. And then people tell you you have to love yourself, so what is all that? It's all the devil's work or what? Selling you what he doesn't have? Bloody love? How can you not love yourself? Try! So whatever you do is out of love. Love is running the whole show. You sit here for love.

Q: We sit here out of love?

K: Yes. Absolutely.

Q: Love for yourself.

K: Yes. The lover is in love with himself. It's all self-love. Self being in love with itself and trying to get to know it, to control it. You are here to control yourself. Because you want your beloved to do what you want.

Q: Fuck!

K: Yes. You want to fuck yourself to know yourself.

Q: So when you say that all our interactions are testimonies of love, you mean self-love?

K: Yes, all is there because the self always falls in love again with itself, at first sight. And the first sight is awareness. It becomes aware and it's already in love with itself. Instant love. It's realizing itself out of loving itself.

Q: But when you say all our interactions are testimonies of love.

K: Testimonies? The results of it.

Q: I read in your book...

K: In my book? Forget my book! This book is translated by a German guy from German into English. And then from that translation there was an English man from London translating it into English English. And then from that English English there was an American guy translating it into American English. And every time there was a little difference. And then they wanted me to read it if I like it. And I read just one sentence, and I said it's all fine, but leave me alone. I didn't even read the German one, why should I read the English one? So you can tell me everything that's in the book, because I don't know.

Q: So instead of testimonies, what is your word actually? If the books says that all our interactions are testimonies of love.

K: Testimonies I never used. Not that I can remember.

Q: So what is your word?

K: All this manifestation is by God falling in love with himself and having started to realize himself. This is a realization of what? Of God falling in love with his own image. With an image of himself. That's the result of it. The result of God falling in love with his own image, which is awareness.

Ask yourself: What is the basis of your interest? Where does it come from? Whatever you do is because you are in love with yourself. Even trying not to love yourself, you try to do it out of love. Because you imagine 'maybe without loving myself I would be better off'. That is actually getting rid of the me. The me is like you are in love with yourself and that love controls you. And then you started to hate to love yourself. So that hating to love yourself became a me. An enemy. So this love affair became an enemy. And now you want to get rid of that love affair but as much as you want to get rid of it you confirm that it has to be there. So out of love it turns into hate. Because both is already there. Loving and hating comes together. But what to do? How to get rid of what you are? Because this is what you are. This is your affair with yourself. Realizing yourself in a love affair with yourself. Moment for moment. And the intention is always love. It hurts. And that's the nature of love. Love hurts. Having a relationship with yourself hurts. Because it's too late. It's a re-late-tion-ship. And then you are the captain of that sinking ship. Then you are already in a Titanic. That's why it became so famous. And enlightenment is like the Titanic hitting the iceberg and then the ship sinks. And then the romantic story comes out of it. 'A ship got enlightened. By sinking into the abyss of the deepest ocean it became one with the ocean. So it rusts in peace'.

Q: You said there are not two, right?

K: There are, but there are not. To say there are not two is not enough. You have to say there are, but there are not.

Q: Is it just information?

K: No, there is God realizing himself, there is the lover and the beloved. There is one image of the lover, and one image of the beloved. So there are two Gods. So there are two, but there are not.

Q: Because it's an image?

K: I don't say that. Because if you say 'that's an image', that makes you what is not an image. Then you are different from the image. So then there are two, the image and you. No, that doesn't work. When there is two there are two. When there is none there is none. But you are neither two nor none. So yes and no. You cannot say there are not two. Sounds good. Advaita is not something that says there is not two. What is the true translation of Advaita? Who knows it? That what is never never, that I would call Advaita. But you will never know if it is two or not two or anything. Whatever you call it, it's just another idea.

Q: Perception doesn't care.

K: That what doesn't know itself doesn't care what it is and what it is not. And that what knows itself is too late. That what knows itself tries to make it a concept. It just becomes another concept. And that what never knows itself cannot create any concept out of that what is not there.

Q: So who are you?

K: I am the absolute absence of any presence of any idea of what I am and what I am not.

Q: Every moment?

K: There is no moment in it. There are only moments if I would know what I am. How can there be moments in that? If you ask me, for what I am there is the absolute absence of any presence of anyone who knows or doesn't know what one is or is not. Even the absence of the absence of any presence absence presence presence absence presence presence absence absence, of that what is presence absence absence absence presence absence absence. No idea. Everyone gets already lost after the first 'presence absence'. How to make one gaga.

Q: Lady Gaga.

K: Mr and Mrs Gaga. That's why when I am in Tiru I always say Arunachala-bala-bala. Whatever the pointer of Arunachala is, there is the mountain who doesn't know to be a mountain or not a mountain. Ask Arunachala: what are you? You can also ask your little finger: who are you? There is no answer. Your finger doesn't need to know what is a finger. It has no idea about a finger. Maharaj would always say 'Bombay doesn't know Bombay. But it is still Bombay'. And that one who knows Bombay is a fiction.

Q: You say the finger doesn't know it is a finger. But if you hurt it it does have sensations.

K: It will never react. You react to it. The finger is not reacting. Ask: Did you react? Did it hurt?

Q: But if you prick it...

K: If you get anesthesia there is no reaction of the finger. They can do with the finger whatever they do. The finger would not react. So who is reacting? If perception is disconnected, there is no reaction. You can cut it, you can make mince meat out of it, and it still would not care. Only that owner reacts. This little I. This awareness-I.

Q: Even a small insect reacts.

K: But if you give an insect anesthesia, the insect doesn't react. Matter doesn't react. If you disconnect the spirit from it, there is no reaction of any gross body or matter or anything. That's why when the spirit is out you call the body dead. Because there is no reaction anymore. But this body is still there. Ask a corpse: are you dead? No answer. So what is reacting? Space? Space reacting to space?

Q: So it's spirit that is reacting.

K: Try to show me what is reacting! Show me what is in control! Show me that what is acting and show me that what is reacting!

Q: So this is kind of automatic, consciousness?

K: Automatic? No. I don't know what it is.

Q: There are always two in consciousness.

K: You can call it this energy cluster of what you call me is reacting. What the past created as a cluster of energetic intentions, what is me, reacting to an outside event. Consciousness already is a reaction of that what is, not knowing itself. Consciousness already is a reaction. And in that reaction, reaction happens. As a dream of reaction. All of that is reaction. You cannot find any action in anything. You cannot find energy. You can only experience effects. Reaction. But you cannot find energy. So what is it? What does react? You cannot know what is acting or reacting. You can only experience the effects of it. And effects are ideas. But there is no one who owns them. Where is the ownership of what? Who can claim it? The claiming happens out of that energy. The claimer is already played by that energy. The claimer, the claiming, what can be claimed, is all a play of that energy. But you cannot know what it is. And that what is acting and reacting to that what is acting, all the karma of consciousness, whatever is the doer and the victim of everything, is not two. In consciousness you can say there are not two. So all there is is consciousness. But for what you are it doesn't matter. Even that is concept. It doesn't help you to be what you are. Even that understanding is a misunderstanding. It comes and goes. It's fleeting. If that would be needed for what you are, it would have to be uninterrupted. But even this understanding is in the dream. It will not deliver what you are looking for. And you are not depending on it, that's the beauty of it. So even the deepest insight of that so-called consciousness, how it works, the greatest guy of knowledge, is still an idiot.

Q: So what you say what you are is energy...

K: No, I don't say that. If I would say I am energy, I am different from what is the effect. So I would still make myself different to something else. Whatever you claim to be, even when you say 'I am energy', 'I am life', I am one too many who claims something. And then I make myself different to something else. No. That's why I say there has to be the absolute absence of any presence. Not 'I am now energy'. 'Before I was relative, and now I am not relative, because now I know myself. Before I didn't know myself'. All of that – fuck it all!

Q: Then what is the soul?

K: Bullshit.

Q: So when the soul leaves the body...

K: Bullshit leaves shit. Shit is leaving shit. There is a concept of soul. One concept leaving another concept. Shit leaving shit. Shit happens. There was once shit in shit, and now shit is out of shit. Shit me.

Q: So you are the Absolute as well as the relative?

K: I have no idea if I am the Absolute or not. The Absolute would not be enough. Or too much. The Absolute is already too much or too less for what I am.

Q: You are not the soul, you are not the body, you are not that.

K: Whatever you come up with – shit!

Q: But still I will come up with it.

K: Yes, shit happens. Trying not to come up with shit, you compress your shit. Compressed shit. So enjoy the shit. Enjoy that whatever you can experience: shit, shit, shit, shit, shit. And only shit happens.

Q: I think that would be a good japa: shit, shit, shit.

K: Yes, it's a bhajan. A shit bhajan.

Q: Yes, it's Shivaratri tomorrow.

K: Shit-aratri. I like shit. I love it.

Q: So this love affair we have...

K: Yes, shit loving shit.

Q: Yes, but also creating...

K: Out of shit comes shit. That's why shit is creating shit. What?

Q: What is shit looking for?

K: Shit is in love with shit. Shit is looking for shit.

Q: It gives a shit.

K: Because shit is giving shit, shit is in love with shit.

Q: Is it also selfish?

K: It is selfish shit. Self-is-shit. Selfish shit. Even Self is shit. I have to be totally tabula rasa. If whatever is shit, then even Self is shit.

Q: No wonder these are donation talks!

K: No, even if they have to pay in the West. You think I am different there?

Q: No!

K: If I am like that then more people are coming. There is a video on youtube called 'Advaita de Toilette'.

Q: Who's video?

K: A shit video.

Q: From Karl Renz?

K: From some guy called Karl Renz. I never put anything anywhere. But you see, people like it, they even put it on youtube.

Q: I think someone said if you knew what enlightenment is you wouldn't even come near it with a stick.

K: Yes, because enlightenment - that's why Advaita is the absolute toilet - because there is an absolute flush. And all the shit is gone in one instant.

Q: But how can it be gone?

K: Because it was never there. By you being what you are there was never any shit. But whatever you come up with is shit. But by just being what you are, you are that what is what is. And in that split second it's like an absolute flush. And shit will always try to avoid that flush. Because shit can only survive in shit. So concept can only survive in concept. That's the nature of concepts. Because if there is that what is not a concept, concepts cannot survive. So you as a concept can only survive in concepts. So shit always likes shit. Always creates more shit. Even trying to get less shit, it makes even out of less more shit. It's like I said, the me, the concept and survival of it, will always create more shit. Because only in shit it can survive. So images can only survive in images. And all the images are empty. So by being what you cannot not be, in one split second, you destroy all that can be destroyed, even the idea of Self gets destroyed, just by you being what you are. Because in what you are there is no idea of Self, or Brahman, or anything. Whatever you can name and frame is not there when you are what you are. So it's all absolute fucking empty. But when you are this imaginary I, you will always try to survive. Creating more shit. Even meditating is trying meditation shit. Even self-inquiry is shit. Shit inquiring into shit. Has to be! Sorry. No I am not sorry. That would be too much. I tell you, if I would know what is happiness, I would call it happiness. I would be absolutely happy that all is shit. And absolutely empty. And never needed. All these so-called icons you create in your so-called dream-world of Gods and Self and Absolute and Para Brahman and all of that, in one instant is gone. Just by being what you are.

Q: So deep sleep you say is the best pointer because there is no idea...

K: Deep deep sleep.

Q: I can't talk about it, can't think about it, can't nothing.

K: Now we can talk about it. But in deep deep sleep you don't care anyway. But now you care. But no one cares that you care. Maybe your wife?

Q: No.

K: Not even her. Especially not her!

Q: Isn't the dream state also...

K: What dream state? We didn't talk about the dream state.

Q: You say only deep deep sleep...

K: Yes, deep sleep is not enough. Deep sleep would be different from awake. The deep deep sleep is the Nature of deep sleep. Which doesn't know any Nature. The Nature of Nature who doesn't know any Nature. The Self of the Self doesn't know any Self. But when the Self knows the Self, there are already two Selfs too many. But you cannot avoid it, because you realize yourself always as two. As the lover and the beloved. What to do? So there are two as an experience, but in Reality not. In realization there is always two. Realization always happens as the lover being in love with the beloved. And this love affair is the realization of this dream. But in Reality there is not even one.

Q: And when you say there is nothing...

K: It's too much.

Q: You said there is nothing.

K: Yes, there is nothing when there is nothing.

Q: But with everything else you have been saying you have said the opposite of that word too.

K: Nothing is too much and everything would be too less for what you are. But the trick is, if you are nothing, you are everything. But if you know you are nothing, it's one too many who knows to be nothing. But when you are nothing you don't know any nothing anymore, then you are nothing and everything. But you cannot become nothing and by that become everything. You are already that what is nothing and everything, but not by knowing it. So some like Adyashanti are making such a big thing out of 'you are no thing'. And then you take it personal again. You have to take it personal. Because if you say 'you are no thing', then you are different from things. And then you are again in this trap of differences. So you make an advantage of being no thing. 'I am nothing'. Ha ha ha ha. It's for sure another idea. Because shit needs shit. And then even nothing becomes shit. When there is one who claims to be nothing. But what to do? Shit happens. You cannot avoid it. This whatever you call consciousness, will always define itself. Even in not defining itself it defines itself as that what cannot be defined. So even if you say I am that what cannot be defined, you define yourself as that what cannot be defined. So it's already a definition. Whatever comes from that point is too much. So that's why you have to make it really difficult to say you are the absolute absence of any presence of any absence presence of anyone who is or is not, knowing or not knowing what one is. It has to be a little like rat tail, and then everyone is already lost, thank God.

Q: So you say the absence of the absence...

K: The absence of the absence is still one too many who is the absence of the absence. Even wei wu wei, you have to make a rat tail wei wu wei wu wei wu wei. Even to call it the Omnipresence, is one presence too many. Because Wei Wu Wei called it the Omnipresence of that what is Self.

Just be what you cannot not be. And there is a blankety blank. There is no need of any bla bla bla. Otherwise it becomes an intellectual exercise. In German I would call it intellectual 'Extrascheiss'. 'Scheiss' in German means shit.

Q: Karl, when you were talking about the absence presence absence presence whatever, the word 'sameness' came to mind...

K: Sameness I don't buy so much. If you say absolutely Self, only Self is, that's maybe a statement you can make, which is like a result of being what you are. Like Nisargadatta would say 'I am That'. It's a result of being That what never needs to know to be what you are, to be That. So being that unpronounceable whatever it is. Pronouncing itself it would say 'I am That', what never needs to be pronounced. This paradox is then working. It has to be a paradox. So out of the needlessness comes the living word of 'I am That'. Not by any intention, there is no need for it. It just comes out. But out of a needlessness, not of any demand or any need. Because this is the needlessness of realization. So you are that what is Reality realizing itself as 'I am That'. And not you becoming reality and then you realize yourself. No, moment for moment you are That realizing itself uninterrupted. And you cannot not realize yourself. You have to realize yourself. But not as what you are. You are already what you are, realizing itself here and now in whatever it is. But 'this' are all real lies. You can only realize yourself in lies. Never as what you are. What you are will never be realized. You can never realize That. Because it is always realizing itself in lies, in images, in ideas. But never as what it is. So yes, and no.

Q: When they are quoting Ramana and say 'abide in the Self'...

K: Yes, abide in 'am I' or 'I am'. Self abidance is to abide in that what never needs to abide in anything.

Q: So why would he have said 'abide in the Self'?

K: He said abide in that what never needs to abide in anything. So abide in that what is Self but not knowing Self. That's your nature, and that's the easiest you can not do. This is effortlessness. Being what you are. That is self abidance. But whatever you try to do, by any action, will never deliver that.

Q: So not abiding in the Self is the same thing?

K: Abiding in the Self or not abiding in the Self. Ha ha.

Q: You say forget about abiding in the Self and just are.

K: Yes, but it's all pointers. One shouldn't take it so literally.

Q: But that's what I am saying. So it doesn't become an effort or a technique.

K: The thing is always, with Ramesh even, the non-doership is a nice pointer. But if you take it personal you become a non-doer. And then you are in the same trap as before. But you cannot otherwise as take it personally. So out of a doer you become a non-doer. Because you think 'before I was a doer, now I understand I cannot do it, it's all God's will, so I am a non-doer'. It doesn't work.

Q: My experience of that was that even when the idea of not being the doer was there, there was still God and me as a non-doer.

K: It's still a survival technique. You take it personal and you will find a way to stay in whatever understanding. And that's why the Yoga Vashista said you realize something now, but it will be gone again and you will be stupid as before. And whatever you can understand is a misunderstanding. There is no exception. Whatever you can realize is part of the dream and needs to be realized. But that what is real never needs to be realized and never will be unreal. And that what is unreal can only realize the unreal. And that what can be realized in the unreal will always be a fleeting shadow of your understanding or not understanding or whatever we say.

Q: Even the idea of the dream.

K: Even the idea of the dream. For the real there is no idea of the dream. The Real doesn't even know the Real. And by not knowing the Real it doesn't know any unreal. But that what knows the real and the unreal will always be unreal. There is no bridge between that. That's why Ramana said when he was asked 'are you realized'?

'How can I be realized. What I am never needs to realize itself to be what it is, so it's ever realized. It is that what is ever realizing itself, but itself can never be realized. So what you see as Ramana is just an image of it. And who cares if Ramana is realized?' No one. Not even Ramana. And that I like. And now all these disciples of Ramana, who never took any disciples, or never took himself as any guru or master. And now Tiru is full of disciples who claim to know what Ramana meant. And everyone has to be like Ramana. And that's one big reason why I don't sit there anymore. Because it really becomes too much.

Q: Even when you say that consciousness is realizing, there was a notional point where there is no consciousness, and then consciousness becomes the apparent many. But even that is conceptual.

K: Absolutely. It's fleeting. It's part of the dream. I don't say it's real or unreal. It's just a realization.

Q: So no thought can express it?

K: The thought already is an expression. How can an expression express that what it came from? Impossible.

Q: It's already a split.

K: It's already too late.

Q: In duality so to speak.

K: That's why I say 'now it's too late'. Whatever you experience, even the now, is too late. If everything is too late, whatever you experience, then even the now is too late. So who cares? If even the presence of that awareness, of this now, this precious infinite now, is too late for you, so what? And whatever happens happens in this infinite now. But by all these happenings you cannot become more or less than you are. All of that comes and goes and you are still what you are. So what? May it be as it is. Or not. Who cares? You can not find one who cares. That is the ultimate medicine of Nisargadatta, not finding yourself anywhere, because you can not be found. Neither in the world, in spirit, or in awareness, or even beyond. You cannot find yourself. And as you cannot find yourself – 'who' cares? You cannot find anyone who cares. Who is there? But you are looking. You cannot not look. The inquiry continues. But maybe you enjoy the not-finding. That's all. 'Oh, I am not in the world, wonderful!' 'I am not in awareness, wonderful!' 'I am not in the absence, wonderful!' 'I am not in the beyond, not even the beyond, ha ha ha!' 'There is no home for me, thank God'. So I cannot find anyone who is at home. As there was never anyone at home, there isn't anyone who is not at home. There is not even a home for home. For whom.

Q: In your book where you debunk enlightenment, 'The Myth of Enlightenment', I forgot how you put it, but my understanding from that was what I also heard from Ramesh. And I liked it so much because I was hearing the same thing. But I can't remember exactly how you put it. There is no one to be enlightened?

K: Yes. That's the beauty of whatever you are. As there was no one unenlightened in the first place. How can out of, coming out of that who was not there, someone who can get enlightened? Who can get enlightened? First try to find one who is unenlightened. And then we can talk about if that one can get enlightened. But first show me one who is unenlightened. So by not finding anyone who is unenlightened, the whole idea of enlightenment – what is this bloody idea?

Q: So someone could say 'everybody is enlightened'?

K: No. You cannot say that. Then you would confirm that there is one. That is like a trick of teachers who are collecting disciples. They are telling you: 'You are already enlightened'. And everyone is drinking from the nectar of the words of the master who tells me I am already enlightened. Oh my goodness! That makes me really diabetic. That's too sweet. The Taoists I like: 'The truth is never beautiful'. Or not beautiful. And beautiful words you can pronounce forever, and the shit by that the flowers will grow. But it doesn't matter for what you are. The Truth is not nice. It doesn't have any power or anything. The truth is: There is no fucking truth. So whatever needs to be fucked needs to be fucked. But not the truth. That's fucked.

Q: And there is no fucker.

K: You realize yourself as the fucker, the fucking and the fucked. But you are not the fucker who is fucking the fucked. You are that what is experiencing itself as the fucker, the fucking and the fucked.

Q: It's a fact.

K: Factory. Even to say you are that what is Reality is too much. Even to come up with some definition of what you are and what you are not, it's all too much. But what else to do? Just for the party to happen, you pronounce something, and then you destroy it again. That's why everyone complains: 'Sometimes you say that, and then one second later you destroy it again because you say the opposite. Make a decision what you want to say!' 'I don't want to say anything, if you ask me! But if I say something I destroy it the next moment'.

Q: You have to, you got to.

K: I don't have to. But I like it.

Q: But you have to, because it is already misleading, and it could be worse misleading.

K: I like that I mislead the shit.

Q: Exactly! It seems like it is not bad enough, then it would be worse.

K: But why not? It's a good business.

Q: It's double misleading.

K: But who cares about being mislead by oneself? And you will always be mislead by yourself. You are the trapper the trapping and the trapped. And you will always be trapped by what you are.

And the absolute trap is falling in love with this bullshit I. And you cannot not fall in love with it. So the love trap will always be there, if you like it or not. What to do?

Q: So similarly all the so-called 'false gurus', or the ones who are misleading, it's all part of the bullshit, it doesn't matter?

K: That's why I say, shit happens. But I can still call them shit. I don't criticize them with that, because there is no one to criticize. I just call shit shit. As I call this shit shit. Whatever I say is shit, and I like shit. I love shit. Because it is empty. And these empty words can never make me more or less than I am, so I love it. Because I don't need it. It's there anyway, and I cannot get rid of it. So I rather enjoy it. Or not. Who cares? Sometimes there is enjoyment, sometimes not. I don't even have to enjoy it to be what I am.

Q: But there is an effort, whether it is conscious or not, to be clear in the pointers that you are giving.

K: No. I have no idea where it comes from. It's just the back door is open and the front door is open. And I am always wondering what happens. For me it is more like the words are already spoken. Now they get pronounced, but they are already spoken. Unavoidable. So there is no effort in it. It is an effortlessness of realization. Every moment is already there before it is even experienced. There is no effort in anyone. So in that sense, that innocence one is, can never get more or less in all the senses. So get to your senses.

Q: So you talking...

K: I am talking?

Q: Whatever is talking. It has the effect of everyone else sort of falling asleep.

K: That's why I take donations or money, because sleeping pills cost something. No, you can say I talk that to death what can be talked to death. And that what you are, which is in spite of talking or not talking, is just what it is. It's a trick, but it doesn't work.

Q: Nothing works.

K: But it's a nice try. No, what I am actually doing is more like working on the sixth sense of humor. Being the joke and then laughing about that what you are is maybe not so bad. Being the divine comedy or the comedy itself is not so bad. Because you must be joking that you look for that what you are in shit. It's a permanent joke. You are knowledge which is looking for itself in shit. Chit looking in shit, and thinking out of shit, chit comes. It's a joke. That what is knowledge itself thinking it can get itself or know itself in shit. What a joke! Never ending joke.

Q: Why is it so easy for us to be in deep deep sleep?

K: For you nothing is easy. You are just dropped in deep deep sleep by what you are. You can never fall into deep deep sleep. What an idea!

Q: What do you mean by 'deep deep'?

K: Deep deep is the Nature of deep sleep. Deep sleep would be different again from something else. So Nature is always Nature. The Nature of awareness, the Nature of I-amness or spirit, or the Nature of the world. In Nature there is no difference. But it's always experiencing itself in differences. So the deep deep sleep is the Nature of deep sleep.

Q: So the second 'deep' is substituted for the word Nature?

K: You could call it the Essence of deep sleep is deep deep sleep. Or the I am of the I am. The World of the World. It's always that what is the Heart of whatever is. Heart itself, which is expressing itself as a lover, loving, and the beloved. But is not the lover, and not the loving, and not the beloved. It is that what is realizing itself as the father, the spirit and the son. The trinity of Shiva. The absolute Abstract which cannot be abstracted anymore by itself. Because it is that what is abstracting everything but it cannot abstract itself. That is that what is the abstract. But whatever you can abstract from that is not that. Because the Substratum cannot go further. Even the nothing you can drop. But not that. So the Dropper, the absolute Dropper, cannot be dropped. Whatever you can drop you can drop, but not that what you are. And every night you do that, naturally. Every night you drop the world, the spirit, and the awareness, and you are simply That what you are. Which is just the experience of absence. And every morning the presence starts again, as awareness, I-amness, and the world, together. But what you are is in no need of neither that or that. But still it's there.

Q: The individual identity gets dropped?

K: Whatever can be dropped gets dropped. Even the dropper gets dropped. First the world gets dropped, then the dropping, and then the dropper gets dropped. And what is left is the Abstract, which can never drop itself. What you call the Abstract, the Substratum. That what is the Abstract, which doesn't know any Abstract.

Q: So you don't even prescribe any kind of investigation or inquiry?

K: Neither I prescribe nor do I say you shouldn't. I would only say whatever you do or don't do is already done maybe or not. Who cares? But by all of that you cannot attain what you are. And what you are longing for is being that what never needs to long for itself because it is what it is. And that can never be achieved or attained by whatever you imagine. But imagining will still happen. So inquiry continues, but you better be in spite of that. Because in the presence there will be consciousness inquiring into the nature of consciousness, uninterrupted. It will always have the intention of knowing itself.

Q: Isn't that a concept?

K: Yes, it's another concept, but it's just an intention of love. Call it whatever. It's an intention of being happy you can find in everything. If you call it a concept I don't mind. But for me it is not a concept. It's just a lover being in the loving and caring about the beloved. It's just that what I am realizing itself in that loving caring.

Q: Are you saying that's the experience?

K: That is the realization of what I am.

Q: That's the constant experience?

K: It's a constant experience of love, as a lover loving what can be the beloved. Loving caring about itself. In the presence is the absolute uninterrupted experience.

Q: You are saying it's an experience, but there is no experiencer?

K: I don't say that.

Q: You don't say there is a subject experiencing that.

K: By that I don't say anything about what I am and I am not.

Q: Just what is?

K: For me I would even say I don't have to be to be.

Q: That's what I meant by conceptual.

K: Still when you ask me how I experience myself, I would say I experience myself in an infinite love affair with myself. Because in every experience I experience this absolute tendency to know myself. In every experience I experience absolute this loving and caring about myself. And if you ask anybody, this would be the essence of any experience: loving and caring about what you are.

Q: So if you are shouting at someone, you are loving caring?

K: Absolutely.

Q: It's just a different expression of loving.

K: Maybe by shouting at myself, because I talk loud to myself, but I know it will never listen.

Q: Because you don't see another?

K: No. This is like an entertainment with myself. I see expressions which are different. But in these expressions there is no difference in nature. So as I am that, I shout at myself. Sometimes I even kill myself. But I cannot be killed by killing. And I cannot be offended by what I am. But still I experience offense. And I like to offend myself. Absolutely. And I call myself asshole. Because sometimes my Self is an asshole. Absolutely. But an absolute one.

Q: What about jealousy and those kind of feelings?

K: I am absolute jealous of myself sometimes. There is a jealous God. You cannot avoid any experience. If you are jealous you are jealous.

Q: Is even that an expression of love?

K: Of course! How can you be jealous without loving the other one? Or yourself? Sometimes you are even jealous about yourself. You are even jealous that what you are doesn't need to know itself when you are something what needs to know itself. Then you are jealous about yourself. Jealous about God. God is jealous about God who doesn't know God and doesn't need to know God. But if God is God who needs to know God he is jealous about himself that what he is doesn't need to know itself. What a bullshit! But that is the way you realize yourself, in bullshit. And love makes you so crazy. And all that you cannot avoid. You have to realize yourself in all possible ways. You cannot avoid one single bullshit. It's all bullshit, it's all entertainment, no one needs it, and still you can not avoid it. As absolute as you are in Reality is your realization. There is no single aspect you can get rid of. Not one little stupid jealousy you can not experience.

Q: Isn't it the same that is in spite of all that bullshit you are?

K: The nature of that what I call shit is Chit. But that what is Chit doesn't know any Chit or shit. And that what knows Chit and shit, even that Chit is shit. So when there is Chit and shit, when there are these two concepts, both are shit. But still the nature of shit is Chit, not knowing Chit or shit. So if I call you shit, then still your Nature is that what is Chit. So if I call you stupid, even the Nature of stupidity is Knowledge. There is only Knowledge in Reality. The Real is always real. And even the Nature of the unreal is real. But if there are two concepts, the unreal and the real, then it becomes shit-reality. But still the Nature of the unreal is real. And the Nature of the Real is real. But that Reality doesn't know any Reality.

Q: You say it is entertainment.

K: Entertainment has no intention that it should end. In entertainment there is no winner or loser.

Q: Why don't you condemn it, it's a useless affair? Why don't you deny it?

K: Why should I deny what is not even there?

Q: It is a useless affair.

K: But I like useless things.

Q: You like it.

K: Yes, I like it. Personal taste. Useless is fun. The idea of useful, that's...

Q: There is a duality aspect of that uselessness.

K: Of course. You can only experience yourself in duality. I like that I like it. And I like when I don't like it.

Q: You play with your current duality.

K: I play with whatever and it is a play of what I am and it doesn't matter how I play. But in the taste of this guy, entertainment I like more than calling it something else. It has to be a personal taste, because what is my Nature has no taste. The Tastelessness has no taste. But is experiencing itself as a guy who has taste. Ok, it's a tasteless guy. I always say you are the Tastelessness. In German it is an offense if I call someone Tastelessness.

Q: It doesn't matter, but the way it is taken appears to matter. The way you say it it doesn't matter. But if somebody takes it a different way it matters to them.

K: Yes, but I don't care. If I would care I would have problems.

Q: What is really happening is you saying 'don't take it this way, take it that way'.

K: No, I don't say that. Take it whatever way, it doesn't matter.

Q: But if you say 'be what you are'...

K: Be what you cannot not be. I don't tell you 'be what you are'. Because that would make you a difference. Be what you cannot not be, that's all.

Q: You are detaching us...

K: No, I am not detaching anyone. I am even detaching you from detachment. Because you are even in the absence of detachment or the presence of detachment what you cannot not be. I am not detaching anyone here. I have no interest in any bloody detachment. Because who bloody needs to be detached from what?

Q: You are denying the one...

K: I am detaching you from detachment. Because you have to be that what is the Absolute, you are absolutely detached from whatever, because there is no second, that's all. You are detachment itself. How can I detach you? From what? You are That. How can you detach yourself from what? But by being what you can not not be you are what is nothing and everything. Whatever you say or don't say. You are the absence and you are the presence and you are whatever is and is not. But even that is all bullshit. Just be what you cannot not be. And there is no one who needs anything. Never demands anything. No necessity, no demand of anything. Just by being what you can not not be. But the moment you make it a concept again and you want to have it, and then comes this bloody ownership bullshit. And then you suffer about not having it. And then you question 'why and how can I be what I cannot not be?' What a joke! 'How can I be what I cannot not be'? Can you do that? Listen to it! Even pronouncing it you have to laugh. But you will do it, I know. Ramana's 'Be what you are' or 'Be as you are' – you are always: 'How?' It's like someone inviting you to dance. 'How can I dance?' So I have to make it the neti-neti. 'Be what you cannot not be'. That's the neti-neti, absolute neti-neti. 'What you cannot not be'. If I tell you 'be what you are', then you detach from something. Because then you think it has to be something special.

But if I make it a negative negative, then you are that what never needs to be pronounced. Because that what is a positive never needs to be pronounced. But the neti-neti is negative negative negative negative. But what is the positive is always unpronounced.

Q: Sounds good.

K: 'Oh yeah, sounds good'.

Q: Can a person have special powers to kill everything?

K: See? I am not worth the money! Because if after two and a half hours someone has this question, then I didn't work well enough. And I like it, because I like to be absolute irrelevant. Imagine I would create some results here. Imagine someone would get what I say.

www.ingramcontent.com/pod-product-compliance
Lightning Source LLC
Chambersburg PA
CBHW050634170426
43200CB00008B/1019